Buying a Home
in
ITALY

A Survival Handbook

David Hampshire

SURVIVAL BOOKS • LONDON • ENGLAND

First published 1999
Second Edition 2001
Third Edition 2003
Fourth Edition 2008

Copyright © Survival Books 1999, 2001, 2003, 2008
Cover photograph © Darren Green (www.shutterstock.com)
Illustrations and maps © Jim Watson

Survival Books Limited
26 York Street, London W1U 6PZ, United Kingdom
☎ +44 (0)20-7788 7644, 🗐 +44 (0)870-762 3212
✉ info@survivalbooks.net
💻 www.survivalbooks.net

British Library Cataloguing in Publication Data.
A CIP record for this book is available
from the British Library.
ISBN: 1-978-905303-25-4

Printed and bound in India by Ajanta Offset

ACKNOWLEDGEMENTS

My sincere thanks to all those who contributed to the successful publication of the fourth edition of this book, in particular the many people who provided information, and took the time and trouble to read and comment on the draft versions. I would especially like to thank Graeme Chesters (research and updating), Peter Read (editing and proofing), Donna Jackson (checking the Italian), Di Tolland (desktop publishing and photos) and Grania Rogers (photo editing). I would also like to thank Nicola Meecham, Karbalaei Hassan Ali (Farrokh), Mary Jane Cryan, Laura Jane Pancani, Nick Daws, Fulvio Ferri, the staff of Ville e Casali magazine, Luciano D'Alessandro, Gianni Bernabò Di Negro and everyone else who contributed in any way to this and previous editions, who I have omitted to mention. Finally, thanks to Linda Travella of Casa Travella and Louise Talbot of Brian A. French for photographs, and a special thank you to Jim Watson for the cover design, illustrations, cartoons and maps.

THE AUTHOR

David Hampshire was born in England and after serving in the Royal Air Force, was employed for many years in the computer industry. His work has taken him around the world and he has lived and worked in many countries, including Australia, France, Germany, Malaysia, the Netherlands, Panama, Singapore, Spain, and Switzerland. David starting working as a technical author in Australia in the '80s and he became a full-time, freelance writer in 1990. He is the author or co-author or editor of around 20 titles about living & working and buying property abroad. David lives with his partner in England and Panama.

WHAT READERS & REVIEWERS

'If you need to find out how France works then this book is indispensable. Native French people probably have a less thorough understanding of how their country functions.'

Living France

'It's everything you always wanted to ask but didn't for fear of the contemptuous put down. The best English-language guide. Its pages are stuffed with practical information on everyday subjects and are designed to compliment the traditional guidebook.'

Swiss News

'Rarely has a 'survival guide' contained such useful advice – This book dispels doubts for first-time travellers, yet is also useful for seasoned globetrotters – In a word, if you're planning to move to the US or go there for a long-term stay, then buy this book both for general reading and as a ready-reference.'

American Citizens Abroad

'Let's say it at once. David Hampshire's Living and Working in France is the best handbook ever produced for visitors and foreign residents in this country; indeed, my discussion with locals showed that it has much to teach even those born and bred in l'Hexagone – It is Hampshire's meticulous detail which lifts his work way beyond the range of other books with similar titles. Often you think of a supplementary question and search for the answer in vain. With Hampshire this is rarely the case. – He writes with great clarity (and gives French equivalents of all key terms), a touch of humour and a ready eye for the odd (and often illuminating) fact. – This book is absolutely indispensable.'

The Riviera Reporter

'A must for all future expats. I invested in several books but this is the only one you need. Every issue and concern is covered, every daft question you have but are frightened to ask is answered honestly without pulling any punches. Highly recommended.'

Reader

'In answer to the desert island question about the one how-to book on France, this book would be it.'

The Recorder

'The ultimate reference book. Every subject imaginable is exhaustively explained in simple terms. An excellent introduction to fully enjoy all that this fine country has to offer and save time and money in the process.'

American Club of Zurich

HAVE SAID ABOUT SURVIVAL BOOKS

'The amount of information covered is not short of incredible. I thought I knew enough about my birth country. This book has proved me wrong. Don't go to France without it. Big mistake if you do. Absolutely priceless!'

Reader

'When you buy a model plane for your child, a video recorder, or some new computer gizmo, you get with it a leaflet or booklet pleading 'Read Me First', or bearing large friendly letters or bold type saying 'IMPORTANT - follow the instructions carefully'. This book should be similarly supplied to all those entering France with anything more durable than a 5-day return ticket. – It is worth reading even if you are just visiting briefly, or if you have lived here for years and feel totally knowledgeable and secure. But if you need to find out how France works then it is indispensable. Native French people probably have a less thorough understanding of how their country functions. – Where it is most essential, the book is most up to the minute.

Living France

A comprehensive guide to all things French, written in a highly readable and amusing style, for anyone planning to live, work or retire in France.

The Times

Covers every conceivable question that might be asked concerning everyday life – I know of no other book that could take the place of this one.

France in Print

A concise, thorough account of the Do's and DONT's for a foreigner in Switzerland – Crammed with useful information and lightened with humorous quips which make the facts more readable.

American Citizens Abroad

'I found this a wonderful book crammed with facts and figures, with a straightforward approach to the problems and pitfalls you are likely to encounter. The whole laced with humour and a thorough understanding of what's involved. Gets my vote!'

Reader

'A vital tool in the war against real estate sharks; don't even think of buying without reading this book first!'

Everything Spain

'We would like to congratulate you on this work: it is really super! We hand it out to our expatriates and they read it with great interest and pleasure.'

ICI (Switzerland) AG

CONTENTS

1. MAJOR CONSIDERATIONS   17

Why Italy?   17
Buying For Investment   20
Climate   21
Economy   22
Cost Of Property   23
Cost Of Living   24
Permits & Visas   25
Visitors   25
Visas   27
Permits To Stay   28
Residence Permits   29
Working   30
Retirement   31
Language   32
Health   33
Pets   36

2. WHERE TO LIVE?   41

Geography   41
Regions   43
Location   71
Getting There   77
Getting Around   86

3. YOUR DREAM HOME 93

Research 94
Avoiding Problems 94
Renting Before Buying 99
Hotels & Hostels 101
Home Exchange 101
House Hunting 102
Estate Agents 103
Property Prices 107
Fees 111
Types Of Property 113
Italian Homes 116
Buying A New Home 118
Buying A Resale Home 119
Buying An Old Home 120
Community Properties 121
Retirement Homes 126
Garages & Parking 126
Timeshare & Part-Ownership Schemes 127
Inspections & Surveys 130
Renovation & Restoration 135
Building Your Own Home 142
Selling Your Home 143
Selling Your Home Yourself 144

4. MONEY MATTERS 149

Italian Currency 149
Importing & Exporting Money 150
Banks 153
Mortgages 156

5. THE PURCHASE PROCEDURE 161

Conveyancing 161
Contracts 163
Completion 167

6. MOVING HOUSE 171

Shipping Your Belongings 171
Pre-Departure Health Check 173
Immigration 173
Customs 175
Embassy Registration 176
Finding Help 176
Moving In 177
Checklists 178

7. TAXATION 181

Fiscal Code 181
Income Tax 182
Property Tax 187
Capital Gains Tax 188
Inheritance Taxes 189

8. INSURANCE 193

Health Insurance 194
Household Insurance 198
Holiday & Travel Insurance 200

9. LETTING 205

Rules & Regulations 206
Location 206

Swimming Pool   207
Letting Rates   208
Furnishings   208
Keys   209
Cleaning   209
Using An Agent   209
Doing Your Own Letting   210
Information Packs   213
Maintenance   213
Security   214
Increasing Rental Income   214

10. MISCELLANEOUS MATTERS   217

Crime   217
Heating & Air-Conditioning   218
Home Security   220
Postal Services   222
Shopping   223
Telephone Services   229
Television & Radio   236
Utilities   240

APPENDICES   253

Appendix A: Useful Addresses   253
Appendix B: Further Reading   256
Appendix C: Useful Websites   261
Appendix D: Weights & Measures   263
Appendix E: Maps   268
Appendix F: Airline Services   273
Appendix G: Glossary   277

INDEX   289

Villas, Portofino, Liguria

IMPORTANT NOTE

Readers should note that the laws and regulations for buying property in Italy aren't the same as in other countries, and are also liable to change periodically. I cannot recommend too strongly that you check with an official and reliable source (not always the same), and take expert legal advice before paying any money or signing any legal documents. Don't, however, believe everything you're told or read, even – dare I say it – herein!

To help you obtain further information and verify data with official sources, useful addresses and references to other sources of information have been included in most chapters, and in **Appendices A to C**. Important points have been emphasised throughout the book in bold print, some of which it would be expensive or foolish to disregard. **Ignore them at your peril or cost!** Unless specifically stated, the reference to any company, organisation, product or publication in this book does not constitute an endorsement or recommendation.

AUTHOR'S NOTES

- Frequent references are made throughout this book to the European Union (EU), which at the time of writing, which comprise Austria, Belgium, Bulgaria, Cyprus, the Czech Republic, Denmark, Estonia, Finland, France, Germany, Greece, Hungary, Ireland, Italy, Latvia, Lithuania, Luxembourg, Malta, the Netherlands, Poland, Portugal, Romania, the Slovak Republic, Slovenia, Spain, Sweden and the United Kingdom, and the European Economic Area (EEA), which includes the EU countries plus Iceland, Liechtenstein and Norway.

- All prices are shown in euros (€) unless otherwise stated. Prices quoted should be taken as estimates only, although they were mostly correct when going to print and fortunately don't usually change overnight. Although prices are sometimes quoted exclusive of value added tax (IVA) in Italy, most prices shown are inclusive of tax, which is the method used when quoting prices in this book unless otherwise stated.

- Names of major Italian cities are written in English and not Italian, e.g. Rome (Roma), Milan (Milano), Naples (Napoli), Padua (Padova), Sienna (Siena), Turin (Torino), Florence (Firenze), Genoa (Genova) and Venice (Venezia).

- Times are shown using am for before noon and pm for after noon. Most Italians don't use the 24-hour clock. All times are local, so you should check the time difference when making international calls.

- His/he/him also means her/she/her (please forgive me ladies). This is done to make life easier for both the reader and (in particular) the author, and isn't intended to be sexist.

- The Italian translation of many key words and phrases is shown in brackets in italics.

- Warning and important points are shown in **bold** type.

- The following symbols are used in this book: ☎ (telephone), 📄 (fax), 💻 (Internet) and ✉ (email).

- Lists of **Useful Addresses, Further Reading** and **Useful Websites** are contained in **Appendices A, B** and **C** respectively. Other appendices include: **Weights & Measures**; **Maps**; **Scheduled Airline Services**; and a comprehensive **Glossary** of property terms.

Grand Canal, Venice

INTRODUCTION

If you're planning to buy a home in Italy or even just thinking about it, this is **THE BOOK** for you! Whether you want a palazzo, farmhouse, cottage or apartment, a holiday or a permanent home, ***Buying a Home in Italy*** will help make your dreams come true. The aim of this book is to provide you with the information necessary to help you choose the most favourable location and most appropriate home to satisfy your personal requirements. Most importantly, it will help you avoid the pitfalls and risks associated with buying a home in Italy.

You may already own a home in another country; however, buying a home in Italy (or in any 'foreign' country) is a different matter altogether. One of the most common mistakes many people make when buying a home abroad, is to assume that the laws and purchase procedures are the same as in their home country. **This is rarely, if ever, the case!** Buying property in Italy is generally safe, particularly when compared with some other countries. However, if you don't follow the rules provided for your protection, a purchase can result in a serious financial loss, as some people have discovered.

For many people, buying a home in Italy has previously been a case of pot luck. However, with a copy of ***Buying a Home in Italy*** to hand you'll have a wealth of priceless information at your fingertips – information derived from a variety of sources, both official and unofficial, not least the hard won personal experiences of the author, his friends, colleagues and acquaintances. This book doesn't contain all the answers – but what it will do is reduce the risk of making an expensive mistake that you may bitterly regret later, and help you make informed decisions and calculated judgements, instead of costly mistakes and uneducated guesses – forewarned is forearmed! Most important of all, it will help you save money and will repay your investment many times over.

Buying a home in Italy is a wonderful way to make new friends, broaden your horizons and revitalise your life – and it provides a welcome bolt-hole to recuperate from the stresses and strains of modern life. I trust that this book will help you avoid the pitfalls and smooth your way to many happy years in your new home in Italy, secure in the knowledge that you've made the right decision.

Buona fortuna!

David Hampshire
November 2007

The Vatican, St. Peter's Basilica and Sant'Angelo Bridge, Rome

1.
MAJOR CONSIDERATIONS

Buying a home abroad is not only a major financial commitment, but also a decision that can have a huge influence on other aspects of your life, including your health, security and safety, your family relationships and friendships, your lifestyle, your opinions and your outlook. You also need to bear in mind any restrictions that might affect your choice of location and type of property, such as whether you will need (or be able) to learn another language or dialect, whether you will be able (or permitted) to find work, whether you can adapt to and enjoy the climate, whether you will be able to take your pets with you, and, not least, whether you will be able to afford the kind of home (and lifestyle) that you want. In order to ensure that you're making the right move, it's as well to face these and other major considerations before making any irrevocable decisions.

WHY ITALY?

Italy is one of the most beautiful countries in Europe, and possibly the most alluring, with more than its fair share of ravishing landscapes and stunning towns. It's a country of huge variety, offering something for everyone: magnificent beaches for sun-worshippers; beautiful unspoiled countryside for nature-lovers; a wealth of magnificent ancient cities and towns for history enthusiasts (virtually every town is a history book of battles and religious milestones); an abundance of mountains and seas for sportspeople; vibrant nightlife for the jet set; fine wines for oenophiles and superb cuisine for gourmets; a profusion of painting, sculpture and music for art lovers; and tranquillity for the stressed. Few other countries in the world offer such an exhilarating mixture of beauty, culture, history, sophistication and style.

When buying property in Italy, you aren't simply buying a home, but a lifestyle. As a location for a holiday, retirement or permanent home, Italy has few rivals, and in addition to the wide choice of properties and generally good value, it offers a fine climate for most of the year, particularly in the centre and south.

Despite the many excellent reasons for buying a home in Italy, it's important not to be under any illusions about what you can expect from a home there. The first and most important question you need to ask yourself is **exactly** why do you want to buy a home in Italy? For example, are you seeking a holiday or a retirement home? If you're seeking a second home, will it be used mainly for long weekends or for longer stays? Do you plan to let it to offset some of the mortgage and running costs? How important is the property income? Are you

primarily looking for a sound investment or do you plan to work or start a business in Italy?

Often buyers have a variety of reasons for buying a home in Italy; for example, many people buy a holiday home with a view to living there permanently or semi-permanently when they retire. If this is the case, there are many more factors to take into account than if you're 'simply' buying a holiday home that you will occupy for only a few weeks a year, when it may be wiser not to buy at all! If, on the other hand, you plan to work or start a business in Italy, you will be faced with a whole different set of criteria.

Can you really afford to buy a home in Italy? What of the future? Is your income secure and protected against inflation and currency fluctuations? In the '80s, many people purchased holiday homes in Italy by taking out second mortgages on their family homes and stretching their financial resources to the limit. Not surprisingly, when the recession struck in the early '90s, many people had their homes repossessed or were forced to sell at a huge loss when they were unable to maintain the mortgage payments.

Italians aren't very mobile and move house much less frequently than the Americans and British, which is reflected in the fairly stable property market. Nevertheless, since 2004 property prices have increased countrywide by some 25 per cent, compared with average inflation of around 2 per cent per annum, and in some cities, fashionable resorts and regions (such as the Italian lakes, the Italian Riviera and Tuscany) prices rise faster than average, which is usually reflected in much higher purchase prices (see **Cost Of Property** on page 23).

You shouldn't expect to make a quick profit when buying property in Italy, as you need to recover the high costs associated with buying a home when you sell. You should look upon a property purchase as an investment in your family's future happiness, rather than merely in financial terms.

Unless you know exactly what you're looking for and where, it's sensible to rent a property for a period until you're more familiar with an area. As when making any major financial decision, it isn't wise to be in too much of a hurry. Many people make expensive (even catastrophic) errors when buying homes in Italy, usually because they don't do sufficient research and are too hasty, often setting themselves ridiculous deadlines (such as buying a home during a long weekend break or a week's holiday). Not surprisingly, most people wouldn't dream of acting so rashly when buying a property in their home country! It isn't uncommon for buyers to regret their decision after some time and wish they'd purchased a different kind of property in a different region – or even in a different country!

☑ **SURVIVAL TIP**

Before deciding to buy a home in Italy, it's wise to do extensive research (see page 105), study the possible pitfalls (see page 106) and be prepared to rent for a period (see page 111).

Advantages & Disadvantages

There are both advantages and disadvantages to buying a home in Italy, although for most people the benefits far outweigh the drawbacks.

Advantages

- guaranteed summer sunshine in most areas;
- good value (provided you avoid the most fashionable areas), particularly if you want a country house with a large plot;
- the solidity and spaciousness of rural homes;
- unparalleled design and a huge variety of architectural styles;
- a stable property market;
- safe purchase procedures (provided you aren't reckless);
- the integrity of (most) licensed estate agents and notaries;
- superb food and excellent wines at reasonable prices;
- ease and low cost of access (at least for most western Europeans);
- good rental possibilities (in many areas);
- excellent local tradesmen and services;
- a gentle, slow pace of life in rural areas;
- the warmth and bonhomie of Italian people;
- the timeless splendour of Italy on your doorstep.

Disadvantages

- the relatively high purchase costs associated with buying property;
- the high crime rate in some urban areas;
- traffic congestion and pollution in most towns and cities;
- the threat of severe storms and earthquakes in some regions;
- overcrowding in popular tourist areas;
- overbearing bureaucracy (which was invented to prevent Italians having paradise on earth!);
- an unstable national government (over 60 since 1945!);
- the relatively high running costs of a home compared with some other countries
- high taxes for residents and an increasing cost of living;
- water shortages in many regions (particularly during the summer);

You should also bear in mind the following pitfalls that await anyone purchasing property abroad:

- Unexpected renovation and restoration costs (if you don't do your homework);
- The risk of overpaying for a home and being unable to sell it and recoup your investment;
- The possibility of over-stretching your finances (e.g. by taking on too large a mortgage);
- The heavy workload associated with owning a large home and garden;
- The expense of getting to and from Italy if you don't live in a nearby country (or a country with good air connections).

BUYING FOR INVESTMENT

In recent years, Italian property has been an excellent investment, particularly in Tuscany, Umbria, the Italian Riviera (Liguria), and the major cities such as Florence, Milan, Naples, Rome and Venice, where prices have risen fastest. There are various kinds of property investment. Your family home is an investment, in that it provides you with rent-free accommodation. It may also yield a return in terms of increased value (a capital gain), although that gain may be difficult to realise unless you trade down or move to another region or country where property is cheaper. Of course, if you buy property other than for your own regular use, e.g. a holiday home, you will be in a position to benefit from a more tangible return on your investment. There are four main categories of investment property:

- **A holiday home**, which can provide your family and friends with rent-free accommodation while (hopefully) maintaining or increasing its value; you may be able to let it to generate extra income.
- **A home for your children or relatives**, which may increase in value and could also be let when not in use to provide an income.
- **A business property**, which could be anything from a private home with bed and breakfast or guest accommodation to a shop or office.
- **A property purchased purely for investment**, which could be a capital investment or provide a regular income, or both. In recent years, many people have invested in property rather than shares or savings to provide an income on their retirement.

A property investment should be considered over the medium to long term, i.e. a minimum of five and preferably 10 to 15 years. Bear in mind that property isn't always 'as safe as houses' and investments can be risky in the short to medium term. You must also take into account income tax if a property is let (see property taxes on page 187). Capital gains tax is no longer payable in Italy, although you may be liable for income tax on any profit made if the property isn't your main residence (see page 229). You also need to recoup purchase costs of around 12 to 15 per cent when you sell (see **Fees** on page 127).

Before deciding to invest in a property, you should ask yourself the following questions:

- Can I afford to tie up capital in the medium to long term, i.e. at least five years?
- How likely is the value of the property to rise during this period?
- Can I rely on a regular income from my investment? If so, how easy will it be to generate that income, e.g. to find tenants? Will I be able to pay the mortgage if the property is empty and, if so, for how long?
- Am I aware of all the risks involved and how comfortable am I with taking those risks?
- Do I have enough information to make an objective decision?

When buying to let, you must ensure that the rent will cover the mortgage (if applicable), running costs and void periods (when the property isn't let). Bear in mind that rental rates and letting seasons vary with the region and town, and an area with high rents and occupancy rates today may not be so fruitful next year. Gross rental yields (the annual rent as a percentage of a property's value) are from around 5 to 10 per cent a year in most areas (although gross yields of 15 per cent or more are possible) and net yields (after expenses have been deducted) 2 to 3 per cent lower. Yields vary considerably with the region or city, and the type of property.

See also **Mortgages** on page 156, **Taxation Of Property Income** on page 187, **Location** on page 71 and **Chapter 9** (Letting).

CLIMATE

Italy generally has a temperate climate influenced by the Mediterranean and Adriatic seas, and the protective Alps encircling the north. The islands of Sicily and Sardinia and southern Italy enjoy a mild Mediterranean climate, as does the Italian Riviera. Italy has warm dry summers and relatively mild winters in most regions, although there's a marked contrast between the far north and the south of the country. Rome is generally recognised as the dividing point between the cooler north and the hotter southern regions. The best seasons throughout the country are spring and autumn, when it's neither too hot nor too cold in most regions.

Summers are generally very hot everywhere, with average temperatures in July and August around 24°C (75°F). Thunderstorms are common in inland areas. Summers are short and not too hot in alpine and the northern lake areas; the Po Valley has warm and sunny summers but can be humid. Summers are dry and hot to sweltering the further south you go (too hot for most people), although sea breezes alleviate the heat in coastal areas. In Rome and further south the *scirocco* wind from Africa can produce stifling weather in August with temperatures well above 30°C (86°F).

Winters are relatively mild in most areas, with some rainy spells. However, they're very cold (but usually sunny) in alpine regions, where snowfalls are frequent. The first snowfall in the Alps is usually in November, although light snow sometimes falls in mid-September and heavy snow can fall in October. The Alps shield northern Lombardy and the lakes area (including Milan) from the extremes of the northern European winter (although Turin is colder, for example, than Amsterdam). Fog is common throughout northern Italy from autumn through to February and winters can be severe in the Po Valley, the plains of Lombardy and Emilia Romagna.

Venice can be quite cold in winter (it often snows there) and it's often flooded (*acqua alta*). Florence is cold in winter, while winters are moderate in Rome, where it rarely snows. The Italian Riviera and Liguria experience mild winters and enjoy a Mediterranean climate, as they're protected by both the Alps and the Apennines. Sicily and southern Italy have the mildest winters, with daytime temperatures between 10ºC and 20ºC (50ºF and 68ºF).

Rainfall is moderate to low in most regions and is rare anywhere in summer. The northern half of the country and the Adriatic coast are wetter than the rest of Italy. There's a lot of rain in the central regions of Tuscany and Umbria in winter, although they suffer neither extreme heat nor cold most of the year. There's a shortage of water in many areas during summer, when the supply is often turned off during the day and households are limited to a number of cubic metres per year.

Average daytime maximum/minimum temperatures in Centigrade (and Fahrenheit) for selected cities are shown below.

Weather forecasts (*previsioni del tempo*) are broadcast on television and radio and published in daily newspapers.

Earthquakes

Italy is susceptible to earthquakes and volcanic eruptions (see **Geography** on page 41). There has been a government campaign in recent years to inform people and allay their fears about earthquakes,

although it has probably had the opposite effect! Officially, some 3,000 towns (out of a total of 8,000) are under constant threat from earthquakes. These contain some 10m homes, at least two-thirds of which aren't earthquake-proof (even those that are supposedly 'earthquake-proof' often aren't). See also **Natural Phenomena** on page 75.

The regions most at risk from earthquakes are Calabria, Friuli-Venezia Giulia, Marche and Sicily. The area extending from Tuscany to Basilicata (with the exception of Puglia) has a medium to high risk, while all other regions are low to medium or low risk.

ECONOMY

When you're contemplating buying a property abroad, the financial implications of the purchase are usually one of your main considerations. These include the state of not only the Italian economy, but also that of your home country (or the country where you earn your income). The state of the economy in your home country (and your assets and job security there) may dictate how much you can afford to spend on a property, whether you can maintain your mortgage payments and the upkeep of a property, and how often you can afford to visit Italy each year.

City	Average Temperatures High/Low ºC (ºF)			
	Spring (April)	Summer (July)	Autumn (Oct)	Winter (Jan)
Brindisi	18 (64)/11 (52)	29 (84) 21 (70)	22 (72)/15 (59)	12 (54)/6 (43)
Cagliari	19 (66)/11 (52)	30 (86)/21 (70)	23 (73)/15 (59)	14 (57)/7 (45)
Milan	18 (64)/10 (50)	29 (84)/20 (68)	17 (63)/11 (52)	5 (41)/0 (32)
Naples	18 (64)/9 (48)	29 (84)/18 (64)	22(72)/12 (54)	12 (54)/4 (39)
Palermo	20 (68)/11(52)	30 (86)/21(70)	25 (77)/16 (61)	16 (61)/8 (46)
Rome	19 (66)/10 (50)	30 (86)/20 (68)	22(72)/13 (55)	11 (52)/5 (41)
Venice	17 (63)/10 (50)	27 (81)/19 (66)	19 (66)/11(52)	6 (43)/1 (34)

For example, in 2002 and early 2003, the German recession meant that many prospective German property owners could no longer afford to buy in Italy and numerous property owners were unable to travel as often as they wished, and interest rate increases in the UK in 2007 deterred some potential British buyers. Your home country's economy is also important if you plan to retire to Italy and will be primarily living on a pension.

If you intend to live and work in Italy, or more importantly, plan to run a business, the state of the Italian economy will be a major consideration. Italy's economy has traditionally been one of the world's strongest, but in recent years growth has been slow (around 2 per cent in 2006). There are several serious problems facing the country's economic situation, including chronic public debt, political fragmentation and large differences in wealth between regions. Although privatisation has boosted the state coffers, successive governments have failed to make the most of the profits. Small and medium-size enterprises are the backbone of the Italian economy, and the government is establishing high-tech areas (mainly in Sicily) with some success in an attempt to modernise the economy.

Italy adopted the Euro in 2002, along with 11 other EU countries, and European Central Bank (ECB) interest rates. Although the general perception was that inflation was rampant in the year following the change-over, officially it was 3 per cent, and in 2007 it was under 2 per cent.

COST OF PROPERTY

One of the major considerations for anyone contemplating buying a home in Italy is whether they can afford to buy there and, if so, what kind of home can they afford and where? Foreign buyers have traditionally been attracted by the relatively low cost of property compared with many

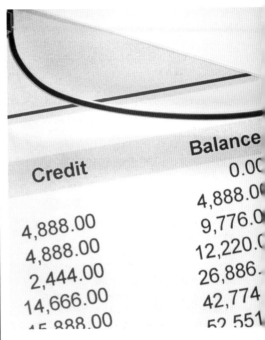

other European countries, particularly in rural areas. However, prices have risen considerably in the last few years, particularly in the cities and regions such as Tuscany, and property in the most popular areas is no longer the bargain it once was, which can come as quite a shock to newcomers.

Nevertheless, property in Italy remains good value compared with many other countries, particularly rural properties with a large plot, although (with the exception of remote areas, mostly in the south) there are few bargains left. A slice of *la dolce vita* needn't cost the earth, with habitable cottages and terraced village homes available from around €125,000, modern apartments from around €175,000 and large country homes from €300,000. If you're seeking a home with a large plot and a swimming pool, however, you will need to spend at least €600,000 (depending on the area); for those with the financial resources the sky's the limit, with luxury apartments in

Rome and Venice, and villas on the Italian Riviera costing from at least €1m. For more details of property prices, see page 107.

If you're seeking a holiday home and cannot afford to buy one outright, you may wish to investigate a scheme that provides sole occupancy of a property for a number of weeks each year rather than buying a property. Schemes available include part-ownership, leaseback and timesharing (see **Timeshare & Part-Ownership Schemes** on page 127).

☑ SURVIVAL TIP

Don't rush into any of these schemes without fully researching the market and before you're absolutely clear what you want and what you can realistically expect to get for your money.

COST OF LIVING

No doubt you would like to try to estimate how far your Euros will stretch and how much money (if any) you will have left after paying your bills. Inflation in Italy in mid-2007 was around 2 per cent and the country has enjoyed a relatively stable economy in recent years. Salaries are generally reasonable and Italy has a high standard of living, although the combined burden of social security, income tax and indirect taxes make Italian taxes among the highest in the EU.

Anyone planning to live in Italy, particularly retirees, should take care not to underestimate the cost of living, which has increased considerably in the last decade. Italy is a relatively expensive country by American and even British standards, and is one of the most expensive in the EU, although there's a huge disparity between the cost and standard of living in the prosperous north and central regions of Italy, and those in the relatively poor south.

The cost of living in Italy's major cities is much the same as in cities in the UK, France and Germany. Luxury and quality products are expensive, as are cars, but wine and spirits are inexpensive. However, you should be wary of cost of living comparisons with other countries, which are often wildly inaccurate and usually include irrelevant items which distort the results.

Food costs almost twice as much in Italy as it does in the US, but is similar overall to most other western European countries, although you may need to modify your diet. Around €500 will feed two adults for a month, excluding fillet steak, caviar and alcohol (other than a moderate amount of inexpensive beer or wine). It's possible to live frugally in Italy if you're willing to forego luxuries and live off the land. Shopping for selected 'luxury' and 'big-ticket' items (such as stereo equipment, electrical and electronic goods, computers, and photographic equipment) abroad can also yield significant savings.

It's difficult to calculate an average cost of living in Italy, as it depends on an individual's circumstances and lifestyle. In the Mercer Cost of Living Survey 2007 (🖥 www.mercer.com/costofliving) of the world's 143 most expensive cities, Milan was the highest ranked Italian city at number 11 and Rome was in 18th place. Some other rankings included London (2nd), Hong Kong (4th), Paris (13th), New York (15th), Dublin (16th), Madrid (26th), Athens (29th), Glasgow (36th), Munich (39th), Birmingham, UK (41st), Los Angeles (42nd) and Brussels (44th).

Somewhat surprisingly, Italian cities don't rate highly in international quality of life surveys; for example, in the Mercer Human Resource 2007 Quality of Living survey of the 50 top cities in the world, Milan was the only Italian city ranked, in 49th place.

PERMITS & VISAS

Before making any plans to buy a home in Italy, you must ensure that you will be permitted to use the property when you wish and for whatever purpose you have in mind. This includes ensuring that you have the required permits and visas. While foreigners are freely permitted to buy property in Italy, most aren't allowed to remain in the country longer than three months per year without an appropriate permit or visa, which may limit your enjoyment of a holiday home.

If there's a possibility that you or a family member will wish to work or live permanently in Italy, you should ensure that this will be possible before making any plans to buy a home there (see also **Working** on page 30).

☑ **SURVIVAL TIP**

Italy is a very, very bureaucratic country – among the worst in the western world (if not the worst) – and, despite the fact that it's a member of the EU, the documentation necessary (even for EU nationals) to work or live there is pernicious. It can take many months to obtain a residence or work visa.

Immigration is a sensitive issue in Italy and in recent years the country has been flooded with refugees and illegal immigrants (*clandestini*) from Africa, Eastern Europe (particularly Albania, Turkey and the former Yugoslavia) and Asia (particularly China). Italian immigration laws change frequently and new legislation may alter some of the information contained in this chapter. You shouldn't base any decisions or actions on the information contained herein without confirming it with an official and reliable source, such as an Italian consulate. Permit infringements are taken seriously by the authorities and there are penalties for breaches of regulations, including fines or even deportation for flagrant abuses.

When in Italy, you should always carry your passport, permit to stay or residence permit (if you have one); these serve as an identity card (*carta d'identità*), which Italians must carry by law. Foreign residents can obtain an identity card from their local registry office. You can be asked to produce your identification papers at any time by the Italian police or other officials and, if you don't have them, you can be taken to a police station and interrogated.

VISITORS

European Union (EU) nationals don't require a visa for stays of up to 90 days. Citizens of the following countries don't require a visa for stays of between 30 and 90 days depending on the country (check with your local Italian embassy or consulate): Andorra, Argentina, Australia, Benin, Bolivia, Bosnia-Herzegovina, Brazil, Burkina Faso, Canada, Chile, Colombia, Costa Rica, Croatia, Ecuador, El Salvador, Fiji, Guatemala, Guyana, Honduras, Iceland, Israel, Ivory Coast, Japan, Kenya, (South) Korea, Latvia, Liechtenstein, Macedonia, Malaysia, Maldives, Mexico, Monaco, New Zealand, Nicaragua,

Niger, Norway, Paraguay, Samoa, San Christopher and Nevis, San Marino, Singapore, Switzerland, Togo, Trinidad and Tobago, Uruguay, the USA and Venezuela. **All other nationalities require a visa to visit Italy for any period.**

Citizens of many EU countries can visit Italy with a national identity card, while others require a full passport. However, while identity cards are accepted at all points of entry to Italy, the Italian authorities may not accept them when applying for a permit to stay. If you're an EU national and wish to remain in Italy for longer than 90 days, it's therefore highly recommended to enter with a full passport.

Italy is a signatory to the Schengen treaty (named after the small town in Luxembourg where the original seven members signed the treaty), along with 14 other countries (Austria, Belgium, Denmark, Finland, France, Germany, Greece, Iceland, Italy, Luxembourg, the Netherlands, Norway, Portugal, Spain and Sweden). The Schengen countries issue a new kind of visa for visitors, called the 'Schengen visa' (see 🖳 www.eurovisa.info/ SchengenCountries.htm), which allows the holder to move freely between Schengen countries.

To obtain a Schengen visa, you must hold a passport or travel document recognised by all the Schengen member states, and valid for at least three months beyond the validity of the visa. You can apply for a Schengen visa, which is valid for 90 days within a six-month period, from the consulate of the country that's your main destination or the one you intend to visit first. A visa application guide (in English, Chinese and Spanish) is available online (🖳 www.schengenvisa.cc/download_application.html).

A Schengen visa isn't the appropriate visa if you wish to remain in a member state, including Italy, for longer than 90 days, study, take up employment or establish a trade or profession (see **Visas** below). If you wish to stay longer than 90 days, you must obtain an extension of your visa from the local police headquarters, although this isn't a right and cannot be taken for granted (you need a good reason and proof of financial resources) and must obtain a permit to stay (see page 32). However, if your passport hasn't been stamped (which is likely, particularly for EU nationals), the authorities have no way of knowing when you entered the country, so the system is 'flexible'.

Italian immigration authorities may require non-EU visitors to produce a return ticket and proof of accommodation, health insurance and financial resources. When you stay with friends in Italy (rather than, for example, at a hotel or campsite) for longer than three days, you're officially required to register with the local police, although in practice few short-stay visitors comply with this. Failure to register is punishable by a fine of up to around €220.

EU nationals who visit Italy to seek employment or start a business have 90 days in which to find a job or apply for a

permit to stay (see page 32), although if you haven't found employment or have insufficient funds, your application will be refused. If you're a non-EU national, it isn't possible to enter Italy as a tourist and change your status to that of an employee, student or resident, and you must return to your country of residence and apply for the appropriate visa.

VISAS

EU nationals don't require visas for visits to Italy, but require a permit to stay (see page 32) if they plan to remain longer than 90 days. Non-EU nationals need a 'residence visa' (*visto per ragioni di dimora*) to enter Italy with a view to staying longer than 90 days and may need one for a visit of a shorter duration (see **Visitors** above). Application should be made at an Italian consulate abroad well in advance of your planned departure date. Visas may be valid for a single entry only or for multiple entries within a limited period. A visa is in the form of an adhesive sticker (not a stamp) inserted in your passport, which must be valid until at least three months **after** the visa expires.

Visas are issued for a multitude of reasons, each of which has its own abbreviation (*sigla*). These include tourism (A), business (B), religion (C), diplomatic service (D), domicile (DM), joining family (F), dependent work (L-1), self-employment (L-2), artistic work (L-3), medical care (M), mission (MS), study (S), sporting activity (SP), re-entry (R), transit (T), airport transit (TA) and visiting family (V).

Non-EU nationals who plan to take up residence in Italy without working (e.g. retirees and those of independent means) may apply for an 'elective residence visa' (*residenza elettiva*). However, elective residence visas are awarded by Italian consulates at their discretion and, although no minimum amount of income is stated, non-EU nationals with capital over

€250,000 and property owners in Italy stand a far greater chance of being granted a visa than those with less capital and no property. If you're granted an elective residence visa, you must report to the local police within eight days of your arrival in Italy to be issued with a permit to stay (see below).

The type of visa issued depends on the purpose of your visit and the length of your stay, and determines the type of permit to stay that's issued after you arrive in Italy.

☑ **SURVIVAL TIP**

If you plan to stay in Italy for longer than six months, you must ensure that you obtain a visa that's valid for at least a year; otherwise you'll be able to obtain a permit to stay (see page 32) for only six months and won't be able to renew it..

Some of the documentation you may need to apply for a visa, mainly concerning permission to work, must be obtained in Italy. Although your prospective employer normally handles this on your behalf, your presence in Italy can help to speed up the process. If you plan to open a business or work freelance, you must also register at the local tax office (*intendenza di finanza*) and chamber of commerce (*camera di commercio*) or professional registrar (*albo dei professionisti*), and present the documents from these agencies together with your visa application. This can be a costly and time-consuming process, as once the documentation is obtained you must return to your country of residence to apply for the visa. Nevertheless, it may be worthwhile if you want to ensure that you have all the necessary documents to obtain your visa and permits to stay and work.

Another reason you may decide to visit Italy to obtain documents in connection with a visa application, is simply to obtain proof that you've been in Italy. This evidence may be important, as the Italian government is continually changing the immigration laws. For example, a law passed by the Italian government in October 1998 included a remedy clause (*sanatoria*) stating that all non-EU citizens who could prove their presence in Italy before 27th March 1998 could apply for a permit to stay without having to obtain a visa from their country of residence. This wasn't the first time a new immigration law included this kind of clause, nor will it be the last.

Having obtained the necessary paperwork, an application for a visa must be made to your local Italian consulate with jurisdiction over your place of residence. It may be possible to make an application by post, but in other cases you're required to visit in person. If you decide to apply in person (or have no choice), bear in mind that there are invariably long queues at consulates in major cities (take a thick book).

Proof Of Financial Resources: Proof of financial resources or financial support may take the form of bank statements, letters from banks confirming arrangements for the regular transfer of funds from abroad, or letters from family or friends guaranteeing regular support. Letters should be notarised. Students may submit a letter from an organisation or institution guaranteeing accommodation or evidence of a scholarship or grant. Retirees should take their pension book or copies of recent pension cheques. Proof of financial resources isn't required by someone coming to Italy to take up paid employment.

PERMITS TO STAY

All foreigners (*extracomunitari*) planning to remain in Italy for longer than 90 days must apply for a 'permit to stay' (*permesso di soggiorno* or *carta di soggiorno*) at the local police headquarters (*questura*) within eight days of their arrival.

The latest immigration law (passed in October 1998) changed the name of permits to stay for EU citizens from *permesso di soggiorno* to *carta di soggiorno*, even though the substance of the permit has remained the same. However, this isn't common knowledge and not all local police headquarters are aware of the change in name. Don't be surprised, therefore, if you apply for a *permesso di soggiorno* and receive a *carta di soggiorno* or vice versa. To avoid confusion, the more commonly used term, *permesso di soggiorno*, is used throughout this chapter to refer to all types of permits to stay.

☑ **SURVIVAL TIP**

A permit to stay *isn't* a residence permit (see page 33), which must be applied for after you have your permit to stay, if you wish to become a formal resident.

It can take up to three months to obtain a permit, which can be issued only for the purpose stated in your visa. There are many types of permit to stay, including the following:

● *Permesso di soggiorno per turismo* – for tourists. Technically anyone visiting Italy for over a week who isn't staying in a hotel, boarding house or an official campsite should apply for one, although in practice this rarely happens;

● *Permesso di soggiorno per lavoro* – a work permit for an employee (see **Working** below);

● *Permesso di soggiorno per lavoro autonomo/indipendente* – for independent or freelance workers;

- *Permesso di soggiorno per dimora* – for foreigners establishing residence in Italy who don't plan to work or study (see **Retirement** below).

RESIDENCE PERMITS

Obtaining your permit to stay (see above) doesn't constitute residence. To obtain registration as a resident (*residenza anagrafica*) you must apply to the registry office (*ufficio anagrafe*) at your local town hall (*comune*). To obtain a residence permit (*certificato di residenza*) you require a 'suitable' address. Although all addresses are potentially suitable for residence, some rental contracts forbid you to use an apartment's address for this purpose. Such rental contracts are mainly used with foreigners, so that landlords can regain possession of their property more easily should they wish to do so. Eviction of any person from their legal residence is almost impossible in Italy, and landlords don't want to take any unnecessary risks with foreigners.

A residence permit for an EU national is valid for at least five years and is automatically renewable, while a student's permit is valid for one year only, but is renewable. Members of your family are issued with a residence permit for the same period as the principal applicant. A residence permit remains valid, even if you're absent from Italy for up to six months, or you're doing military service in your country of origin. If you change residence within Italy, you must declare it at the police headquarters of your new residence within 15 days of moving home. Your new address is entered on your residence permit.

Unlike most other EU countries, anyone staying in Italy for longer than 183 days per year **isn't** legally required to apply for residence. However, despite the hassles, having the right of residence (*il diritto di soggiorno*) entitles you to:

- ship your personal effects from abroad without paying duty or VAT;
- buy land or property;
- buy and register a car;
- open a resident's bank account;
- apply for a driving licence;
- obtain an identity card (*carta di identità*);
- obtain health care from the local health authority;
- send your children to a state school.

If you're officially resident, you pay considerably lower taxes when you purchase a property intended as your main residence. When you're resident in Italy (with a residence permit), you must provide a 'certificate of residence' for certain transactions, such as converting your driving licence and obtaining a residential electricity contract.

WORKING

If there's a possibility that you or any family members may want to work in Italy, you must ensure that it will be possible before buying a home. If you're a national of an EU member country (your passport must show that you have the right of abode in an EU country), you don't require official approval to live or work in Italy, although you still require a permit to stay (*permesso di soggiorno per lavoro*).

A non-EU national wishing to work in Italy requires an 'entry visa for reasons of work' (*visto d'ingresso per motivi di lavoro*), which you must obtain in your home country or country of residence, and an authorisation to work issued by the local Department of Labour office (Ispettorato Provinciale del Lavoro) where the business is registered. This must, in turn, be authorised by the local police headquarters, who stamp it *nulla osta* (literally 'nothing hinders') on the back. This document must be obtained by your prospective employer in Italy and be sent to you in your country of residence for presentation at an Italian consulate with your other documents. Be warned, however, that for non-EU nationals, obtaining authorisation to work is a highly bureaucratic and time-consuming process. It can take a year or more, and unless you're employed by an Italian company in your home country or are already living in Italy, it's rare to find an employer in Italy who's willing to go to the trouble involved.

Italy has restrictions on the employment of non-EU nationals, which were strengthened in the late 20th century due to the high unemployment rate (around 9 per cent in 2003, falling to 7 per cent in 2006). The 1998 Immigration Law introduced a quota system, which restricts the number of freelance people of any nationality and category allowed into the country each year. Uncertainty in the interpretation of the new rules, especially in consulates abroad, is making it difficult and long-winded for foreigners to work in Italy legally. However, thousands of non-EU nationals are being employed due to a severe shortage of semi-skilled and skilled workers in the north (the north-east in particular). Employers are putting pressure on the government for immigration quotas to be handled by the regions, according to local employment needs, while the politicians would prefer to create jobs for southern Italians.

Before moving to Italy to work, you should dispassionately examine your motives and credentials and ask yourself the following questions:

● What kind of work can I realistically expect to find in Italy?

● Are my qualifications and experience recognised in Italy?

● Are there jobs in my profession or trade in the area where I wish to live?

● How good is my Italian? Unless your Italian is fluent, you won't be competing on equal terms with Italians (you won't anyway, but that's a different matter). Most Italian employers aren't interested in employing anyone without, at the very least, an adequate working knowledge of Italian.

The answers to these and many other questions can be quite disheartening, but it's better to face them **before** moving to Italy than afterwards. While hoping for the best, you should plan for the worst and have a contingency plan and sufficient funds to last until you're established.

Many people turn to self-employment or start a business to make a living, although this path is strewn with pitfalls for the newcomer. See *Living and Working in Italy* (Survival Books) for information. Many foreigners don't do sufficient homework before moving to Italy.

RETIREMENT

Retired and non-active EU nationals don't require a visa before moving to Italy, but an application for a permit to stay (*permesso di soggiorno per dimora*) must be made within eight days of your arrival. Non-EU nationals require an 'elective' residence visa (*residenza elettiva*) to live in Italy for longer than 90 days (see page 31). All non-employed residents must prove that they have an adequate income (*reddito*) or financial resources to live in Italy without working. You're usually considered to

have adequate resources if your income is at least equal to the basic Italian state pension of around €8,000 per year for each adult member of a family (although you're unlikely to be able to live on it!). This can be a regular income such as a salary or pension, or funds held in a bank account. When you make your visa application, you should include evidence of income, including bank statements, annuities and pensions.

All foreign residents (including EU residents) who don't qualify for medical treatment under the Italian national health service (*servizio sanitario nazionale/SSN*) must have private health insurance, and be able to support themselves without resorting to state funds. EU nationals in receipt of a state pension are usually eligible for medical treatment under the *SSN*, but require form E-121 from their home country's social security administration as evidence.

If you're an EU national and have lived and worked in Italy for over three years,

you're entitled to remain there after you've reached retirement or re-retirement age, although if you retire before the official retirement age you won't be entitled to a state pension.

LANGUAGE

Although Italian is the national language of Italy, large minorities speak German (in Alto Adige), French (in the Val d'Aosta), Slovene and Ladino. There are also some 600 regional dialects, many of which are difficult or impossible to understand (e.g. Neapolitan and Sicilian), even for fluent Italian speakers. Sardinian is virtually a separate language and has more in common with Catalan (the language of Catalonia in Spain) than Italian.

Standard Italian (*italiano standard*) is, however, taught in all state schools and almost everyone can understand it (although elderly people may know only their regional dialect). French is widely understood and English is spoken in the major cities and tourist centres. The ability to speak English confers prestige in Italy and anyone with a smattering (most waiters) are keen to show it off. However, English isn't spoken as widely in Italy as in many other European countries, particularly in the south of the country, and you shouldn't expect to find English speakers in rural areas.

Unlike the French, Italians appreciate any attempt to speak their language, however tortured. Italian is a relatively easy language to learn (if that can ever be said of any language!), as it's pronounced exactly as it's written – although Italians often express themselves with their hands! It has many similarities to French and Spanish (with which it shares many words) and you will have a head start if you can speak either of these languages. Even the most non-linguistic (and oldest) person can acquire a working knowledge of Italian.

All that's required is a little hard work and some help and perseverance.

If you don't speak Italian fluently, you may wish to enrol in a language course. If you want to make the most of your time in Italy, you should start learning Italian as soon as possible, i.e. before you buy a home there. For people living in Italy permanently, learning Italian isn't an option but a necessity, particularly in areas where little or no English is spoken.

Your business and social enjoyment and success in Italy will be directly related to the degree to which you master Italian.

You won't just 'pick it up' (apart from a few words), but must make an effort to learn. Teaching Italian is a huge business in Italy, with classes offered by language schools, Italian colleges and universities, private and international schools, foreign and international organisations, town councils, cultural associations, vocational training centres, clubs and private teachers. Tuition ranges from introductory courses for complete beginners, through specialised business or cultural courses to university-level courses leading to recognised diplomas.

There are many language schools (*scuole di lingua*) throughout Italy offering a wide range of classes depending on your language ability, how many hours you wish to study a week, how much money you want to spend and how quickly you wish to learn. Language classes roughly fall into the following categories:

Category	Hours Per Week
Standard	Up to 20
Intensive	20 – 30
Total immersion	40+

The cost of a one-week (40 hours) total immersion course is from around €200, depending on the school. Courses vary in length from four months to a year and can be attended either in small groups or individually. Many language schools also offer a variety of other courses, ranging from translation and interpreters' courses to business, cooking, literature and history of art. Schools offer a variety of language diplomas (including their own internal qualifications), but only a few offer the *Certificato d'italiano come Lingua Straniera (CILS)* qualification, which is recognised as an entry-level, Italian-language qualification for non-EU students wishing to study at Italian universities.

A quicker, though more expensive, way to learn Italian is to have private lessons. Italy has the highest number of teachers in Europe and, because they're also among the worst paid, there's no shortage of people prepared to give private lessons. Depending on where you live in Italy, there's a wide variation in rates, from around €15 per hour in some central and southern regions to €35 or more per hour in Rome and Milan with a qualified teacher. Good places to look for a suitable teacher or to place an advertisement include local newspapers, and university and public notice boards. Friends, neighbours and colleagues may be able to recommend a teacher. In some areas, the local youth advisory service (*Informagiovani*) provides free conversation classes for foreign students.

A guide to many language schools, institutions and organisations offering Italian-language tuition is provided by the Associazione Scuole di Italiano come Lingua Seconda (ASILS), Ufficio di Presidenza, Via Fiorentina 36, 1 – 47021 Bagno di Romagna (☎ 0942 23441, ⌨ www.asils.it) and from the Italian Cultural Institute in many countries, including the UK (39 Belgrave Square, London SW1X 8NX, UK, ☎ 020-7235 1461, ⌨ www. icilondon.esteri.it).

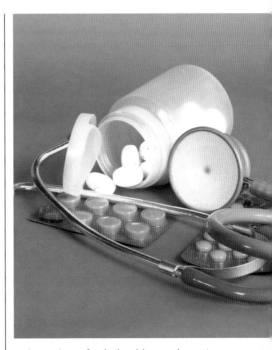

A number of scholarships and grants are available from the Universities for Foreigners in Sienna and Perugia, and some private language schools in Italy for foreign students wishing to attend short-term language courses. For information, contact the cultural sections of Italian embassies abroad. A good directory of Italian-language schools is available via the internet (⌨ www.it-schools.com), covering most regions of the country and with links to many schools.

HEALTH

One of the most important aspects of living in Italy (or anywhere else for that matter) is maintaining good health. The Italians are generally healthy and have one of the highest life expectancies in Europe (around 83 for women and 77 for men). The incidence of heart disease in Italy is among the lowest in the world, a fact attributed in part to their healthy Mediterranean diet (which includes lots of fresh fruit and vegetables, garlic, olive oil and red wine), as is the incidence of cancers. However, the country has a high incidence of smoking-related health problems – the percentage of smokers in Italy is among the highest in the EU – and liver (*fegato*) problems as a result of too much alcohol are also fairly common.

There are no special health risks in Italy and no immunisations are required unless you arrive from an area infected with yellow fever. Babies are issued with a vaccination record (*libretto delle vaccinazioni*) and children must have certain vaccinations in order to attend school. You can safely drink the water (unless there's a sign to the contrary, e.g. *acqua non potabile*), although it sometimes tastes awful. Many people prefer bottled water (when not drinking red wine, which tastes much better!).

The most prevalent health problems among expatriates include sunburn and sunstroke, stomach and bowel problems (due to the change of diet and more often, water, but also caused by poor hygiene), and various problems caused by excessive alcohol consumption (including a high incidence of alcoholism). Other health problems are caused by the high level of airborne pollen in spring in some areas (which particularly affects asthma and hay fever sufferers), and noise and traffic pollution, particularly in Italy's major cities.

If you aren't used to Italy's hot sun, you should limit your exposure and avoid it altogether during the hottest part of the day, wear protective clothing (including a hat) and use a sun block. Too much sun and too little protection will dry your skin and cause premature ageing, to say nothing of the risks of skin cancer. Care should also be taken to replace the natural oils lost from too many hours in the sun, and the elderly should be particularly careful not to exert themselves during hot weather.

Italy's largely mild climate is therapeutic, particularly for sufferers of rheumatism and arthritis and those prone to bronchitis, colds and pneumonia. Italy's slower pace of life is also beneficial for those who are susceptible to stress (it's difficult to remain uptight while taking a *siesta*), although it often takes foreigners some time to adjust. The climate and lifestyle in any country has a marked affect on mental health, and people who live in hot climes are generally happier and more relaxed than those who live in cold, wet climates (such as northern Europe).

☑ **SURVIVAL TIP**

The quality of healthcare and healthcare facilities in Italy varies from poor to excellent depending on the town/city and the region, and whether you have private health insurance.

Italian doctors and other medical staff are well trained; the best Italian doctors are among the finest in the world (many pioneering operations are performed in Italy), as are the best hospitals. On the other hand, the worst public hospitals are among the poorest in the EU. There's a stark contrast between public and private health facilities in Italy, which has a disintegrating public health service that's over-stretched and under-funded, particularly in Rome and southern regions (where corruption is rife).

Hospital facilities are limited in some areas, particularly the south, and nursing care and post-hospital assistance in Italy are well below what most northern Europeans and North Americans take for granted. There are usually long waiting lists for specialist appointments and non-urgent operations. Italy's provision for disabled travellers is also poor, and wheelchair access to buildings and public transport is below average for Western Europe.

Not surprisingly, healthcare costs per head in Italy are among the lowest in the EU and the country spends a relatively small percentage of its GDP on health. Nevertheless, Italy's national health service (*servizio sanitario nazionale/SSN*) provides free or low cost healthcare to residents and their families, plus university students and retirees (including those from other EU countries). The public health service provides free hospital accommodation and treatment, medical tests and specialist consultations, and pays up to 90 per cent of the cost of prescription medicines, most of which cost around €20. The *SSN* pays for 75 per cent of out-patient and after-care treatment, and provides limited dental treatment. Many medical expenses can be totally or partially deducted for tax purposes, including the cost of spectacles, hearing aids and visits to medical specialists, therefore you should retain all medical receipts.

Newcomers who earn money in Italy must register with their local Azienda di Sanità Locale (ASL), often referred to under their previous name, Unità Sanitaria Locale (USL), and obtain a national health number as soon as possible after their arrival (you will receive a health card or *tessera sanitaria*). ASLs can provide a list of local doctors, public health centres and hospitals. You will need to register with a doctor (*medico convenzionato*).

The country has comparatively few dentists per head of population and treatment can be astronomically expensive (patients also need to be wary of unnecessary treatment). There are English-speaking and foreign doctors in resort areas and major cities.

If you don't qualify for healthcare under the public health service, it's essential to have private health insurance (in fact, you won't usually get a residence permit without it), although free emergency treatment is usually available for the uninsured. Visitors to Italy should have holiday health insurance (see page 237) if they aren't covered by a reciprocal arrangement.

If you're a retired EU national planning to live permanently in Italy, you need form E121. EU citizens who retire early before qualifying for a state pension can receive free health cover for two years by obtaining form E106 from their country's social security department. If the temporary cover expires before you reach retirement age, you must make voluntary social security contributions or take out private health insurance (see page 237).

It's possible to have medication sent from abroad, when no duty or value added tax is usually payable. If you're visiting a holiday home in Italy for a short period, you should take sufficient medication to cover your stay. In an emergency a local doctor will write a prescription that can be filled

at a local chemist's or a hospital may refill a prescription from its own pharmacy. It's also wise to take some of your favourite non-prescription medicines (e.g. aspirins, cold and flu remedies, lotions, etc.) with you, as they may be difficult or impossible to obtain in Italy or be much more expensive. If applicable, take spare spectacles, contact lenses, dentures and a hearing aid with you.

When you've had a surfeit of Italy's good life, a variety of health 'cures' are available at spas (*terme*) and health farms, which are also of benefit to those who suffer from arthritis and similar health problems (treatment is partly paid for by the national health service).

Health (and health insurance) is a particularly important issue for anyone retiring to Italy. Many people are ill-prepared for old age and the possibility of health problems.

There's a shortage of welfare and home-nursing services for the elderly in Italy, either state or private, and foreigners who are no longer able to care for themselves are often forced to return to their home countries.

There are few state residential nursing homes in Italy or hospices for the terminally ill, although there are a number of private, purpose-built retirement developments.

PETS

If you plan to take a pet (*animale domestico*) to Italy, it's important to check the latest regulations. Make sure that you have the correct papers, not only for Italy, but for all countries you will pass through to reach Italy. Particular consideration must be given before exporting a pet from a country with strict quarantine regulations, such as the UK. If you need to return prematurely with a pet to a country with strict quarantine laws, even after a few hours in Italy, your pet must go into quarantine, e.g. for six months in the UK.

In March 2000, the UK introduced a Pet Travel Scheme (PETS), which replaced quarantine for qualifying cats and dogs. Under the scheme, pets must have a microchip inserted in their neck, be vaccinated against rabies, undergo a blood test and be issued with a health certificate ('passport') confirming that all the foregoing have been carried out. **Bear in mind that the PETS certificate may not be issued until months later.** The scheme is restricted to animals imported from rabies-free countries and countries where rabies is under control – around 25 European countries plus Bahrain, Canada, the USA and others.

The microchip, rabies vaccination and blood test costs pet owners around £200/€300, plus £60/€90 a year for annual booster vaccinations and around £20/€30 for a border check. Shop around and compare fees from a number of veterinary surgeons. To qualify, pets must travel by sea via Dover, Plymouth or Portsmouth, by train via the

Channel Tunnel or via Gatwick or Heathrow airports (only certain carriers are licensed to carry animals).

British pet owners must contact their Local Animal Health Office to obtain an Application for a *Ministry Export Certificate for Dogs, Cats and Rabies Susceptible Animals* (form EXA1). Contact details are available via the Pet Travel Scheme run by the Department for Environment, Food and Rural Affairs (DEFRA), Animal Health (International Trade) Area 201, 1A Page Street, London SW1P 4PQ, UK (☎ 0870-241 1710, 🖳 www.defra.gov. uk/animalh/quarantine). The completed form should be sent to DEFRA at the above address. DEFRA will contact the vet you've named on the form and he will perform a health inspection. You will then receive an export health certificate, which must be issued no more than 30 days before your entry into Italy with your pet.

A maximum of five pets may accompany travellers to Italy. A rabies vaccination is usually required, although this doesn't apply to accompanied pets (including dogs and cats) coming directly from the UK or for animals under three months old. A rabies vaccination is necessary if pets are transported by road from the UK to Italy via France. If a rabies vaccination is given, it must be administered not less than a month or more than 12 months prior to export. There's generally no quarantine in Italy but, if a pet has no rabies certificate, it can be quarantined for 20 days.

A health inspection must be performed by a licensed vet (*veterinario*) before you're issued with an export health certificate (bilingual, Italian-English) that's valid for 30 days after stamping. Certificates can be obtained from Italian consulates abroad and can also be downloaded from Italian consulate websites. Animals may be examined at the Italian port of entry by a veterinary officer.

Some animals require a special import permit from the Italian Ministry of Agriculture, and pets from some countries are subject to customs duty. Parrots are subject to special restrictions. Further information is available from the Italian customs authorities (🖳 www.agenziadogane.it).

If you're transporting a pet to Italy by ship or ferry, you should notify the shipping company. Some companies insist that pets are left in vehicles (if applicable), while others allow pets to be kept in cabins. If your pet is of a nervous disposition or unused to travelling, it's best to tranquillise it on a long sea crossing. Pets can also be transported by air and animals are permitted to travel to most airports. A useful guidebook to hotels and guesthouses accepting dogs, *In Italia con cane e gatto* (Touring Club Italiano/TCI) is available from book shops. The French hotel chains Etap and Ibis accept visitors with pets.

At the age of three months, a dog must be registered at the local 'dog bureau' (*anagrafe canina*) and some municipalities issue dog tags. Italian regulations require dogs to be microchipped as a means of registration, which must be done by a veterinary surgeon. Dogs and cats don't need to wear identification discs in Italy and there's no system of licensing (a dog tax was abolished because most people claimed their dogs were working animals and refused to pay it!). However, it's wise to fit your dog with a collar and a tag containing your name, address and telephone number. Lost dogs are taken to the local pound, and unidentified dogs may be put down if the owner cannot be found.

Although Italy isn't exactly a nation of animal lovers (animals and birds are regarded as something to eat or shoot at), pets are rarely restricted or banned from long-term rental or holiday accommodation (but check when renting an apartment). However, all dogs must be kept on a leash and (if dangerous) muzzled in public areas in towns and on public transport; in some towns large dogs are prohibited from travelling on public transport. Where permitted, you must usually pay full fare on public transport for a dog that isn't carried (e.g. in a container).

If you intend to live permanently in Italy, dogs should be vaccinated against hepatitis, distemper and kennel cough, and cats immunised against feline gastro-enteritis and typhus. Pets should also be checked frequently for ticks and tapeworm.

⚠ Caution

There are a number of diseases and dangers for pets in Italy that aren't found in most other European countries, including the fatal leishmaniasis (also called Mediterranean or sandfly disease), which can be prevented by using sprays or collars.

Obtain advice about this and other diseases from a veterinary surgeon on arrival in Italy. In areas where there are poisonous snakes, some owners keep anti-venom in their refrigerator (which must be changed annually). Take extra care when walking your dog, as some have died after eating poisoned food, which is sometimes laid by hunters to control natural predators. Don't let your dog far out of your sight or let it roam free, as dogs are often stolen in Italy or mistakenly shot by hunters. Poop-scoops must be used in some cities and towns, where you can be fined €30 for not cleaning up after your dog, although most people ignore this law.

Health insurance for pets is available from a number of insurance companies (vets' fees are high in Italy) and it's wise to have third party insurance in case your pet bites someone or causes an accident.

The Ente Nazionale per la Protezione degli Animali (national association for the protection of animals) is the main organisation for animal welfare in Italy; it operates shelters for stray and abused animals, and inexpensive pet hospitals in many cities. A wealth of information (in Italian only) about pet welfare and health in Italy is available from the PetNews website (🖳 www.petnews.it).

Rome

Capri, Campania

2.

WHERE TO LIVE?

Having decided to buy a home in Italy, you must choose the region and what sort of home to buy. If you're unsure about where and what to buy, the best decision is usually to rent for a period (see page 99). You may be fortunate and buy the first property you see without doing any homework and live happily ever after. However, a successful purchase is much more likely if you thoroughly investigate the towns and communities in your chosen area, and compare the types and prices of properties and their relative values. It's a lucky person who gets his choice absolutely right first time; however, there's a much better chance if you do your homework thoroughly.

When choosing a location, take into account its popularity, which will greatly affect prices. Instead of Tuscany, for example, where prices are soaring, why not consider Emilia Romagna, the Marche or Piedmont, all beautiful regions (many would argue that they're as stunning as Tuscany), but without the inflated prices. If you're buying a holiday home, consider also the accessibility of a region or area from your home country, as well as local transport networks.

The 'best' place to live in Italy obviously depends on your preferences and it's impossible to specify the ideal location for everyone. The aim of this chapter is to identify the positive and possible negative aspects of each region in order to help you choose the region of Italy best suited to you and your family.

GEOGRAPHY

Italy covers an area of 301,245km² (116,319mi²), slightly larger than the UK and around the same size as the USA state of Arizona, and comprises a long peninsula shaped like a boot. The country is 1,200km (750mi) in length and between 150 and 250km (93 to 155mi) in width. Italy has borders with France (488km/303mi), Switzerland (740km/460mi), Austria (430km/267mi) and Slovenia (199km/124mi), and encompasses two independent states within its borders: the Vatican City (47ha/116acres) in Rome, established in 1929, and the Republic of San Marino (61km²/24mi²) within the Marche region.

It's a land of stark contrasts, including towering mountains and vast plains, huge lakes and wide valleys. It has a wide variety of landscape and vegetation, but almost 80 per cent of the country consists of hills and mountains. Italy has two mountain ranges: the Alps and the Apennines. The Alps (*Alpi*) form the country's northern border stretching from the Gulf of Genoa (*Golfo di Genova*) in the west to the Adriatic

Sea (north of Trieste) in the east. The highest peak in the Italian Alps is Monte Rosa (4,634m/15,203ft) on the Swiss border. The Alps are divided into three main groups, western, central and eastern; the eastern group, known as the Dolomites (*Dolomiti*), are regarded by many to be the most beautiful and spectacular. The alpine foothills are characterised by the vast Po Valley and the lakes of Como, Garda and Maggiore.

The Apennines form the backbone of Italy, extending for 1,220km/758mi from Liguria near Genoa to the tip of Calabria and into Sicily. The highest peak in the Apennines is the Corno Grande (2,914m/9,560ft) in the Gran Sasso d'Italia range in Abruzzo. The Apuan Alps (*Alpi Apuane*) in the north-west of Tuscany form part of the sub-Apennines and are composed almost entirely of marble, which has been mined since Roman times. In the south (on the toe of the Italian 'boot') are the Gargano and Sila ranges.

Northern Italy has large areas of forest and farmland, while the south is mostly scrubland; lowlands or plains comprise less than a quarter of Italy's total land

mass. The largest plain is the Po Valley (bounded by the Alps, the Apennines and the Adriatic Sea), a heavily populated and industrialised area. The Po is Italy's longest river, flowing from west to east across the plain of Lombardy in the north into the Adriatic. Its tributaries include the Adige, Piave, Reno and Tagliamento rivers. Other major Italian rivers are the Tiber (Rome) and the Arno (Tuscany). A coastal plain runs along the Tyrrhenian Sea from southern Tuscany through Lazio into Puglia (Tavoliere delle Puglia), while another smaller plain is Pianura Campana near Mount Vesuvius. Italy has a number of great national parks, including Abruzzo in the Apennines and the Alpine Gran Paradiso between Val d'Aosta and Piedmont.

The country is surrounded by sea on all sides except in the extreme north and has a vast and varied coastline of some 8,000km (5,000mi), including its islands (see below). The Ligurian and Tyrrhenian seas bound the west of the peninsula; the Ionian Sea lies off the coasts of Puglia, Basilicata and Calabria in the south; and the Adriatic Sea in the east separates Italy from Slovenia. Coastal areas vary considerably, from the generally flat Adriatic coast to the dramatic cliffs of Liguria and Calabria. Coastal highlights include the Amalfi Coast (south of Naples), the crescent of Liguria (the 'Italian Riviera') and the Gargano Massif (the spur jutting into the Adriatic). Many coastal areas are in danger of being ruined by uncontrolled development and just 10 per cent of the country's coastline (800km/500mi) remains undeveloped.

The country has many islands, which include Sicily (*Sicilia*, situated across the Strait of Messina), the largest and most densely populated island in the Mediterranean, and the islands of Pantelleria, Linosa and Lampedusa between Sicily and Tunisia. The many small islands surrounding Sicily offer excellent opportunities for scuba-diving

and underwater fishing, as well as spectacular scenery. These include the Lipari group of islands (comprising Lipari itself plus Vulcano, Panarea and Stromboli), Ustica, Favignana, Levanzo, Marittimo, Pantelleria and Lampedusa. Italy's (and the Mediterranean's) second-largest island is Sardinia (*Sardegna*), situated in the Tyrrhenian Sea to the west of the mainland and south of the island of Corsica (France). It's the country's most sparsely populated region with a coastline of some 1,300km (800mi), and is one of Italy's most unspoilt regions.

Among Italy's most famous and attractive islands are Capri, Ischia and Procida in the Gulf of Naples, but the seven islands of the Tuscan archipelago (off the Maremma coast) are among the most appealing of all Mediterranean islands, and include Elba, Capraia, Pianosa, Montecristo, Gorgona, Giglio and Giannutri. The beautiful island of Elba (where Napoleon was exiled from May 1814 to February 1815) covers an area of 224km² (86mi²), two-thirds of which is woodland, and has some excellent sandy beaches. Other Italian islands include the virtually unknown (five) Pontine islands, some 32km (20mi) off the coast of Lazio.

Italy has a number of active volcanoes, including Mount Etna on Sicily (3,274m/10,741ft), Stromboli (on the Isle of Eolie off the west coast of southern Italy) and Vesuvius (near Naples). Etna (which started its latest eruptions in spring 2007) and Stromboli are among the world's most active volcanoes, while Vesuvius hasn't erupted since 1944. Italy is also susceptible to earthquakes; a European fault line runs through the centre of the country from north to south down to Sicily. The highest risk areas are in southern Italy, where some 70 per cent of the terrain is susceptible to earthquakes. The country's last major earthquake hit Messina and Reggio di Calabria in 1908 killing some 85,000 people. More recently there have been earthquakes

in Friuli (1976), Irpinia, south-east of Naples (1980), Umbria (1997, when more than 40,000 people were left homeless) and in Molise (2003).

> A map of Italy showing the major cities and geographical features, and the 20 regions and 110 provinces, are shown in Appendix E.

The regions are described below (the Italian names of the regions, where these differ from the English names, are given in brackets).

REGIONS

Abruzzo (*Abruzzi*)

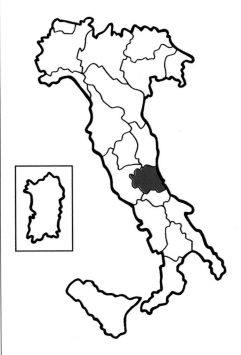

Abruzzo is situated in central Italy bordering Lazio to the west and with a long Adriatic coastline to the east. It contains the provinces of Chieti, L'Aquila (also the name of the capital city), Pescara and Teramo, and used to include Molise to the south, which became an independent region in 1963. The region covers an area of 10,794km² (4,168mi²). Abruzzo is a mountainous region with the highest mountains in central Italy, which are part of the Apennines that form the backbone of the region on the western side. The highest peaks are in the Gran Sasso group, where the Corno Grande reaches a height of 2,912m (9,551ft). The region contains three national parks: Gran Sasso-Laga, Maiella-Morrone, and the national park of Abruzzo, which is home to the endangered species of Marsican brown bears (which are unique to Italy), as well as wolves, deer, chamois, and many other mammals and birds.

Abruzzo is sparsely populated (1.3m people, with a density of 116 people per km²), due to its mountainous terrain and high emigration. However, its folk traditions endure through a myriad of rituals, festivals and pilgrimages, and the local dialect is still widely spoken. There has been an increase in prosperity in recent years thanks to state aid, new industry, and the harnessing of water power to create electricity. The area between Pescara and Chieti is the region's economic centre, with the highest per capita income in southern Italy and relatively low unemployment (around 8 per cent). Abruzzo has traditionally been dominated by a mountain economy and is noted for sheep farming – the migration of sheep towards the southern regions of Puglia and Lazio is a centuries old tradition. The region is also famous for its handicrafts. L'Aquila (which means 'The Eagle'), the region's capital, is a university city noted for its rich cultural life. It was founded in the 13th century by people drawn from 99 smaller centres, an event commemorated by a 99-spout fountain. In the 1400s, L'Aquila was the second most important city in the Spanish Kingdom of

Naples and is one of the smallest (and the youngest) capital cities in Italy.

The region contains a wealth of attractive historic towns, including Atri, Lanciano, Penne and Vasto, while other interesting towns include Chieti, Lanciano, Pescara, Scanno (noted for its traditional copperware), Sulmona (known for its sugar-covered almonds or *confetti*) and Teramo. Pescara (whose name comes from the word *pesca* meaning fishing, once the main activity of the area) is a popular holiday resort and the only city in the region with a population of over 100,000. Other resorts include Francavilla al Mare, Guilianova, Montesilvano, Roseto degli Abruzzi, Silvi Marina and Vasto. Roccaraso and Pescasseroli in the Simbruini mountains are popular ski resorts with Romans, but their long, cold winters and tortuous roads don't make them popular with foreigners.

Property

Traditional local architecture consists of roughly-built stone houses with small windows, usually built in groups on hillsides, while in towns severe stone *palazzi* are common. The price of old buildings in need of renovation is quite low compared with the rest of Italy,

although the region isn't popular among foreigners and entire abandoned villages can be purchased. Property prices start at €1,150 per m², although rural buildings for restoration are considerably cheaper.

Communications

Abruzzo has excellent communications, particularly with Rome due to the recent opening of the A24 motorway. The nearest international airport is Rome and there's a regional airport at Pescara (see **Airports** on page 80).

Basilicata (*Lucania*)

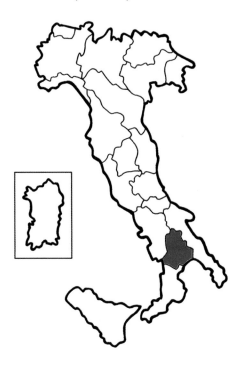

Basilicata contains the provinces of Matera and Potenza; the town of Potenza is the regional capital. It's the least-populated region of central and southern Italy and is one of the poorest and least developed regions of the so-called *Mezzogiorno*, with one of its lowest per capita incomes

and an unemployment rate of over 20 per cent. The population of Basilicata is around 610,000, and its area 9,991km² (3,858mi²). It has a harsh terrain consisting of rugged mountains (rising to over 1,800m/6,000ft in the west) between Calabria and Apulia, and coastlines on both the Tyrrhenian and Ionian seas.

The region's main economy is agriculture (mostly olives, livestock and sheep farming) and. although only some 8 per cent of the land is suitable for cultivation, 40 per cent of the population is employed in farming, often on tiny parcels of land. Agricultural workers outnumber industrial workers, although there has been a flourish of industrial development in recent years, which has brought some welcome prosperity. The production of arts and crafts for the tourism industry is also an important industry.

Basilicata has seen the widespread migration of its young to the north for many decades and consequently many villages (particularly those in inhospitable, mountain areas) are dying, inhabited almost exclusively by the elderly. The region is also noted for its widespread corruption, inefficiency and organised crime, and is susceptible to earthquakes.

The main city of Matera (60,000) is noted for the primeval beauty of its cave dwellings (*i Sassi*), which seem to grow from the surrounding tufo stone. These historic dwellings, where peasants used to sleep with their animals, are now protected and an increasingly popular property option, among both foreigners and Italians. *Sassi* prices start at around €1,300 per m². If a cave needs restoring, you will need to spend a further 50 per cent, but government grants are available for up to half the price of restoration, although the process and paperwork involved may try your patience!

Property

Basilicata isn't a popular tourist destination and is of little interest to foreign property buyers, although it may be ideal for those wishing to 'get away from it all'. Nevertheless, there are some splendid resorts on the two small strips of coast (such as Maratea on the Tyrrhenian coast), where there are few foreign property owners. Other resorts include Bagnara Calabra, Copanello, Diamante, Paola, Pizzo, Praia a Mare, Scalea, Scilla and Soverato. Interesting historic towns include Venosa, with its Roman and medieval remains, and Melfi, once a Norman stronghold. Property is cheap and prices start at €675 per m², rising to €1,350 per m² in Matera.

Communications

The region has poor rail and road communications with the rest of the country, although road links have improved in recent years. The nearest international airport is Naples and the nearest regional airport Bari (see **Airports** on page 80).

Calabria

Calabria (known as *Brutium* in Roman times) contains the provinces of Catanzaro, Cosenza and Reggio di Calabria. The regional capital is Catanzaro, founded by the Byzantines in the 9th and 10th centuries, while the city of Reggio di Calabria (the region's largest) has Greek origins. Other important towns include Cosenza, Crotone and Vibo Valentia. Calabria's population is around 2m and its area 15,077km² (5,822mi²); it's the southernmost region of the peninsula (the island of Sicily is further south). It's dubbed the 'blue and green' region and is the most unspoilt region of Italy, noted for its crystal clear seas that wash the deserted coastline.

Calabria forms the toe of the Italian boot and boasts magnificent coastlines (reflected in names such as the Costa Viola) on both the Ionic and Tyrrhenian seas, served by a coastal road and railway line. High mountains plunge into the sea, creating an intricate and varied coastline with a medley of small bays, long sandy beaches and lush vegetation. The mountainous interior is relatively inaccessible, with the Sila mountains in the north and the Aspromonte in the south, with its vast forests. The mountains offer superb scenery and many attractive villages (with houses of grey stone and terracotta roofs), where traditional handicrafts are produced. The national parks of Calabria and Pollino were created to protect the natural resources of the forests. Historic towns include Corigliano, Calabro, Castrovillari (a Swabian stronghold) and Rossano, the Greek settlements of Locri and Gerace, and the picturesque coastal town of Tropea.

The southern region of Italy consists largely of flat land and large fertile plains (less than 9 per cent of the land), where olive and citrus groves contrast with ugly industrial developments, such as those at Lamezia Terme.

Calabria is an impoverished region that saw mass overseas migration in the early

20th century, and to northern Italy and the rest of Europe in the '60s and '70s. The region has very high unemployment (around 25 per cent) and the lowest per capita income in Italy, although in recent years the economy has received a welcome boost from tourist developments on the coast.

⚠ **Caution**

Crotone and Reggio di Calabria have a frightening criminal reputation and kidnapping is commonplace. Due to the poor economy, organised crime (the local 'mafia' is known as the *Ndrangheta*) is rife, although foreigners aren't prime targets.

Property

Tourism is an important industry with coastal properties priced at about €1,850 per m² in Tropea and Scalea, two of the area's most sought-after resorts, although property isn't usually built to the same standards as in northern Italy.

Communications

The construction of a motorway link to the north and new railway lines has reduced the region's isolation and the it's increasingly popular with tourists, particularly Italians. Basic infrastructure such as hospitals and schools, however, is poor. There's a regional airport at Reggio di Calabria, although the nearest international airport is Palermo in Sicily (see **Airports** on page 80).

Campania

Campania (named *Campania Felix* by the Romans) contains the provinces of Avellino, Benevento, Caserta, Naples (*Napoli*) and Salerno. The city of Naples (population 1.1m) is the regional capital and, indeed, the unofficial capital of the whole of southern Italy. The population of Campania is around 5.8m in an area of 35,208km² (13,595mi²). Agriculture is an important local industry, employing around a quarter of the workforce; other important industries include livestock (e.g. buffalo for the production of mozzarella cheese), canning, textiles, and handicrafts such as leather, coral, inlaid wood and ceramics. The region has a high unemployment rate (around 25 per cent).

The area around Naples includes one of the most beautiful coastlines in Italy and the Gulfs of Naples, Salerno and Policastro are home to a number of world-famous resorts, including Positano, Ravello, Sorrento and Vietri sul Mare. Among Italy's most famous and attractive islands are Capri, Ischia and Procida in the Gulf of Naples. The Isle of Capri has been immortalised in song (as has the Bay of Naples) and the island of Ischia, with its thermal baths, including the Terme di Poseidon, is a favourite among northern visitors. Sorrento, famous for its lemon groves, is the largest and most popular Neapolitan resort.

The region is steeped in history and contains a wealth of Roman ruins, including Pompeii and Herculaneum in the shadow of Mount Vesuvius, whose eruption destroyed the towns in AD79. Their excavation provides a fascinating insight into how the ancient Romans lived. Other interesting towns include Padula (with its charterhouse), Sessa Aurunca, Santa Maria Cápua Vetere and Teano. The national parks of Cilento, Valle di Diano and Vesuvius were created in 1991 to protect areas of natural beauty from property speculators. The imposing Greek temples of Paestum in the south are among the best-preserved Greek architecture in the world and there's also a magnificent royal palace and park (rivalling Versailles) at Caserta.

Naples is famous for the vitality of its citizens, but also for corruption and the mafia (the *Camorra* is the Neapolitan branch of the mafia), although in recent years the city's administrators have tried to improve its image to attract more tourists. The city's extreme

poverty is the main reason for the high rate of petty crime (known as *microcriminalità*), such as thefts and purse-snatching. Naples is considered by many to be a 'third-world' city, infamous for its traffic congestion (said to be the worst outside Cairo) and outrageous driving habits.

Naples is also a major tourist centre, boasting splendid Greek and Roman art treasures, such as those in the Museum of Capodimonte, and a breathtaking natural setting. The 19th century phrase 'see Naples and die' (coined in the days of the Grand Tour) referred to its unique charm, not forgetting its poverty, overcrowding and crime. A quarter of Campania's population lives around Naples, a third of which is under 14. Among the city's traditions are its devotion to San Gennaro (the local patron saint) and to soccer (*calcio*).

Property

The property market is buoyant, although property on the islands in the archipelago of Capri, Ischia and Procida is prohibitively expensive, and little is available. On the Amalfi coast, prices start at €2,500 per m², while inland prices fall dramatically to as little as €750 per m². In stark contrast with the immaculately painted villas and *palazzi* in the wealthier resort areas, there are numerous half-abandoned villages in the interior, and an abundance of poorly-designed and shoddily-built apartment blocks dotted along the coast. The region is noted for its high risk of earthquakes and landslides, particularly on the overbuilt coast.

Communications

Naples is an important rail and road junction with good communications to the north and south. Its airport has frequent flights to Rome and Milan and internationally (see **Airports** on page 80), while the motorway south from Salerno to Reggio Calabria is toll-free in recognition of the region's poverty. The tiny island of Procida, held by the English navy in 1799, is connected by regular ferries to the mainland, as are the neighbouring islands of Capri and Ischia.

Emilia Romagna

Emilia Romagna contains the provinces of Bologna (also the name of the regional capital city), Ferrara, Forli, Modena, Piacenza, Parma, Ravenna, Reggio Emilia and Rimini. It's one of the country's largest regions with an area of 22,075km² (8,524mi²) and a population of 4.2m, and takes its name from the *Via Aemilia*, the ancient Roman road to Rome, and the Romagna, name of the former Papal State. The region has an outstanding artistic heritage dating from Etruscan, Roman, Byzantine and Renaissance times. Emilia Romagna encompasses the tiny Republic of San Marino on top of Mount Titano, famous nowadays for duty-free shopping, philately and its Formula 1 grand prix race.

Situated between Lombardy and Tuscany, Emilia Romagna is a rich and fertile region with many important industries. The northern area consists of a flat and featureless wheat prairie, while in the south are the foothills of the Apennines. The country's major river, the Po, forms a delta with the marshy area known as the Valli del Comacchio (famous for its eels) before emptying into the Adriatic. The intensely cultivated land is given over to large-scale farming, and Emilia Romagna is the country's main producer of grain, sugar beet, soft fruit, tomatoes, grapes and rice.

The capital city of Bologna (population 400,000) is a beautiful and proud city with outstanding Renaissance architecture, covered porticos and towers. It's known as '*La Dotta*' (the erudite) on account of its university, which was founded in 1088 and is one of the oldest in the world.

Bologna has a rich gastronomic heritage and claims the best cuisine in Italy, including pasta (tortellini, lasagne and fettuccini), mortadella, *prosciutto di Parma* (fine cured ham), parmesan cheese and Lambrusco wines. It's a lively, congenial, cultivated and relatively tourist-free city, although it's also one of Italy's most expensive places to live. A thriving industrial area surrounds Bologna and only some 3 per cent of the region's population is unemployed.

Parma has a Romanesque cathedral and baptistery, and a charming opera house with strong connections with Verdi, who lived at nearby Sant'Agata. Modena is home to the quintessentially Italian car manufacturer, Ferrari, and is noted for its fine cuisine, exquisite Romanesque cathedral and the Este Gallery. Ferrara has a number of fine palaces associated with the Este family, and Ravenna, with its many fascinating Romanesque buildings and mosaics, is the resting place of Italy's most famous poet, Dante. It was also the ancient capital of the Western Roman Empire during its decadence under Gothic and Byzantine domination. Small towns of interest include Carpi (known for works in scagliola – imitation stone or plaster mixed with glue), Cesena (home of the Malatesta dynasty), Comacchio, Correggio, Faenza (famous for ceramics) and Mirandola. The region contains a wealth of attractive historic town centres with arcaded streets, brick *palazzi*, cobbled plazas and splendid cathedrals.

The wide sandy beaches along the Adriatic coastline are home to number of thriving resorts, including Cattolica, Cervia, Cesenatico, Milano Marittima, Rimini and Riccione, popular with young Italians and foreigners.

Property

Property in the region costs from €2,300 per m² in Porto Ganbaldi to €4,250 per m² in Riccione-Terme, although in rural areas inland prices are lower. The region doesn't contain many derelict properties at bargain prices, as it has one of the highest standards of living in Italy, evidenced by the wealth of prestigious country properties with sky high prices (few of which come on the market).

Communications

Emilia Romagna has excellent road, rail and air links with the rest of Italy. Bologna has an international airport (see **Airports** on page 80) and is a major rail junction, with good rail and road links with the north and Rome.

Friuli-Venezia Giulia

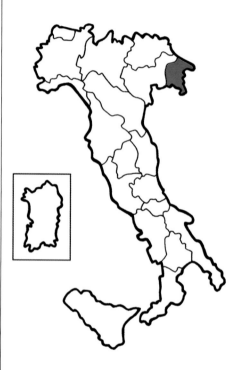

The region of Friuli-Venezia Giulia contains the provinces of Gorizia, Pordenone, Trieste (also the capital city) and Udine, covering an area of 7,844km² (3,029mi²) with a population of around 1.2m. It's situated in the north-east of the country bordering Austria and Slovenia to the north and east, the Adriatic to the south and the Veneto region to the west. Friuli was occupied by the Romans under Julius Caesar and is short for *Forum Iulii* or Julian Forum. The region was partitioned between

Italy and Yugoslavia in the aftermath of the second world war and its population is ethnically mixed – more middle European than Italian. The region is one of five in Italy accorded semi-autonomous status.

The mountainous north contains peaks as high as 2,750m (9,000ft) and is famous for the heroic first world war battles in Carso, Gorizia and Udine. There are some plains in the south around the coasts of the Gulf of Trieste, which are dotted with sandy beaches such as those at Grado and Lignano Sabbiadoro. The region is crammed with artistic treasures from the Roman, Byzantine and Romanesque-Gothic eras, and is one of the most cosmopolitan and culturally sophisticated in Italy. Among the many attractive cities of historic importance are Aquileia, with its Roman monuments and Byzantine mosaics, Grado ('golden island') with its elegant beaches, and Cividale dei Friuli, founded by Julius Caesar.

Trieste is the largest port on the Adriatic and was once the principal port of the Austro-Hungarian empire. It's a splendid, ancient city, designed on a grid pattern, with superb neo-classical 18th century architecture in the city centre (Borgo Teresiano) and some elegant Art Nouveau buildings. It occupies an idyllic setting on a promontory featuring Miramare castle and the nearby resorts of Sistiana and Duino. The German poet Rilke, the exiled Irish writer James Joyce and the Italian novelist Italo Svevo (Ettore Schmitz) were the initiators of Trieste's literary tradition, which continues to this day. Trieste is also an international centre for scientific research and education (the United World College).

The Friuli-Venezia Giulia region is noted for its San Daniele ham, wine production (Pinot and Refosco), grain, fruit orchards, dairy produce and livestock. Industries include shipbuilding at Monfalcone and Trieste, textiles, chemicals, cutlery,

forestry, furniture, and lead and zinc mining. The reconstruction after a devastating 1988 earthquake gave a huge boost to the local economy, and the reconstruction funds were wisely used to modernise industry. Unemployment is around 5 per cent.

Udine has the highest rainfall in Italy and winters in Trieste are noted for some very cold days with strong winds known as the *bora*. In contrast, summers are mild and pleasant, without the very high temperatures found in many other regions. In a recent survey Udine was voted the best place to live in Italy.

Property

Property is reasonably priced and in the towns often features pretty Venetian architecture, while stone chalets with slate roofs are common in the mountains. On the Lagoon of Marano there are traditional fishermen's houses built of reeds with cone-shaped roofs, which are sometimes let for rustic holidays. Prices range from €1,025 to €2,900 per m², depending on location.

Communications

The region's communications are good: ferries leave from Trieste for the southern Adriatic and Greece, motorways link Trieste with Milan, Turin and Venice, and there's a rail link with Austria via the Tarvisio Pass and an international airport in Trieste (see **Airports** on page 80).

Lazio (*Latium*)

Village, Cinque Terre, Liguria

(and capital of Italy) is Rome, where over half of Lazio's population (2.7m) is concentrated. Situated in the centre of the peninsula, Lazio has borders with all five regions of central Italy, plus Campania in the south. Its coastline is washed by the Tyrrhenian Sea and crossed by the River Tiber, while to the east are the high peaks of the Abruzzi. Lazio has pretty rolling hills, gracious villas, walled hill towns, vineyards, olive groves and hazelnut orchards. Some three-quarters of the population is employed in the service sector, particularly tourism and work connected with the central government. Agriculture also thrives and is an important industry in the hinterland around Rome and the south towards Latina. Unemployment is around 10 per cent.

The region of Lazio contains the provinces of Frosinone, Latina, Rieti, Rome (*Roma*) and Viterbo, and covers an area of 17,224km² (6,651mi²) with a population of 5.3m. The regional capital

Rome (the 'eternal city') is built on seven hills and was the unofficial capital of Christianity and the seat of the Papal States long before it became the capital of a united Italy in 1870. It's one of the world's great historic cities, with a wealth of monuments and buildings from Roman times to the Renaissance and Baroque periods. Other reasons for visiting Rome are its plethora of parks, fountains, and priceless art treasures, such as those housed in the Vatican museum. Romans are famous for their *joie de vivre*. A sage once said that 'every day you spend in Rome adds a year to your intellectual life' and the city attracts people from around the globe.

Rome has the second-largest number of foreign residents in Italy after Milan, which is reflected in the number of schools, activities, and associations for foreigners.

Many new hotels were built for the Holy or Jubilee Year of 2000, although it's becoming increasingly difficult to find reasonably priced accommodation within easy reach of the centre. Unfortunately the days of *la dolce vita* (as portrayed in Fellini's celebrated film of that name) are long gone and Rome is heavily polluted by traffic fumes, which have degraded the quality of the city's air and life.

Hill towns in the Castelli area (where Romans go for Sunday excursions) include Castel Gandolfo (the Pope's summer residence), Frascati (famous for its wine), Genzano, Rocca di Papa and Tivoli (site of Hadrian's Villa and the Villa d'Este, with its famous fountains immortalised by Liszt). Seaside resorts to the south include Anzio, Circeo, Gaeta, Sabaudia, San Felice, Sperlonga, Terracina and the island of Ponza (accessible by hydrofoil from Formia). The Pontine islands, Ponza and Ventotene lie 32km (20mi) off the coast and are served by a summer ferry service from Anzio (a town made famous by the Allied landings in 1943 during WWII).

North of Rome are Santa Marinella and Santa Severa, and the inland lakes of Bolsena, Bracciano and Vico, much loved by English and German expatriates. In the Tuscia-Viterbese area, the towns of Cerveteri, Tarquinia and Tuscania, and the stone necropolis of Norchia near Vetralla are reminders of the mysterious Etruscan people who once inhabited this area. Viterbo's medieval quarter is the best preserved in Europe. This area is slowly but surely being discovered by foreigners (Tuscia has been dubbed 'Tusciashire', just as Chianti has been called 'Chiantishire'), many of whom prefer it to Tuscany on account of its relatively low property prices and proximity to Rome. Other interesting towns in the region include Agnani, Caprarola (with its magnificent Palazzo Farnese), Civitavecchia (the busy port of Rome), Ferentino and historic Palestrina.

Property

The region's architecture is typified by the many fortified hill towns with their tall, narrow houses built of grey peperino stone and tufo rock. Property prices are highest in the areas surrounding Rome, as many Romans commute from the coast or have weekend retreats in the countryside. Prices in Rome have risen considerably over the last decade and properties in the city cost from €4,000 to €10,000 per m², although prices are considerably cheaper on the outskirts. The Aventino, Cassia, EUR, Flaminia and Parioli areas are favoured by foreigners for their proximity to international schools, and quality apartments in these areas run from €3,150 to over €6,500 per m².

Communications

As you would expect, Lazio has a good network of roads (all of which lead to Rome!), and excellent rail and air links with other regions and internationally (see **Airports** on page 80).

Liguria

The region of Liguria contains the provinces of Genova, Imperia, La Spezia and Savona and has a population of some 1.6m, 90 per cent of whom live on the coast (which puts a huge strain on the infrastructure). The capital is Genoa (*Genova*) with a population of over 600,000. Liguria is one of Italy's smallest regions, covering an area of 5,417km² (2,092mi²) but extending the entire length of the coast of the Ligurian Sea, from the French border to Tuscany, with one of the steepest and most dramatic coastlines in Italy. It's noted for its mild year-round climate and natural beauty.

The coastal area is known as the Italian Riviera and is a holiday playground for the world's rich and famous. It actually consists of two Rivieras: the Riviera di Ponente to the west of Genoa and the Riviera di Levante, the more cosmopolitan and glamorous, to the east. The Gulf of La Spezia (with Lerici and Portovenere) is known as the 'gulf of poets' in memory of Byron and Shelley, who lived and died there. It's famous for the beautiful resorts of Cinque Terre and Sarzana, while further up the coast are Camogli (with its pastel houses), Chiavari, Portofino (which has a perfect harbour), Rapallo, San Fruttuoso and Santa Margherita. Few tourists venture into the interior, which is dotted with beautifully preserved medieval villages that have maintained their charm and peaceful character. Among the many historic towns worth a visit are Albenga and Ventimiglia, where there's a famous market.

The coastal strip from Genoa to the French border is an area of great beauty, although it's overdeveloped and overrun with tourists in some parts. It was made popular by the British (who built the magnificent Hanbury Gardens) and Russian émigrés in the 1920s, attracted by the best climate in northern Italy, sheltered from the cold eastern winds by the Maritime Alps and the Ligurian Apennines.

Genoa is the largest industrial zone and port in Italy, and is flanked by Savona and La Spezia and their large commercial ports. Genoa is rich in culture and history, and was the birthplace of Christopher Columbus and one of the five great maritime republics of Italy in the 13th century. The port area, which had become run down, has recently been renovated and new attractions constructed, including a magnificent aquarium.

The architecture of Liguria is typified by attractive turn-of-the-century villas, often with pastel plastered walls or *trompe l'oeil* paintings.

Agriculture is limited to olive groves, vineyards and flowers, particularly in the Riviera dei Fiori (Riviera of Flowers) area

Riomaggiore, Liguria

around Diano Marina, San Remo (famous for its song festival and casino) and Alassio, where flower nurseries are a major business and roses bloom all winter. These are favourite holiday destinations, with both summer visitors and retirees in winter.

Property

Property is expensive along the coast, but homes in inland villages are reasonably priced. The market is sharply divided around Genoa, the western part of Liguria offering much cheaper properties along the narrow coastal plain, while the eastern half has sky high prices in its rocky coastal villages. Prices on the Italian Riviera have risen considerably in recent years, and the resorts of Levanto and San Remo are very expensive, although less so than the equivalent on the French Riviera further to the west. Prices range from between €2,500 and €4,500 per m² for a quality apartment with a view in a top resort such as Portofino. In the Cinque Terre villages, prices can be as high as €5,000 per m².

Communications

Liguria is served by Nice (France) and Genoa airports (see **Airports** on page 80),and also has excellent road and rail connections.

Lombardy (*Lombardia*)

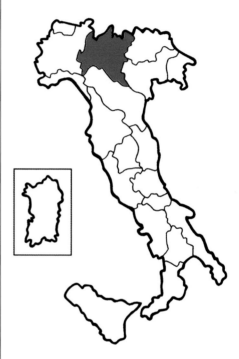

Lombardy is situated in the north of Italy (bordering Switzerland) and contains the provinces of Bergamo, Brescia, Como, Cremona, Mantua (*Mantova*), Milan (*Milano*, also the region's capital city), Pavia, Sondrio and Varese. It's one of Italy's largest regions, covering an area of 23,854km² (9,211mi²) with a population of 9.48m. Lombardy is an important commercial region and the industrial heartland of Italy, the area around Milan producing some 40 per cent of Italy's GDP. One of the main industries is textiles, particularly silk (Como) and wool (Biella), while Milan is the country's financial centre and its wealthiest city (with its most expensive property and highest cost of living).

Geographically, Lombardy is the most varied region in Italy with the vast alluvial plain of the River Po (Italy's longest river) valley in the south, and gently rolling hills rising to the dramatic peaks of the Alps in the north, interspersed with the famous lakes of Como, Garda, Maggiore and d'Iseo. The lakes area is popular for both principal and holiday homes, and their stunning backdrop of mountains has inspired composers, painters and writers for generations, including Rossini, Shelley, Verdi and Wordsworth. In the mountains are numerous ski resorts, including Alta Badia, Cervinia, Cortina, Courmayeur, Gressoney, Livigno, Madonna di Campiglio, Ponte di Legno, Sestrére, La Thuile and Val Gardena.

Among the most attractive lake towns are Bellagio, which has a breathtaking setting on Lake Como, Desenzano, Gardone Riviera, Limone sul Garda (where a special micro-climate creates winters mild enough for wine production and botanical gardens), Salò and Sirmione. It's a favourite area with retirees, as the hills protect the lakefront from northern winds.

Milan (population 1.3m) is the financial and economic centre of Italy, and also the heart of its communications and fashion industry. It's renowned for its rich cultural life and numbers among its many attractions the Brera gallery, Leonardo's famous fresco of the Last Supper in the church of Santa Maria delle Grazie, the La Scala opera house, Sforzesco Castle, and a myriad of museums and galleries. Milan is one of Italy's foremost shopping cities with a wealth of elegant (and expensive) shopping streets such as the Galleria and Via Montenapoleone. The symbol of Milan is the imposing Gothic cathedral (the third-largest in Europe) with its Madonnina set amid a forest of spires, pinnacles and flying buttresses. Milan is also noted for its cuisine and boasts some of Italy's best restaurants, where one can try the local *risotto alla milanese*. Milan has the highest foreign population in Italy.

Other fine cities in Lombardy include Bergamo, Brescia, Crema, Mantua (*Mantova*), Monza (with a royal villa and famous Formula One racetrack) and Vigevano, each with its own unique character. Tourists and residents alike are attracted to Stelvio national park and popular mountain resorts such as Aprica, Bormio, Caspoggio, Chiesa, Livigno, Madesimo, Ponte di Legno, Santa Caterina, Stelvio and Valfurva.

Property

Property in Lombardy is among the most expensive in Italy, particularly in Milan (with its wealth of *palazzi* with elegant patio-courtyards), where prices start at around €7,500 per m², the lakes area and the more fashionable ski resorts, such as Cortina. As these prices suggest, property in Lombardy is in high demand among foreign buyers, who, some years, buy as much as 10 per cent of property in the region. With the opening of a new motorway, the towns of Arona, Baveno, Stresa and Verbania are now within 45 minutes of Milan and have seen increasing numbers of Milanese buying principal homes. Prices here are around €1,500 per m² for homes in need of restoration and €1,900 to €3,150 per m² for restored properties.

Communications

Lombardy is served by two international airports in Milan (Linate for some European flights and Malpensa for inter-continental flights and some European flights – see **Airports** on page 80) and has superb road and rail connections, both nationally and internationally.

A new motorway has brought the towns of Arona, Baveno, Stresa and Verbania within 45 minutes of Milan (see **Property** above).

Marche

Marche, Pennabilli

The region of Marche contains the provinces of Ancona (also the name of the regional capital city), Ascoli Piceno, Macerata and Pesaro. The region's population is around 1.55m, mostly concentrated along the coast and in the main valleys, in an area of 9,693km² (3,743mi²). Situated between Umbria and the Adriatic coast, Marche is little known to most foreigners and one of Italy's best kept secrets. The landscape is reminiscent of Tuscany with lush vegetation, rolling hills and charming hill towns such as Urbino, home to the painter Raphael with its Ducal Palace of the Montefeltro dynasty. Other interesting towns include Ascoli Piceno (with a magnificent main square surrounded by porticos), Camerino (a tiny university town), Fano, Fabriano (famous for its paper and salami), Fermo,

Jesi, Loreto (with its famous sanctuary), Macerata, Pesaro (with a fine historic centre), Recanati (home of the poet Leopardi), San Leo and Tolentino.

Marche has a long Adriatic coastline with high cliffs along the Conero Riviera, wide sandy beaches and many attractive resorts, which include Civitanova, Fano, Gabicce, Pesaro, Porto Recanati, San Benedetto del Tronto and Senigallia. The region is famous for its excellent coastal fish restaurants, white Verdicchio wine and, in Ascoli Piceno, stuffed *olive all'ascolana*. Marche is one of Italy's most attractive regions, with friendly people, an unhurried pace of life and stunning landscapes (the national park of Monti Sibillini is a walker's paradise). Once poor, it now enjoy a relatively high standard of living due to recent industrialisation, low unemployment and little crime.

Property

The local architecture includes gracious *palazzi*, white stone farms and cottages, and a wealth of attractive villages with interesting architecture. Relatively expensive apartments are common on the coast, whereas prices for property in the remote hinterland are quite reasonable. It's possible to buy rural property in need of renovation, but access is often poor due to the dearth of sealed roads and other services. In the countryside of Camerino, Osimo or Urbino, a farmhouse requiring restoration costs from €950 per m² (much less than in Tuscany or Umbria), while on the coast you can expect to pay between €1,600 and €3,600 per m² for an apartment in a popular resort such as Senigallia or Sirolo. Bargains, however, can still be found, both on the coast and inland.

Communications

Communications are good along the coast, which is served by the A14 motorway, but poor inland due to the Apennine mountains and a series of parallel valleys that make it difficult to travel east-west. A railway line runs along the coast and there's a regional airport at Ancona (see **Airports** on page 80).

Molise (*Molize*)

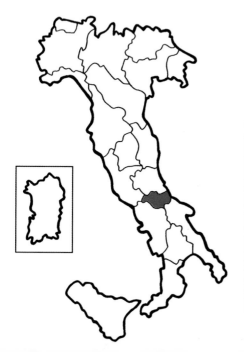

Valley, Molise

Molise, which until 1963 was part of Abruzzo, contains just two provinces: Campobasso (also the name of the regional capital city) and Isernia, which still bears the scars of a 1984 earthquake. Molise covers 4,439km² (1,714mi²) and has a population of around 320,000. It's a poor and backward area with a high unemployment rate where the orderliness of the north and the poverty of the south meet. Its traditions, customs and dialects are influenced by Croatia and Albania, its neighbours across the Adriatic. Agriculture and livestock are the main industries in the wide river valleys, which are cultivated with grains, cereals, grapes, fruit and potatoes, although most land is too steep for farming. There are some cottage and food processing industries near the port of Termoli and natural gas has recently been discovered in the region.

Property & Communications

Molise is isolated from the main paths of communication and isn't a popular area among foreign property buyers, for either permanent or holiday homes. The only good road and rail links are along the coast, which is served by the Bologna-Taranto motorway and the Bologna-Lecce railway. The nearest international and domestic airport is Naples (see **Airports** on page 80).

Piedmont (*Piemonte*)

Piedmont (the name means the land at the foot of the mountains) contains the provinces of Alessandria, Asti, Cuneo, Novara, Turin (*Torino*, also the name of the regional capital city) and Vercelli. The region has an area of 25,398km² (9,807mi²) and some 4.4m inhabitants, mostly concentrated in the densely populated industrial plains. Historically, Piedmont was the fountain-head of Italian unity at the time of the Risorgimento under the Savoy family and boasts elegant baroque architecture, excellent

cuisine (Turin is noted for its chocolate and sweets) and wines, including Barolo, Barbera, Barbaresco, Asti Spumante, Cinzano and Martini. Langhe, a pretty hilly region south of the Po, is famous for its wines, truffles and gastronomy.

> Along with Val d'Aosta, Piedmont is the least Italian region of Italy, where educated people have traditionally spoken French. Most people also speak the Piedmontese dialect, which has a poetic tradition.

Piedmont is similar in character and climate to its neighbour Lombardy: surrounded by the Alps with vast flat plains, through which flows the River Po. It's a land-locked region but shares Lake Maggiore with Lombardy. Among the region's many resort towns are Arona, Stresa and Verbania, while Orta San Giulio on Lake Orta and Viverone on the lake of the same name are picture paradises. The southern zone includes the provinces of Alessandria, where Borsalino hats are made, and Vercelli, a rice-growing area.

Piedmont is part of the industrial triangle formed by Genoa, Milan and Turin and an important economic centre with relatively low unemployment. The region's major industries are car manufacturing in Turin (FIAT), textiles, wool and clothing (notably high fashion, particularly in the Biella area).

Turin (population 1m) is a noble and elegant city with fine shops and important museums, and is dominated by the FIAT conglomeration, which has its headquarters there. It's a relatively wealthy, cosmopolitan city with wide boulevards reminiscent of Paris, although it lacks the charm and sophistication of many of Italy's other major cities. Turin's many historic palaces, such as Superga

smaller towns are generally good value. In recent years, the purchase of wine estates has become popular among foreign buyers, although whether they make a success of their wine remains to be seen!

Communications

The region has excellent communications and is well served by international trains, motorways and the international airports of Turin, Genoa (Liguria) and Milan (Lombardy – see **Airports** on page 80).

Puglia (*Apulia* or *Le Puglie*)

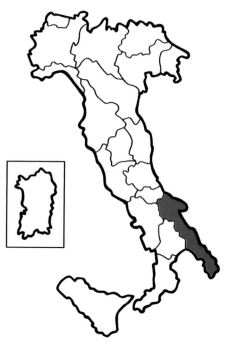

and Stupinigi (which Juvarra designed for the Savoy family), contrast with Art Deco buildings and elegant modern villas with surrounding parklands. Turin is also a centre of pilgrimage, as it's the home of the Holy Shroud (*Sacra Sindone*), the cloth in which Christ's body was reputedly wrapped when removed from the cross. Situated near the Alps, Switzerland and the Italian Riviera, Turin is less polluted than Milan.

Piedmont contains many winter sports resorts (mainly in the north-west), including Claviere, Sauze d'Oux and Sestriere, and the Gran Paradiso national park on the border with Val d'Aosta, where the rare ibex can be found.

Property

The architecture is varied, with grey stone houses with slate (*ardesia*) or stone tiled roofs in mountainous areas. A property at Sauze d'Oux costs around €2,500 per m², while in Sestriere the same home may be as much as €4,500 per m². The Langhe area is more reasonably priced, and houses in

Puglia contains the provinces of Bari (also the name of the regional capital city and now a chic resort), Brindisi, Foggia, Lecce and Taranto. It covers an area of 19,356km² (7,474mi²) with a population of some 4.1m. Puglia forms the heel of the Italian boot, jutting into the Ionian and Adriatic Seas towards Albania and forming the Gulf of Taranto to the west. The original inhabitants were probably from Illyria and Greece, and Hannibal and Frederick II were just two of the many invaders who passed through and left their mark (Puglia's ports were also stopping off points for the Crusaders in the Middle Ages). More recent 'invaders', who are claimed to have caused an increase in crime in the region, include Albanian and Kurdistan refugees, who frequently (literally) wash up on the shores of Puglia.

The region has low rainfall and chronic water shortages and therefore only crops resistant to drought are successful. An adequate water supply is essential in this region. The huge Tavoliere plateau near Foggia is a rich grain-growing plain producing around half of Italy's durum wheat (for pasta); other important crops include olives, of which Puglia supplies around half the country's needs, almonds and grapes (for wine). There's some heavy industry at Bari, Barletta, Brindisi and Taranto, but the region has a high unemployment rate.

The Gargano peninsula in the north-east has a steep, rocky coastline and peaks rising to around 1,000m (over 3,000ft); it encompasses a national park, where wooded crags thrust into the sea towards the tiny Tremiti Islands. Here lie the historic sanctuary of Monte San Angelo, attractive towns such as Peschici and Vieste, and tourist amenities such as the holiday villages at Pugnochiuso. The impressive grottos or Caves at Castellana are a major tourist attraction, as are the 13th century fortress of Castel del Monte in Andria and the marine grotto of Polignano.

Property

The cities of Bari, Brindisi, Foggia, Lecce and Taranto contain superb examples of Baroque and Romanesque architecture.

Unique local forms of architecture include white-washed houses with dark conical roofs known as *trulli*, which are found only in Alberobello, and isolated, walled country farmsteads (*masserie*).

Traditional country and coastal properties include attractive, whitewashed cube-shaped houses. In general, property is reasonably priced except in the centre of cities; centrally-located property in Ostuni or Vieste costs from €1,250 to €2,250 per m², although prices in Barletta rise to €2,750 per m². The property market is currently buoyant, although foreign buyers are thin on the ground, and the few that venture this far south tend to favour Brindisi, Gargano and Lecce.

Communications

A motorway and railway line run along the Adriatic coast, but connections to the west are difficult due to the Apennine mountains. The region's main domestic airports are Bari and Brindisi (see **Airports** on page 80). Regular ferries to Greece and the former Yugoslavia operate from Brindisi and Otranto.

Sardinia (*Sardegna*)

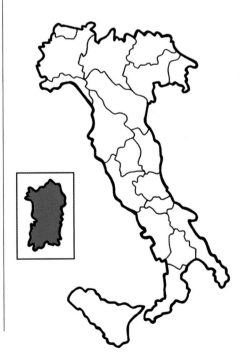

Sardinia contains the provinces of Cagliari (the regional capital), Nuoro, Oristano and Sassari. The island's rich and colourful history dates back to the time of the Phoenicians. It was later a Roman colony, and was also invaded in turn by Ostrogoths, Byzantines, Vandals, Saracens and Normans (1061), later becoming part of the maritime republics of Pisa, Genoa and the Aragonese. From 1718, Sardinia was ruled by the house of Hohenstaufen, the Piedmontese house of Savoy and finally became part of a united Italy. Some of the towns reflecting this patchwork history are Iglesias (Pisa republic), Bosa (Spanish), Alghero (Catalan), Castelsardo (Genoa republic) and Carloforte (Piedmontese).

Sardinia is the second-largest island in the Mediterranean (after Sicily), 267km (166mi) long and 120km (75mi) wide, covering an area of 24,090km² (9,302mi²), situated just 6.5km (4mi) from Corsica (France) across the Strait of Bonifacio. The island is noted for its rugged mountain terrain, which reaches a height of 1,833m (6,017ft) on Monti Gennargentu. Its inhabitants (the population is 1.66m) consider it to be a tiny continent rather than an island, as it contains a huge variety of geography, despite its small area. Within a few hours' drive of Porto Cervo are landscapes similar to the Seychelles, an 'African' desert, 'Australian' beaches, prehistoric sites and modern areas reminiscent of North America.

It's Italy's most sparsely populated region with (unusually) the largest concentration of people in the interior, where traditional, sheep-rearing communities have largely ignored the 1,287km (800mi) coastline until fairly recently. Sardinians are a proud and traditional people, and there are five different dialects on the island, reflecting its varied history. Sardinia is largely undeveloped with problems similar to those of southern Italy, such as low investment, poor services and communications, high unemployment (around 20 per cent), low incomes and a high crime rate (including frequent incidences of kidnapping). There's some industry in Cagliari, Nuoro and Porto Torres, but the economy is mainly based on sheep-rearing and tourism – over a million Italians visit the island in the summer months.

Water shortages are commonplace, and the island has high levels of radon gas (see page 76).

Property

Property on the island is generally considered to be a very good investment and Sardinia is expected to become one of the most popular places to purchase property in Italy in the future. Many foreigners purchase homes here for the breathtaking, mountainous landscape, the sea of varying colours, the beaches of fine white sand and rocky coves, and the excellent food. There are charming resorts in the south, such as Santa Margherita di Pula, Capo Boi and Villasimius, where property prices start at €1,800 per m².

At the top end of the scale, the resorts on the Costa Smeralda in the north-east are among the most exclusive in the Mediterranean, and a popular playground of Europe's rich and famous.

This exclusive area with its golf courses, marinas and elegant villas was developed by the Aga Khan in the '70s and boasts prices in Porto Rotondo and Porto Cervo of millions of Euros for its elegant villas. Elsewhere the architecture is simple stone houses, and the city and town architecture has little of the flair common on the mainland.

Communications

Sardinia is 200km (124mi) from mainland Italy, with which it has regular air connections (see **Airports** on page 80), and is served by ferries from Genoa, Civitavecchia (the port of Rome, from where a fast ferry reaches the island in three hours), Naples, Palermo, Tunisia and France. It's the only region of Italy without any motorways, although most roads are of good quality.

Sicily (*Sicilia*)

with a wealth of remarkable architecture, particularly Norman and Baroque. It was the most important Carthaginian colony in the Mediterranean for five centuries and Palermo's 700,000 inhabitants have an enduring bond with its ancient traditions. Other major cities include Catania, with a population of around 300,000, Messina, a modern city entirely rebuilt after being destroyed by an earthquake in 1908, and the ancient city of Agrigento with its magnificent Greek temples.

The island has witnessed successive waves of invaders, including Greeks, Carthaginians, Saracens and Romans (who made it their granary), Byzantines, Arabs, Normans, Angevins, Aragonese and Bourbons, all of whom left their mark and contributed to the unique quality of this extraordinary island. Among the rich Greek remains are the temple complexes of the Valley of the Temples, Agrigento, Syracuse (with its theatre), Segesta and Selinunte, all of which are better preserved than

Sicily contains the provinces of Agrigento, Caltanissetta, Catania, Enna, Messina, Palermo, Ragusa, Syracuse (*Siracusa*) and Trapani, and has a population of 5.1m. Sicily's rich and complex history is evident in the capital Palermo, a splendid city in the grand manner; opulent and vital,

There are large sandy beaches on the southern coast, where Cefalu near Palermo is a favourite coastal resort, as are Acireale, Acitrezza, Mondello and Tindari. Other beautiful towns include Agrigento, Syracuse and Taormina, (overlooked by Mount Etna's still active volcano) and the attractive smaller centres of Monreale, Erice, Noto, Gela, Modia and Marsala, famous for its Marsala wine – a tradition begun by English families residing in the area. Many small islands surround Sicily, offering spectacular scenery and excellent facilities for scuba-diving and underwater fishing. These include Favignana, Lampedusa, Levanzo, Marettimo, Panarea, Pantelleria, Stromboli, Ustica, Vulcano and the islands of Lipari. Sicily is an earthquake zone and water shortages are common.

any ancient theatres in Greece. Roman relics are best seen in the villa of Piazza Armerina, with its exceptional mosaics (which include women in bikinis!). Sicily has a fascinating mixture of architectural styles, including numerous Arab influences, while the cathedral of Monreale is the most significant Norman building in the whole of Italy.

Sicily is the largest and most densely populated island in the Mediterranean. It's a land of stark contrasts between the breathtaking coastal scenery and run-down coastal resorts, city slums and polluting industries; the interior's wealth of greenery, including eucalyptus, citrus and olive trees, prickly pear cactus and vines, and the sparse population of the island's interior, and teeming urban conurbations on the coastal belt. Sicily has more autonomy than most other Italian regions for historical and ethnic reasons, although it's also synonymous with the mafia (*cosa nostra*), whose 'GNP' is reckoned to be around 12 per cent of Italy's! It's the most powerful and richest criminal organisation in the world and makes Sicily a dangerous place for police, magistrates and judges. Another problem is unemployment, which is the highest in Italy.

Property

The island is noted for its cube-shaped houses with flat roofs and also for its flimsily-built modern buildings and concrete jungle resorts. You should be wary of new-looking buildings on the coast, which may be illegal and subject to demolition orders in the future, as under Sicilian law any construction built after 1967 within 250m (800ft) of the beach is illegal.

Sicily is tipped to become one of Italy's most popular regions with foreign buyers. Coastal homes may be purchased from around €650 to €1,850 per m² in Syracuse up to €3,150 per m² for a good property on the coast at Taormina, which is popular with British property buyers. Palermo (prices from €1,150 to €2,500) has many attractive properties available for restoration and government grants can be obtained for restoration costs, although the grants can (and do!) take up to three years to be approved.

Some property on the island is linked to organised crime, a link that will become clear when you're negotiating the price and when enquiries are made about whether you have fire insurance, which – needless to say – you should accept and pay for!

Communications

Communications and road links are poor to adequate but improving. Palermo's and Catania's international airports have good links with the rest of Italy and internationally (see **Airports** on page 80), and there are regular ferries to the mainland taking around 15 minutes (from Villa San Giovanni to Messina). The crossing time will be reduced to just a few minutes when the bridge (set to have the world's longest suspended span at 3.3km/2mi) across the Strait of Messina between Villa San Giovanni and Messina, which has been planned for some 25 years and has recently been approved, is completed in around 2009.

Tuscany (*Toscana*)

Tuscany covers 22,990km² (8,877mi²) and contains the provinces of Arezzo, Florence (*Firenze*), Grosseto, Leghorn (*Livorno*), Lucca, Massa Carrara, Pisa, Pistoia and Sienna. Tuscany's population of around 3.6m is concentrated along the coast and between Florence (the regional capital, with a population of 400,000) and Pisa, an area where cultural tourism is the major industry (unemployment is relatively low at around 5 per cent). Florence, birthplace of the Renaissance, is one of the world's most beautiful cities. Cradle of Italian art and science; it's a living museum and the most popular cultural site in Europe, containing a wealth of art, bridges, churches, palaces and statues (including Michelangelo's *David* in the Uffizi gallery). Due to its popularity, Florence is in danger of being overwhelmed by tourists, who number over 7m a year.

Sienna is Florence's great historical rival, the largest surviving medieval town in Europe and home of the famous Palio horse race. Other notable Tuscan cities, each with its own remarkable cathedral (*duomo*), include Arezzo, Leghorn, Lucca, Pisa (with its famous 13th century leaning tower), Pistoia and Prato.

In few places in the world have man and nature blended so harmoniously as in Tuscany, with its rare combination of pleasant climate, stunning scenery, beautiful towns and cities, cultural heritage, culinary delights and fine wines. The countryside has a unique charm, with gently rolling hills, farmhouses, vineyards, olive and cypress groves, and soft colours. It's criss-crossed with white roads (*strade bianche*) and dotted with the stone farmhouses (*casali*) that many foreigners find irresistible, particularly if they've seen the film *Stealing Beauty* or read the book *Under the Tuscan Sun* by Frances Mayes.

The most famous area of Tuscany is Chianti, the oldest officially designated wine-growing region in the world. It's marvellous walking country and has been dubbed 'Chiantishire' due to the large number of Anglo-Saxon visitors and summer residents (there are some 4,000 houses owned by foreigners – mainly American, British and German).

One of Italy's most expensive wines is produced in the Montalcino area (it costs from around €80 per bottle!), and the finest olive oil (and other fine wines) are to be found in the 'golden' triangle bounded by Florence, Sienna and Volterra. Truffles (*tartufi*) are found in Val d'Orcia and San Giovanni Val d'Arno.

Among the region's best coastal resorts are the Argentario peninsula, Forte dei Marmi, Lido di Camaiore, Marina di Castiglioncello, Marina di Pietrasanta and Viareggio, which is blessed with wide, sandy beaches. The island of Elba (where Napoleon spent his 'hundred days' from May 1814 to February 1815) has some excellent sandy beaches, although two-thirds of its 224km² (86mi²) is composed of woodland. It's Italy's third-largest island (after Sicily and Sardinia) and is reached by ferry from Leghorn and Piombino. Other islands of the Tuscan archipelago include Capraia, Giannutri, Giglio, Gorgona, Montecristo (where Dumas set his classic tale) and Pianosa.

On the Maremma coast (in the middle of the Tuscan coast) are the Maremma and Uccellina parks, the latter consisting of 25,000 acres of wild and beautiful unspoilt countryside. Nearby is Monte Argentario, a peninsula attached to the mainland by three isthmuses containing the coastal resort towns of Orbetello, Porto Ercole and Porto Santo Stefano. The area is noted for its beautiful villas and marinas (such as Cala Galera) and is a fashionable summer holiday retreat among wealthy Romans and Florentines. Other popular holiday areas on the southern Tuscan coast include Ansedonia, Punta Ala (with its marina and golf course) and Talamone. There are famous spas at Bagni di Lucca, Bagno Vignone, Casciana, Chianciano, Montecatini, San Casciano Bagni, Saturnia and Terme.

Property

Tuscany's architecture is typified by its stone farmhouses and stunning fortified hilltop towns with a profusion of towers and turrets, such as Cortona, Monteriggioni and San Gimignano. The region is noted for its fine villas and *palazzi*, painted in traditional Tuscan red, farmhouses (*casali*), stone village houses, and warm-coloured stone and terracotta roofs. Property in central Tuscany is among the most expensive in the country, particularly anywhere within an hour of the cities of Florence, Sienna or Pisa. 'Chiantishire' is one of the world's most expensive rural residential areas and there are currently few rural homes available there, although townhouses and apartments can be found in villages and towns. Less expensive properties can be found north of Lucca, in Lunigiana and around Arezzo. Prices in the region start at €750 per m² (usually for little more than a

remote ruin) and reach €8,750 per m² in a popular area of Florence such as Poggio Imperiale.

Communications

Tuscany boasts an excellent rail and road network, although traffic jams on motorways in the region are commonplace, and it has major international airports at Florence and Pisa (see **Airports** on page 80), while Leghorn is a busy port.

Trentino-Alto Adige

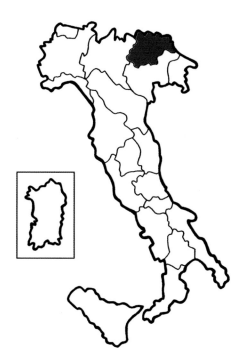

Trentino-Alto Adige contains the autonomous provinces of Bolzano and Trento, each with a capital city of the same name (these are also the two regional capitals and have equal status). The population of around 970,000 speaks Italian, German and Ladino, plus a variety of dialects. Trentino-Alto Adige was part of the Austro-Hungarian Empire until 1918, and German is still taught in schools. The region has one of the lowest population densities in Italy, a third of inhabitants living in small mountain villages, and it has one of the country's lowest unemployment rates.

Trentino-Alto-Adige is Italy's northernmost region and is dominated by the Alps, which divide Italy from Austria. The cuisine has a distinctly Austrian flavour with *knodel, krapfen* and *strudel* existing alongside *polenta* and spaghetti. There's a definite Tyrolean influence in the Baroque architecture, the carved and painted palace facades, and the large wood and stone chalets. The Dolomite mountains are a heady mixture of dense forests, alpine lakes and fascinating rock formations, and are a magnet for visitors from around the world.

Tourism is the region's most important industry and tourists flock year round to the resorts of Bressanone, Brunico, Canazei, Madonna di Campiglio, Merano, Moena, Ortisei, San Candido, San Martino di Castrozza, Santa Cristina, Selva di Val Gardena, Val di Fassa and Vipiteno. Agriculture is also important, particularly in Val di Non (famous for its apple orchards), while the region's vineyards produce mostly white wines such as Gewürztraminer, Riesling, Sylvaner and Terlaner. Dairy farming is another important industry.

Radon gas (see page 76) is present in some areas of Trentino-Alto Adige.

Property

Trentino-Alto Adige is noted for its fine estates and castles (*castelli*). Property in the most popular mountain resorts is in high demand and is among Italy's most expensive outside the major cities. Prices start at €1,600 per m² in less popular regions and rise to €5,500 per m² in central Bolzano.

Communications

The region has a good road and rail network, and is linked with Austria via the Brenner

Pass. It's served by airports in Milan, Venice and Verona (see **Airports** on page 80).

Umbria

Umbria contains the provinces of Perugia (also the name of the regional capital city) and Terni. It's one of Italy's smallest regions, covering an area of 8,455km² (3,265mi²) with a population of around 880,000. Despite lying on a major earthquake fault line, Umbria is one of the few areas where the countryside hasn't been largely deserted by the population. River valleys such as that of the Tiber are cultivated with grain, olive groves and terraced vineyards, and there's some industry around Foligno, Narni, Perugia and Terni. Umbria, which consists largely of forest and farmland, is quintessentially Italian and is known as the 'green heart of Italy' or the 'land of woods and saints'.

It's a land-locked region, less accessible, dramatic and glamorous than its neighbour Tuscany, but with fewer tourists and foreign property owners.

> The spiritual beauty of the countryside is reflected in hilltop towns such as Todi, which has become a fashionable spot with a large enclave of foreign artists and writers since an American university voted it one of the world's most attractive towns.

Perugia, the region's capital and largest city, is a fine old Etruscan town with a famous University for Foreign Students specialising in courses in Italian art, culture and language. Assisi is the home of Saint Francis (Italy's patron saint), whose life is commemorated in the immortal frescoes of Giotto (which were badly damaged in an earthquake in 1997) in the Basilica di San Francesco. Spoleto is famous for its annual music, drama and dance festival, called the Festival of Two Worlds. Other famous towns include Città della Pieve (the home of Perugino), Città di Castello, Deruta (famous for its ceramics), Foligno, Gubbio (a medieval 'film set'), Narni, Norcia, Orvieto (with its magnificent cathedral and fine wines) and Panicale.

Property

The local architecture is sombre but attractive, featuring light-coloured stone and similar in style to Tuscany. Towers are a typical feature of the region's hilltop villages and farmhouses, which cost from around €1,500 per m² near Bevagna to €2,750 per m² near Assisi. More people are discovering the region's unspoilt, backwater charms; it's particularly popular with British, Dutch and German property buyers – so much so that few rural properties come onto the market.

Communications

Communications in the region are fair and improving. There's a domestic airport at Perugia (see **Airports** on page 80) and the toll-free E45 *superstrada* connects with the A1 motorway and also the Civitavecchia-Rome motorway, making it a fast journey to Rome and Fiumicino international airport. From Perugia it's also possible to make day trips to the sea and the sandy beaches of the Etruscan Riviera via the E45 to Orte, or via the Orte-Viterbo *superstrada* to Tarquinia.

Val D'Aosta

Castle of Fenis, Val D'Aosta

The autonomous region of Val D'Aosta contains only one province, Aosta, and is the smallest (3,263km²/1,260mi²) and most sparsely populated region in Italy, with a population of just 125,000. It's also Italy's wealthiest area, with a very low unemployment rate. The regional capital and only large city is Aosta, founded by the Romans in 25BC and named after Emperor Augustus. It contains a wealth of Roman remains, including the city walls, theatre and a triumphal arch. In the 11th century it came under the domination of the Savoy family, but was always considered autonomous. Officially bi-lingual (Italian and French), the region also boasts several dialects, including a Provençal *patois* and Walser, a German dialect.

Thanks to the region's landscapes and outstanding natural beauty, tourism is the largest industry, attracting over 700,000 visitors annually. The region's mountains include Monte Bianco (Mont Blanc), Europe's highest mountain at 4,810m/15,780ft, whose peak is in France, the Matterhorn (4,478m/14,691ft, peaking in Switzerland), Monte Rosa (4,633m/15,200ft) and Monte Cervino, which draw skiers year round (there's glacier skiing in the summer). The Gran Paradiso national park contains an abundance of forests and wild flowers and many rare animals, including lynx and stambecchi (goats with large horns), and plants.

The Val D'Aosta is one of the favourite Italian winter sports areas and in winter people flock to the main resorts of Cervinia, Courmayeur (the most popular), Breuil-Cervinia and Gressoney.

Other industries include iron mining near Cogne, crafts (e.g. wood carving) and livestock breeding.

Property

Sturdily built and well-designed wooden and stone chalets (*rascards*) are typical of the region. The property market is currently buoyant and prices are generally higher than in neighbouring Piedmont, top properties costing up to €6,250 per m² in chic Courmayeur (where a three-bedroom villa can cost up to €1.3m), €4,500 per m² in Cervinia, and around €2,850 per m² in Saint Vincent (noted for its casino).

Communications

The region has excellent motorway connections with Milan and Turin, and with Switzerland and France (via the Gran San Bernardo pass and the Monte Bianco tunnel), and is also well served by international airports in neighbouring regions – particularly Turin (see **Airports** on page 80).

Veneto

The Veneto region contains the provinces of Belluno, Padua (*Padova*), Rovigo, Treviso, Venice (*Venezia*, also the name of the regional capital city), Verona and Vicenza, and has a population of 4.7m. It has a huge variety of terrain from mountainous to marshy plains and coasts, including the Venice lagoon. The north-eastern area takes in part of the Dolomite

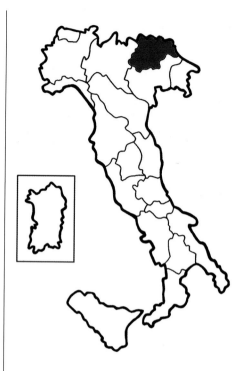

mountains (including the fashionable winter resort of Cortina d'Ampezzo) and the coastal resorts of Bibione, Caorle, Lido di Jesolo and Sottomarina (near Chioggia). There are also a number of popular resorts (such as Sirmione) on the eastern bank of lake Garda near Verona. The vast alluvial plain in the south is formed by many rivers (including the Po) that empty into the Adriatic and is cultivated with vineyards, cereals, fruit trees, sugar beet, tobacco, and potatoes. Dairy farming and fishing are also important industries (the unemployment rate is just 3 per cent).

The region's many historic cities include Verona, best known as the setting for the Romeo and Juliet legend, with its Roman Arena (where opera is performed in summer during the Verona festival), and Padua (*Padova*) with its great basilica of Saint Anthony. The Marca Trevigiana boasts the beautiful towns of Conegliano and Asolo, the ancient hill town where Elizabeth Barret Browning and Eleanora Duse once lived, famous for its frescoed facades. *Urbs Picta* is a nickname for Treviso in the foothills of the Dolomites, containing a wealth of Renaissance palaces and arcades. Local culinary specialities include *radicchio* (red salad), risotto and *polenta*, and local wines include Cartizze, Merlot, Prosecco, Rabosa Cabernet and Recioto.

The pearl of Veneto is, of course, its capital Venice (population 300,000), considered by many to be the most beautiful and romantic city in the world, with its network of canals, bridges, car-free streets and small squares.

The city is a living museum with its many splendid structures, including the Doges' Palace, Saint Mark's Square and the Bridge of Sighs. However, Venice has become a victim of its own popularity and is invaded by some 9m tourists a year (there's talk of limiting their numbers). Other problems include the winter flooding (*acqua alta*) that's a constant threat to the city's buildings, many of which are decaying and in danger of sinking into the sea; in late 2002, work finally commenced on the flood barriers to the lagoon, the first stage of which will cost over €450m. Venice is the most expensive city in Italy, where the population has fallen by around two-thirds in the last 25 years, and the business community is shrinking due to the high cost (some 40 per cent higher than on the mainland) of transporting raw materials along the waterways.

Property

The wonderful Venetian architecture and sumptuous *palazzi* (of which there are some 5,000, built between the 15th and 19th centuries), built of pink Verona or Istrian stone, have always been a strong attraction for wealthy foreigners, who happily pay between €4,000 and €10,000

per m² for a unique home. There are also numerous apartments and converted ground floor storerooms (*magazzini*) on the market, although these are susceptible to flooding. Less expensive properties can be found on the islands in the lagoon, such as Burano, Murano and Torcello, where prices start at around €2,500 per m².

Communications

The region has excellent road and rail links with Milan and central Europe, and Venice airport handles a number of international flights (see **Airports** on page 80).

LOCATION

The most important consideration when buying a home is usually its location – or, as the old adage goes, the three most important considerations are location, location and location! A property in a reasonable condition in a popular area is likely to be a better investment than an exceptional property in a less attractive location. There's no point in buying a dream property if you can't get to it or it's next door to a power station. Italy offers almost every type of property imaginable, but location is as important to your enjoyment of a home, as whether it's a palace or a hovel.

The wrong decision regarding location is one of the main causes of disenchantment among foreigners who purchase property abroad.

Where you buy a property will depend on a range of factors, including your preferences, your financial resources and whether you plan to work in Italy. If you already have a job in Italy, the location of your home will probably be determined by your place of employment. However, if you intend to look for employment or start a business, you must live in an area that allows you the maximum scope. It's unwise to assume that you will find employment in a particular area. If, on the other hand, you're looking for a holiday or retirement home, you can live virtually anywhere, although accessibility and proximity to shops and other services are crucial.

When seeking a permanent home, don't be too influenced by where you've spent an enjoyable holiday or two; a town or area that was fine for a few weeks' holiday, may be far from suitable as a permanent residence.

If you have little idea about where you wish to live, read as much as you can about the different regions of Italy (see page 50 and **Appendix B**) and spend some time looking around your areas of interest. The climate, lifestyle and cost of living can vary considerably from region to region, and even within a region. Before looking at properties, it's important to have a good idea of the type of property you're seeking and the price you wish to pay, and to draw up a shortlist of the areas or towns of interest. If you don't do this, you're likely to be overwhelmed by the number of properties to be viewed. Estate agents usually expect serious buyers to know where they want to buy within a 30 to 40km (20 to 25mi) radius and some even expect clients to narrow it down to specific towns and villages.

The 'best' place to live depends largely on its proximity to your place of work, schools, country or town, shops, public transport, sports facilities, beaches (or other attractions), bars and restaurants. There are beautiful areas to choose from throughout Italy, most within easy travelling distance of a town or city and the coast. Don't, however, believe the times and distances stated in advertisements and estate agents' brochures. According to some agents' magical mystery maps, everywhere in the north is handy for the ski slopes or the Italian lakes and anywhere in the south is a stone's throw from a beach or airport.

When looking for a home, bear in mind travelling times and costs. If you buy a remote country property, the distance to local amenities and services could become a problem, particularly if you plan to retire to Italy. If you live in a remote rural area, you will need to be much more self-sufficient than if

you live in a town and you will have to use a car for everything, which will add significantly to the cost of living. If you will be working in Italy, obtain a map of the area and decide the maximum distance you wish to travel to work, e.g. by drawing a circle with your workplace in the middle. The cost of motoring is high in Italy and is an important consideration when buying a home there.

If possible, you should visit an area a number of times over a period of a few weeks, both on weekdays and at weekends, in order to get a feel for the neighbourhood (walk, don't just drive around!). A property seen on a balmy summer's day after a delicious lunch and a few glasses of *vino,* may not be nearly so attractive on a subsequent visit *senza* sunshine and the warm inner glow. If possible, you should also visit an area at different times of the year, e.g. in both summer and winter, as somewhere that's wonderful in summer can be forbidding and inhospitable in winter (or vice versa). If you're planning to buy a winter holiday home, you should be sure to view it in the summer, as snow can hide a multitude of sins. In any case, you should view a property a number of times before deciding to buy it.

☑ **SURVIVAL TIP**

If you're unfamiliar with an area, most experts recommend that you rent for a period before deciding to buy (see Renting on page 111). This is particularly important if you're planning to buy a permanent or retirement home in an unfamiliar area. Many people change their minds after a period and it isn't unusual for families to move once or twice before settling down permanently.

Obtain a large scale map of the area where you're looking, which may even show individual buildings, thereby allowing you to mark the places that you've seen. You could do this using a grading system to denote your impressions. If you use an estate agent, he will usually drive you around and you can then return later to those that you like most at your leisure – provided you've marked them on your map!

There are many points to consider regarding the location of a home, as detailed below, and you should take into account the present and future needs of all members of your family.

Accessibility

Is the proximity to public transport, e.g. an international airport, port or railway station, or access to a motorway important? Don't, however, believe all you're told about the distance or travelling times to the nearest motorway, airport, railway station, port, beach or town, but check for yourself. Being on a local bus route is also advantageous.

Amenities

What local health and social services are provided? How far is the nearest hospital with an emergency department? What shopping facilities are there in the neighbourhood? How far is it to the nearest town with good shopping facilities, e.g. a supermarket? How would you get there if your car was out of action? Bear in mind that many rural villages are dying and have few shops or facilities, so they aren't a good choice for a retirement home.

Climate

For most people the climate (see page 23) is one of the most important factors when buying a home in Italy, particularly a holiday or retirement home. Bear in mind both the winter and summer climate, the position of the sun, the average daily sunshine, rainfall and wind conditions. You may also wish to check whether the area is noted for fog, which can make driving hazardous. The orientation or aspect of a building is vital; if you want morning or afternoon sun (or both) you must ensure that balconies, terraces and gardens are facing south.

Community

Do you wish to live in an area with many of your fellow countrymen and other expatriates, or as far away from them as possible? If you wish to integrate with the local community, you should avoid foreign 'ghettos' and choose an area or development with mainly local inhabitants. However, unless you speak fluent Italian or intend to learn, you should think twice before buying a property in a village. The locals in some villages resent 'outsiders' buying up prime properties, particularly holiday homeowners, although resident foreigners who take the time and trouble to integrate into the local community are usually warmly welcomed. If you're buying a permanent home, it's important to check your prospective neighbours, particularly when buying an apartment. For example, are they noisy, sociable or absent for long periods? Do you think you will get on with them? Good neighbours are invaluable, particularly when buying a second home.

Crime

What is the local crime rate, e.g. burglaries, stolen cars and crimes of violence? In some areas (e.g. major cities and resorts), the incidence of burglary is high and home insurance is higher than in low-crime areas. Is crime increasing or decreasing? Bear in mind that professional crooks like isolated houses, particularly those full of expensive furniture and other belongings, which they can strip bare at their leisure. You're much less likely to be a victim of theft if you live in a village, where strangers stand out like sore thumbs.

Employment

How secure is your job or business and are you likely to move to another area in the near future? Can you find other work in the same area, if necessary? If you may need to move in a few years' time, you should rent rather than buy, or at least buy a property that will be relatively easy to sell without losing (too much) money. What about your partner's and children's jobs or job prospects?

Garden

If you're planning to buy a large country property with an extensive garden or plot, bear in mind the high cost and amount of work involved in its upkeep. If it's to be a second home, who will look after the house and garden when you're away? Do you want to spend your holidays mowing the lawn and cutting back the undergrowth? Do you want a home with a lot of outbuildings? What are you going to do with them? Can you afford to convert them into extra rooms or guest or self-catering accommodation and, if so, is there a demand for accommodation in the area (see **Chapter 9**).

Local Council

Is the local council well run? Unfortunately, many are profligate and simply use any extra income to hire a few more of their cronies or spend it on grandiose schemes, and many local councillors abuse their positions to further their own ends. If the municipality is efficiently run, you can usually rely on good local social services and sports and other facilities. In areas where there are many foreign residents, the town hall (*comune*) may have a foreign residents' department.

Natural Phenomena

Check with the registry office (*ufficio catasto*) in the local *comune* whether an area is particularly susceptible to natural disasters such as floods (which are common in Italy), storms, forest fires and landslides. If a property is located near a coast or waterway, it may be expensive to insure against floods, which are a constant threat in many areas.

Earthquakes and earth tremors are commonplace in many parts of Italy, due to the fault line that runs through the country, from north to south. The highest risk areas are in the south, but there are few regions that can be considered safe. In areas of risk (e.g. Tuscany, Sicily and the southern mainland), there are strict regulations requiring all buildings (new and restored) to incorporate structural reinforcement, e.g. strengthening of walls and roofs with ironwork. However, such regulations were introduced only in 1981 and many buildings constructed in the '60s and '70s weren't built to withstand earth tremors. On the other hand, buildings constructed in the last 20 years also aren't guaranteed to be earthquake-proof; in 2003, an earthquake demolished a modern village school in Molise while the older properties in the vicinity were practically unaffected.

In areas with little rainfall, which includes most of Italy in summer and in particular Puglia, Sardinia and Sicily, there are often severe water restrictions and high water bills.

Noise

Noise can be a problem in some cities, resorts and developments. Although you cannot choose your neighbours, you can at least ensure that a property isn't located next to a busy road, railway line, airport, industrial plant, commercial area, discotheque, night club, bar or restaurant (where revelries may continue into the early hours). Look out for objectionable properties which may be too close to the one you're considering, and check whether nearby vacant land has been 'zoned' for commercial activities or tower blocks. In community developments (e.g. apartment blocks) many properties are second homes and are let short term, which means you may have to tolerate boisterous holidaymakers as neighbours throughout the year (or at least during the summer months). In estate agents' speak, a popular (*popolare*) area may be noisy, while a residential (*residenziale*) area is usually quiet.

Parking

> ☑ SURVIVAL TIP
>
> If you're planning to buy in a town or city, is there adequate private or free on-street parking for your family and visitors? Is it safe to park in the street?

In some areas it's important to have secure off-street parking if you value your car. Parking is a problem in many towns and most cities, where private garages or parking spaces are rare and can be very expensive. Bear in mind that an apartment or townhouse in a town or community development may be some distance from the nearest road or car park. How do you feel about carrying heavy shopping hundreds of metres to your home and possibly up several flights of stairs? Traffic congestion is also a problem in many towns and tourist resorts, particularly during the high season.

Property Market

Do houses sell well in the area, e.g. in less than six months? Generally, you should avoid neighbourhoods where desirable houses routinely remain on the market for six months or longer (unless the property market is in a severe slump).

Radon

Radon is a naturally occurring radioactive gas formed underground by the radioactive decay of uranium, which is present in small quantities in rocks and soils, and is particularly prevalent in parts of Sardinia and Trentino-Alto Adige. After surfacing in the open air, radon is quickly diluted to harmless concentrations. However, when it enters an enclosed space, such as a house, it can build up to potentially harmful concentrations. The acceptable limit for radon concentration (known as the 'reference level') is 200 Becquerels per cubic metre of air ($200Bq/m3$). It has been shown that prolonged exposure to concentrations of radon above this level increases the chance of contracting lung cancer, and in a few homes in Italy there's a significant health risk for occupants.

You can have a test carried out to check the level of radon in a building or on a plot. In areas that are particularly at risk, you should contract the services of a surveyor or *geometra* to carry out tests. There are several websites providing regional radon maps, although there appears to be no national survey. For example, the website

for Trentino-Alto Adige (⌨ www.provincia. bz.it – in several languages, including English) has a useful map showing high-risk areas; look for 'GeoBrowser' in the 'Maps and Cartography' section.

Sports & Leisure Facilities

What is the range and quality of local leisure, sports, community and cultural facilities? What is the proximity to sports facilities such as a beach, golf course, ski resort or waterway? Although properties in or close to ski and coastal resorts are usually considerably more expensive, they also have the best letting potential. If you're interested in a winter holiday home, which area should you choose? While properties in the Alps are relatively expensive, they tend to appreciate faster than properties in many other areas and generally maintain their value in recessions.

Tourists

If you live in a popular tourist area, it will be inundated with tourists in summer. They won't only jam the roads and pack the public transport, but may also occupy your favourite table at your local bar or restaurant (heaven forbid!). Although a 'front-line' property on a beach or in a marina development may sound attractive and be ideal for short holidays, it isn't always the best choice for permanent residence. Many beaches are hopelessly crowded in the high season, streets may be smelly from restaurants and fast food outlets, parking impossible and services stretched to breaking point, and the incessant noise may drive you crazy. Some people prefer to move inland or to higher ground, where it's less humid, more peaceful and you can enjoy panoramic views. On the other hand, getting to and from hillside properties can be difficult and the often poorly maintained roads (usually narrow and unguarded) are for sober, confident drivers only; many country roads are suitable only for 4WD vehicles.

Town or Country?

Do you wish to be in a town or do you prefer the country? Inland or on the coast? How about living on an island? Bear in mind that if you buy a property in the country, you will probably have to tolerate poor public transport (or none at all), long travelling distances to a town of any size, solitude and remoteness. You won't be able to pop along to the local *panetteria*, drop into the local bar for a glass of your favourite tipple with the locals or have a choice of restaurants on your doorstep. In a town or large village, the market will be just around the corner, the doctor and chemist close at hand and, if you need help or run into any problems, your neighbours will be close by.

In the country you will be closer to nature, will have more freedom (e.g. to make as much noise as you wish) and possibly complete privacy, e.g. to sunbathe or swim *au naturel*. Living in a remote area in the country will suit nature lovers looking for solitude who don't want to involve themselves in the 'hustle and bustle' of town life (not that there's much of this in Italian rural towns). If you're after peace and quiet, however, make sure that there isn't a busy road or railway line nearby or a local church within 'donging' distance. Bear in mind that many people who buy a remote country home find that the peace of the countryside palls after a time, and they yearn for the more exciting city or coastal nightlife. If you've never lived in the country, it's wise to rent before buying. Although it's cheaper to buy in a remote or unpopular location, it's often much more difficult to find a buyer when you want to sell.

GETTING THERE

Although it isn't so important if you're planning to live permanently in Italy and stay put, one of the major considerations when buying a holiday home is the cost of getting to and from Italy. In particular, you should consider the following questions:

● How long will it take you to get to a home in Italy, taking into account journeys to and from airports, ports and railway stations?

● How frequent are flights, ferries or trains at the time(s) of year when you plan to travel?

● Are direct flights or trains available?

● Is it feasible to travel by car?

- What is the cost of travel from your home country to the region where you're planning to buy a home in Italy?

- Are off-season discounts or inexpensive charter flights available?

☑ SURVIVAL TIP

Strikes in the transport sector, particularly air traffic control and the railways, are commonplace in Italy and you should check in advance before you make travel plans.

If a long journey is involved, you should bear in mind that it may take you a day or two to recover. Obviously, the travelling time and cost of travel to a home in Italy will be more important if you're planning to spend frequent long weekends there rather than a few long stays each year. You should include the price of getting to and from Italy in your budget when considering a property purchase, particularly if you're planning to make several visits a year.

If you plan to let a property, it will be more popular if it's within easy reach of an airport with a range of flights, particularly budget flights, from the UK, for example. Always allow plenty of time to get to and from airports, ports and railway stations in Italy, particularly when travelling during peak hours, when traffic congestion can be horrendous.

Airline Services

There are direct international scheduled flights to all major cities in Italy (there are direct flights from the UK to around 26 Italian cities, for example – see **Appendix F**) and many other towns are served by domestic flights. International airlines serving Italy include Italy's partly state-owned national airline, Alitalia (see below),

Air Canada, Air France, American Airlines, British Airways, Continental Airlines, Delta Airlines, Iberia, Icelandair, KLM, Lufthansa, Northwest Airlines, Sabena, SAS, Swissair and US Airways.

Unfortunately, one of the negative aspects of owning a home in Italy is that Alitalia, the national airline, is a basket case and probably the worst major airline in the western world. It makes huge losses and the Italian government has been trying to get shot of it for years without success. However, with losses increasing, it now seems likely that sooner rather than later they will give it away – or pay someone to take it off their hands. Until then, avoid Alitalia like the plague if you have a choice (if you don't, avoid putting anything of value in your checked baggage, as it's likely to get lost). And don't expect any Alitalia staff to speak English or any language other than Italian.

On the plus side (not that there's much), Alitalia has a good safety record and its fares have become more competitive in recent years. Its main hub is at Rome's Fiumicino airport and the airline flies to over 100 cities on six continents. Not surprisingly, it dominates the busy and lucrative Milan-Rome route (even Alitalia can't make a loss on this route!).

The introduction of 'no-frills' flights into the Italian market has been revolutionary and has provided some welcome competition, forcing Alitalia and others to reduce their fares. Budget airlines offer several advantages, including Internet and/or telephone booking, ticket-less flights (no chance of forgetting them) and no seat allocation (an advantage provided you turn up early). Fares can be as low as €15 (from the UK), although they've risen in recent months and flights in high season or on popular routes may be as expensive as those offered by scheduled airlines. Bear in mind that budget airline advertised prices usually don't include airport taxes, which can be high (e.g. €17.50 from Luton in the UK) and you will probably be charged for using a credit card, e.g. €5 to €8. Food and drinks on budget airlines are also expensive.

The instability of the airline business means that airlines frequently merge or go bankrupt, which often results in a reduction of services or the disappearance of routes altogether. Budget airlines also frequently change their routes and prices. You therefore shouldn't invest in a property if you need to rely on cheap flights to a local airport.

Although it's relatively easy to reach regional airports in Italy via Milan or Rome, domestic flights (see page 97) are invariably expensive and time consuming (i.e. flights don't necessarily 'match' incoming international services).

Flights from the UK & Ireland

There's a wide range of flights from UK and Irish airports (Belfast and Dublin in the latter) to many airports in Italy, although some regions are less well served than others (see **Appendix F** for a full list of services). There are usually a number of direct flights every day from London-Gatwick and London-Stansted to a wide range of Italian destinations, and a decent service from Dublin, London-Heathrow and Manchester to various Italian cities. The vast majority of flights go to Milan or Rome, although there are increasing numbers of flights to other Italian destinations. The budget airline market serving Italy from the UK is currently dominated by Ryanair with some 18 destinations, including airports served by few or no other airlines, such as Ancona and Genoa.

Normal scheduled fares to Rome are around £150 single and £300 return. Apex and charter fares cost from around £150 return to Milan or Rome and an additional £20 to £30 to Pisa or Naples. However, fares vary considerably depending on the time of the year, when you book and the airline.

Flights from the US

Several airlines fly direct to Italy from the US, including Alitalia and Delta, although scheduled fares are expensive. Alitalia offer the widest choice of direct flights from the US, including daily flights from Boston, Chicago, Los Angeles, New York and Miami to Milan and to Rome (usually via Milan). Delta flies daily from Chicago, Los Angeles and New York to Rome. Flights take around eight and a half hours from New York to Rome. From Canada, both Alitalia and Air Canada have direct flights to Rome and Milan from Toronto and Montreal. Most European airlines flying from North America to Italy are routed via their European hub rather than flying direct.

The cheapest return fares from the USA are around $500 from New York to Rome rising to $700 in mid- (shoulder) season and to $900 in peak season; add around $100 for flights from Chicago and Miami and $200 from Los Angeles. Charter flights are available from the USA to Italy, but they aren't such good value as in Europe, as scheduled airlines can often beat the prices with special offers and offer greater convenience and fewer restrictions.

Airports

The major international gateways are Rome and Milan, followed by Pisa, Venice and Naples, although more and more cities are becoming accessible by direct international flights, including Florence, Bologna and Perugia. The following is a survey of the main airports serving Italy's 20 regions and the UK airports serving them. The majority of airports provide bus transport to the nearest city, and car hire is also available. Most airport websites have information in English and many offer useful tourist information, including accommodation options as well as basic airport information (several also provide images or aeroplanes taking off and landing, complete with effects, to get you in the mood!).

A table detailing the services between Italian and UK/Irish airports in summer 2007 is contain in **Appendix F**.

Abruzzo

Pescara airport, situated 4km from Pescara city centre, is small and flights are currently only available with Ryanair from London Stansted. Rome's airports are accessible from parts of the region (see **Lazio** below). Flight information can be obtained from ☎ 085-432 4201 and 🖳 www.abruzzo-airport. it.

Basilicata

The nearest international airport is Naples (see **Campania** below).

Calabria

The nearest international airport is Palermo in Sicily (see below).

Campania

Capodichino airport just outside Naples is one of Italy's busiest and has frequent international flights, as well as domestic flights to Milan and Rome. Regular flights to Naples from the UK are available from 11 UK airports (including Belfast and Dublin). Airport information is available on ☎ 081-789 6111 and 🖳 www.portal.gesac.it.

Emilia Romagna

Bologna airport, known as Bologna Marconi, is situated just outside the city and there's a regular bus service to the city taking around 20 minutes. Regular flights to Bologna from the UK are available from Dublin (AerLingus and Ryanair) and London-Gatwick (British Airways). Florence, Milan and Venice airports are accessible from parts of the region (see **Tuscany**, **Lombardy** and **Veneto** respectively below). Airport information is available on ☎ 051-647 9615 and 🖳 www.bologna-airport.it.

Friuli-Venezia Giulia

The region's airport, Ronchi dei Legionari, is located 33km to the west of Trieste and is currently served by only one route from the UK (Ryanair from London-Stansted). Travellers also have the option of Venice (see **Veneto** below), which is served by numerous flights from the UK. Airport information is available on ☎ 04-8177 3224 and 🖥 www.aeroporto.fvg.it.

Lazio

Rome has two airports: Ciampino, situated some 25km (15mi) to the south-east of Rome, which is used mainly for domestic and charter flights, and Fiumicino, Italy's largest catering to over 26m passengers a year. Fiumicino lies around 25km (15mi) west of Rome, almost on the coast, and has excellent facilities. It's connected to Rome's Termini station by a rail shuttle operating every 30 minutes. Most overseas travel agents can book, not only a flight to Fiumicino, but also the shuttle and onward rail travel ticket if required, and provide you with connection times. If you've hired a car, a free shuttle bus takes you to the hire company offices and pick-up point. Rome is well served by regular flights from 14 UK airports (including Belfast and Dublin). Flight information for both Ciampino and Fiumicino is available from 06-65951 and 🖵 www.adr.it.

Liguria

Genoa airport (Cristoforo Columbo International Airport) is built on an artificial peninsula 6km (4mi) to the east of the city. There are currently only flights from London-Stansted (Ryanair). Flight information is available from ☎ 010-60151 and 🖥 www.airport.genova.it.

Nice airport (in France) may provide a useful alternative for visitors travelling to the north-west of Italy. Access from Nice to the Italian Riviera is excellent along the A8 motorway and there's also a bus service from Nice to Genoa. Flights to Nice are available from several British airports. Flight information is available from ☎ 0820-423

333 (from outside France only, cost €0.12 per minute) and 🖥 www.nice.aeroport.fr.

Lombardy

The Lombardy region is served by Milan's two airports: Milan Linate, used for domestic flights and some European flights, is situated 10km/6mi from the city centre; Milan Malpensa, opened in 2000 and situated some 53km/33mi from the city centre, handles inter-continental flights and some European flights. Express trains run every 30 minutes connecting Malpensa airport with Milan's Cadorna railway station, taking around 40 minutes (which will eventually be reduced to 30 minutes). The service operates from 6am to 1.30am and costs €9 one-way.

Flights to Milan are available from numerous airports in the UK and Ireland. Visitors are advised to check which airport and terminal their flight leaves from before travel. Flight information for both Linate and Malpensa is available from ☎ 02-7485 2200 and 🖥 www.sea-aeroportimilano.it.

Marche

The nearest international airport is Rome (see **Lazio** above).

Molise

The nearest international airports are Naples and Rome (see **Campania** and **Lazio** above).

Piedmont

Turin's (Caselle International) airport, is currently served by BA from London-Gatwick, Easyjet from London-Luton and Ryanair from London-Stansted, and the region is also served by airports in Genoa, Milan and Nice (see **Liguria** above and **Tuscany** below). Flight information is available from 🖥 www.turin-airport.com.

Puglia

The nearest international airport is Naples (see **Campania** above).

Sardinia

The island has two international airports: Alghero in the north-west and Olbia in the north-east and within easy reach of the Costa Smeralda. Sardinia is now served by regular flights from six UK airports (including Dublin). Flight information for Alghero airport is available from 🖥 www.aeroportodialghero.com and for Olbia from ☎ 07-8956 3444 and 🖥 www.geasar.it.

Sicily

Sicily has two international airports: Fontanarossa near Catania on the east coast and Palermo, known as Falcone Borsellino, in the north. Six airlines fly to Sicily from Britain. Flight information for Catania is available from 🖥 www.aeroporto.catania.it, and for Palermo from 🖥 www.gesap.it.

Tuscany

The region has two international airports: Florence's Amerigo Vespucci International Airport and Galileo Galilei in Pisa. Florence is currently only served by flights from London-Gatwick (Meridiana) and the airport provides a shuttle bus service, which takes 20 minutes to reach the city centre. Flight information is available from ☎ 055-306 1300 and 🖥 www.aeroporto.firenze.it.

> Pisa is served by flights from 12 UK airports (including Belfast and Dublin). A frequent shuttle bus provides transport to the centre of the city and the railway station, where trains run direct to Florence. Flight information is available from 🖥 www.pisa-airport.com.

Trentino-Alto Adige

The region is served by airports in Milan (see **Lombardy** above), Venice and Verona (see **Veneto** below).

Umbria

The region is served by airports in Florence and Pisa (see **Tuscany** above) and Rome (see **Lazio** above).

Val D'Aosta

The region is served by airports in Milan and Turin (see **Lombardy** and **Piedmont** above).

Veneto

The Veneto region is served by three international airports: Venice-Marco Polo, Venice-Treviso and Verona. Venice is well-served by flights from 11 UK airports (including Belfast and Dublin). Venice-Marco Polo airport offers both bus and water transport to the city, although the journey can take an hour or more. Work started in 2004 on an 8km underwater railway line from the airport to the city centre via the island of Murano, which will reduce the journey time to 12 minutes. The line is expected to be completed by 2010. Flight information is available from ☎ 041-260 6111 and 🖥 www.veniceairport.it.

Verona airport is currently served by flights from six British airports. Flight information is available from ☎ 045-809 5666 and 🖥 www.aeroportoverona.it.

International Rail Services

There are direct trains to Italy from many major European cities and countries, including Austria, France, Germany, the Netherlands, Spain and Switzerland. Italy's railways are connected with those in neighbouring countries by a number of mountain routes linking Milan with Switzerland via the Milan-Simplon Tunnel, Turin with Fréjus in France, Venice to eastern Europe via Tarvisio, and Verona to Austria and Germany via the Brenner Pass. If you take a fast train such as the French *TGV* or Italy's *ETR*, journey times are much reduced. However, some international services run only at night, and daytime journeys may involve a change of train.

You can travel to Italy from London by train via Paris (where you must change trains) and southern France or through Belgium, Germany and Switzerland. However, it's expensive compared to charter flights, and takes much longer.

Travel times from London are around 20 hours to Milan, 24 hours to Rome and 42 hours to Sicily. If you're **very** wealthy, you can take the Orient Express from Paris to Venice, which operates twice weekly from mid-March to mid-November, and travels on to Florence and Rome around ten times a year.

Motorail

Motorail is a European network of special trains, generally overnight, carrying passengers and their cars or motorbikes over distances of up to 1,500km (900mi). Caravans cannot be taken on car trains. Motorail trains with sleeping cars operate on various routes, including Boulogne-Bologna, Boulogne-Rome, Boulogne-Alessandria, Boulogne-Leghorn, Boulogne-Lille-Milan, Brussels-Milan, Dusseldorf-Cologne-Milan-Genoa, Dusseldorf-Cologne-Bolzano, Hamburg-Hanover-Verona, Munich-Rimini, Paris-Milan, 'S Hertogenbosch-Domodossola-Genoa-Milan, 'S Hertogenbosch-Chiasso-Milan, and Vienna-Venice. A wide range of sleeping accommodation is available. Trains don't run every day and operate only during peak months on most routes. The Motorail service tends to be heavily booked from February onwards and it's wise to book well in advance, particularly if you wish to travel during the summer. However, car trains aren't a cheap option and, if you have the time (and inclination), it's much cheaper to drive to Italy.

International Bus Services

You can travel to Italy by bus from many countries; for example, there are direct services from neighbouring countries and from the UK, e.g. London to Bologna,

Florence, Milan, Rome and Turin. London to Milan (with National Express or Eurolines) takes around 21 hours and Rome 30 hours, with return fares around £100 and £110 respectively. There's a 10 per cent reduction for students and fares are around half price for children.

International Ferry Services

Regular international car and passenger ferry services operate between Italy and various countries, including Albania, Croatia, Egypt, France (Corsica), Greece, Israel, Malta, Spain (Barcelona and the Balearics), Tunisia, Turkey and parts of the former Yugoslavia. Ticket prices are usually reasonable, but vary depending on the time of year and are (naturally) most expensive during summer. Some services operate during the summer only and, during the winter, services are severely curtailed on most routes or may be suspended altogether.

Driving to Italy

Many people prefer to drive to Italy, which saves the expense of renting a car on arrival.

If you're driving from the UK, bear in mind that it's almost 1,100km (700mi) from Calais to Milan (taking some 11 hours) and around a further 300km (200mi) to Florence. There are several route options, the fastest of which is via Nancy, Lucerne and Lugano, although you must add high motorway toll fees in France to the cost of your journey. A cheaper option avoiding French motorways is via Belgium and Luxembourg, Strasbourg, Mulhouse in Germany and then to Switzerland and Italy via the Gottard tunnel. However, in order to use Swiss roads you require a Swiss motorway carnet costing around CHF40 (around €25 a year) and available at the border or from the AA (🖳 www.theaa.co.uk) or the RAC (🖳 www.rac.co.uk) in the UK.

Some people prefer to drive through France via secondary roads turning the journey into a mini-holiday as they take their time to enjoy the delights of France on the way. If you choose to drive to Italy, you should take it easy and make regular rest stops or share the driving. If possible, you should avoid Paris and Basle, where traffic congestion is chronic.

☑ SURVIVAL TIP

If you drive to Italy, you must ensure that your car insurance covers travel abroad (most do, although you may need to obtain a 'green card') and you should also have breakdown recovery insurance covering all countries you will pass through, as well as Italy.

Due to the high cost of ferry and road travel and the long travelling time by road between the UK and Italy, you may be better off flying and hiring a car on arrival. Many people who visit Italy frequently or for long periods leave a car at their Italian home.

Crossing the Channel

There's a wide choice of routes for travellers between France and Britain, depending on where you live and the route intended, but only one for Irish travellers. These are (from east to west):

- Dover/Dunkerque (Norfolk Line, 🖳 www. norfolkline-ferries.co.uk);

- Dover/Calais (P&O Ferries, 🖳 www. poferries.com, and Sea France, 🖳 www. seafrance.co.uk);

- Dover/Boulogne (Speed Ferries, 🖳 www.speedferries.com);

- Newhaven/Dieppe (Hoverspeed and Transmanche Ferries, 🖳 www. transmancheferries.com);

- Portsmouth/Le Havre (P&O Ferries);

- Portsmouth/Caen (Brittany Ferries, 🖳 www.brittany-ferries.co.uk);

- Portsmouth/Cherbourg (P&O Ferries);

- Portsmouth/Saint-Malo (Brittany Ferries);

- Poole/Cherbourg (Brittany Ferries);

- Poole/Saint-Malo via Guernsey and Jersey (Condor Ferries, 🖳 www. condorferries.co.uk);

- Weymouth/Saint-Malo via Guernsey and Jersey (Condor Ferries);

- Plymouth/Roscoff (Brittany Ferries);

- Cork/Roscoff (Brittany Ferries).

Fares across the Channel have risen in recent years and, except for special deals or last minute fares, are no longer cheap on any routes. If you're travelling to Italy, you probably won't be able to take advantage of economy returns, which are usually valid for five days only. Fares vary greatly with the time of day and year, with peak fares in the mornings during July and August. Ferry companies offer various deals and discounts for advance bookings and most have loyalty schemes, usually based on points-allocation. Brittany Ferries, Eurotunnel and P&O Ferries have special schemes for property owners abroad, which may be worth joining if you plan to travel to Italy by car on a regular basis, although there are high membership fees and/or restrictive conditions.

Shop around for the best deal, which is probably best done by a travel agent, who has access to fares from all companies or a company specialising in discount Channel crossings, such as Cross-Channel Ferry Tickets (🖳 www.cross-channel-ferry-tickets. co.uk). It's difficult to check fares online as you don't have access to the full range, and can find prices only by using the (time-consuming) booking form or quote facility. Brochures rarely include fares.

Entering Italy

Whichever route you choose to take by road, entry into Italy will inevitably be via a tunnel or mountain pass. Bear in mind that weather and traffic conditions may affect the opening of a tunnel or pass, particularly in winter months, when heavy snow may close a pass or require the use of chains. There's a toll for the use of most tunnels, although some offer discounts for return trips. There are both minimum and maximum speed limits in tunnels, which are usually 40kph (25mph) and 80kph (50mph) respectively. The main tunnels into Italy are:

- **Mont Blanc**, 11.67km (7 mi) long, which reopened in 2002 after a fire in 1999. The tunnel carries around 18,000 vehicles a day and is the most-used tunnel by travellers from the UK. Toll fees for a standard family car are €31.90 one-way and €42.10 when towing a caravan. Further information including traffic conditions, is available from 🖳 www.tunnelmb.net. The maximum permitted speed is 70kph (44mph).

- **Fréjus** (🖳 www.sftrf.fr), 13km (8mi) long, running from south-eastern France to Piedmont. The toll is €31.20 one-way and €41.30 when towing a caravan.

- **San Bernardo** (🖥 www.sitrasb.it), 5.8km (3.6mi) long, from Switzerland to Val d'Aosta. The toll is €22.40 one-way for a car and €34.80 when towing a caravan.

- **Saint Gotthard** (🖥 www.gottard-strassentunnel.ch), 17km (10mi) long, from Goschenen in Switzerland to Airolo in Italy. Toll-free.

The main mountain passes are the Brenner Pass from Innsbruck to Vipiteno (in Trentino-Alto Adige) and the Monte Croce Carnico Pass from Tolmezzo to Lienz (in Friuli-Venezia Giulia), open from June to October only.

Motorway information in France (including toll fees) is available from 🖥 www.autoroutes.fr and general traffic information is available from 🖥 www.bison-fute.equipement.gouv.fr (in French only). Swiss traffic information is available from the Touring Club Switzerland (🖥 www.tcs.ch) or from 🖥www.bs-ing.ch (both in German).

Information about Italian traffic conditions is provided by the Automobile Club Italia (🖥 www.aci.it) and you can also obtain motoring information on ISO Radio (FM 103.3), Jiaradio RTL (FM 102.5) and via the RAI Videotel teletext service.

GETTING AROUND

Public transport (*mezzi pubblici*) services in Italy vary considerably depending on where you live. Public transport is generally good to excellent in Italian cities, most of which have efficient local bus and rail services, supplemented (in Milan, Naples and Rome) by an underground railway (*metrò*) system and (in a few cities) by trams. The Italian railway company (Ferrovie dello Stato/FS) provides a comprehensive and occasionally fast service, particularly between cities served by the super-fast *ETR* trains. Travelling by train can be relaxing, particularly if you have time to enjoy the relatively slow local trains that criss-cross the country. FS offers a range of special tickets and passes for commuters and travellers who book in advance. Most major cities have integrated public transport systems, where the same ticket is valid for buses, trams and the underground.

On the negative side, services are often poorly organised (timetables are usually works of fiction) and beset by strikes, delays and breakdowns. Bus and rail services are poor or non-existent in rural areas and it's generally essential to have a car if you live in the country (most Italians prefer to use their cars for long journeys, rather than fly or use high-speed trains).

Domestic Flights

Some 40 Italian airports are served from Rome and most domestic flights take under an hour. Alitalia dominates domestic flights in Italy, although there are several other carriers – Air Europe (🖥 www.aireurope.it), Airone (🖥 www.flyairone.it) and Meridiana (🖥 www.meridiana.it) – and two regional companies, Air Dolomiti (🖥 www.airdolomiti.it) and Alpi Eagles (🖥 www.alpieagles.com), which provide domestic and some European flights, particularly to Greece. Competition for domestic customers is fierce, particularly on the Rome-Milan and Milan-Naples routes, and during the summer months, when flights to Sardinia are popular.

Travelling by air within Italy can be expensive, although competition has recently driven prices down. Various discounts are available, notably for evening and night flights and for APEX tickets, which must be booked and paid for at least seven days before departure and must include at least one Saturday and Sunday night between the outward and return journeys. Juniors (those aged under 22), students (up to 26), seniors (over 60) and families (consisting of a minimum of three people) can also purchase one-way tickets for half the price of reduced tariffs.

Domestic Rail Services

Trains in Italy are operated by the national company, Ferrovie dello Stato, usually referred to by the initials FS, although you may sometimes see FFSS when it's used in the plural. Italy's rail network is one of the most extensive in Europe, running to around 16,000km (10,000mi) of lines, some two-thirds of which are electrified, and over 3,000 stations. There are also a number of private lines. FS was the first railway in Europe to be nationalised in 1908 (or re-nationalised, as it was originally government owned), but is now 'officially' privatised (the majority of shares are still owned by the government). After years of mismanagement and neglect, all aspects of Italian railways are being modernised; huge investments are being made in infrastructure and rolling stock, particularly high-speed trains, although it still has some way to go to compete with Europe's best.

The rail network extends to all corners of the country, although there's a significant difference between services in the northern and southern parts of the country, the north enjoying more frequent and faster trains and more electrified lines than the south, where there are more single track lines. In an effort to reduce state subsidies, fares have been increased in the last few years, although rail travel is still good value, and cheaper than in most other European countries.

Travelling by train is generally faster, more comfortable and more relaxing than travelling by bus or coach, and in some cases trains are faster than air travel, when the time taken to get to and from airports is included. Fast inter-city train services are the most reliable and the cheapest way to get around Italy (much cheaper than renting a car and paying motorway tolls). Train information is available from the FS central line (☎ 06-44101), the Televideo and Mediavideo teletext services, and from the FS website (🖥 www.ferroviedellostato.it).

Domestic Bus Services

Italy has extensive inter-city and urban bus services and, in fact, has more buses than any other European country, although there's no nation-wide operator. The main long-distance operators are SITA (🖥 www.sitabus.it), which runs services between Basilicata, Campania and Puglia in the south and Lazio, Tuscany and Veneto in central and northern Italy, Autostradale (🖥 www.autostradale.it), which operates

in northern Italy, Lazzi (🖳 www.lazzi.it) in central Italy, and Sena (🖳 www.sena.it) in most regions. Most of the above websites are in Italian only. Each province usually has a local coach company.

Trains are less expensive and usually faster than buses over long distances, but buses can be more direct and faster than local trains, particularly in Tuscany. There are generally good connections between inter-city buses and trains, and bus terminals are usually situated near train stations.

There are excellent bus services in the major cities, some of which also have trams or trolley buses, although private bus services can be confusing and uncoordinated, and they often leave from different locations rather than a central bus station. Services can also be fragmented, localised and sometimes **very** slow. In cities, you usually purchase a ticket (*biglietto*) before boarding a bus; tickets are sold at tobacconists (*tabacchi*), newspaper kiosks, bars (there's usually a *Biglietti* sign), campsite shops and hotel reception desks. A wide range of season and special tickets are available in the major cities, where there are also bus lanes, although Italy's anarchistic motorists tend to use them (illegally), which defeats the object.

In stark contrast to the cities, buses in rural areas are few and far between, and the scant services that exist are usually designed to meet the needs of schoolchildren, workers, and shoppers on market days. This means that buses usually run early and late in the day, with little or nothing in between, and services may cease altogether during the long summer school holiday period (July and August).

Domestic Ferry Services

Italy has a well-developed network of ferries (*traghetti*) and hydrofoils (*aliscafi*), although services are usually severely curtailed outside the summer months. Regular services connect the mainland with Italy's many islands, including Sicily (from Villa San Giovanni), Sardinia (from Civitavecchia and Livorno), the islands of Capri, Ischia and Sorrento (from Naples), and the Aeolian, Pontine, Tremiti and Lipari islands (from various ports). Regular car ferry services also link Naples to Sicily (Palermo and Messina, taking around 20 hours!) and to nearby islands as well as to Genoa, which is also linked to Sardinia and Sicily (Palermo). (The bridge across the Strait of Messina between Sicily will make some ferry services obsolete in around 2009 – see **Communications** on page 70). Ferries and hydrofoils also operate between towns on the major lakes, including Como, Garda and Maggiore.

Restaurant, bar and recreation facilities such as cinemas are provided on the larger, long-haul ferries, where passengers can choose between a cabin (first or second class) and an airline-type, reclining armchair (*poltrona*). Italy's major ferry operators are Grimaldi (🖳 www.grimaldi-ferries.com), Tirrenia (🖳 www.gruppotirrenia.it) and Volaviamare (🖳 www.volaviamare.it).

Italian Roads

The Italian road network is divided into four categories: motorways (*autostrade*), national highways (*strade statali*), provincial roads (*strade provinciali*) and municipal roads (*strade comunali*).

> The country has an excellent motorway network covering around 6,000km (3,700mi), most of which are toll (*pedaggio*) roads, although there are some 1,000km (620mi) of free motorways (*superstrade*) around cities and some other stretches of motorway are toll-free.

The main north-south route is the *Autostrada del Sole* from Milan to Reggio di Calabria (via Bologna, Florence, Rome and Naples), designated the A1 from Milan to Naples and the A3 from Naples to Reggio di Calabria

(the latter stretch being toll-free). Given Italy's mountainous terrain, the country's motorways include many spectacular bridges and tunnels, especially in the Alps in the north of the country.

Motorway tolls depend on the height of your car or the wheel-base and number of axles, and the company operating the toll. The rate per kilometre varies but is usually around 5¢ or 6¢. On most motorways you collect a ticket when you join and pay when you leave. On some stretches, however, there are fixed charges that are payable in advance. Credit cards are usually accepted, but don't take it for granted. When paying by credit card, look for a lane with a large sign showing a depiction of credit cards.

Some companies offer season tickets at reduced rates and you can buy a *Viacard* (like a telephone smartcard) costing €25, €50 or €75 at some motorway tolls, restaurants, petrol stations, and at certain banks and most tobacconists. This makes paying tolls easier and faster, as you can use reserved lanes. Alternatively, you can obtain a *Telepass*, a sensor (known as an On Board Unit/OBU) installed on your windscreen that records the distance you travel on toll roads when you pass through *Telepass* gates. You're billed by direct debit from a bank account – quarterly if you spend less than €258, monthly for higher amounts. There are several options for both *Telepass* and *Viacard*, and the *Telepass* website (💻 www.telepass. it) offers the useful *ProfiloPass* facility, whereby you can find out your best option depending on how often you travel. *Viacards* and *Telepasses* aren't available on all motorways.

If you plan to travel long distances on the motorway network, the Autostrade Spa website (💻 www.autostrade.it) will prove invaluable. It provides comprehensive information in English about routes, tolls, service stations, traffic forecasts and interactive maps.

State roads (*strade statali*) are major roads indicated by blue signs and shown on maps with the prefix 'SS' followed by a number. They are often multi-lane, dual-carriageway roads and, although slower than motorways, are toll-free. Many state roads follow the routes originally planned by the ancient Romans, including the famous consular roads with illustrious names such as Via Appia, Via Pontina and Via Flaminia.

Provincial roads (*strade provinciali*), also with blue signs, are shown on maps as 'SP'. They vary considerably in quality and may be little more than rough tracks in some areas. The lowest grade are community roads (*strade comunali*) with white signs, which are 'maintained' (or not) by the local communes (e.g. towns) they serve. Motorways, state roads and most provincial roads are numbered, while other roads aren't.

If you drive in northern Italy in winter, when snow and ice are commonplace, take it easy! In bad conditions you will notice that most Italian drivers slow down considerably and even habitual tailgaters leave a larger gap than usual (at least a couple of metres!). Even a light snowfall can be treacherous, particularly on an icy road. When road conditions are bad, you should allow two to three times longer than usual to reach your destination (if you're wise, you'll stay at home). Bear in mind that many mountain passes are closed in winter – check with the Automobile Club Italia

☑ **SURVIVAL TIP**

Dial the emergency number (113) to report an accident or breakdown. On motorways, there are emergency phones every 2km (1.25mi), some of which have separate buttons for breakdowns (indicated by a spanner) and injuries (indicated by a red cross). Simply press the appropriate button and wait for help to arrive.

Road conditions can be checked 24 hours a day by calling the Automobile Club Italia (☎ 06-49981, 💻 www.aci.it).

Portofino, Liguria

3.

YOUR DREAM HOME

O nce you've considered possible locations for your dream home in Italy, you must decide on the type of property that will best suit your requirements, and consider the purchase options and the fees associated with buying.

When buying a home anywhere, it isn't wise to be in too much of a hurry – and Italy is no exception. Although it's a common practice, mixing a holiday with property purchase isn't wise, as most people are inclined to make poor decisions when their mind is fixed on play rather than business. Some people make expensive (even catastrophic) errors when buying a home in Italy, usually because they don't do sufficient research and are simply in too much of a hurry – often setting themselves ridiculous deadlines such as buying a home during a long weekend or a week's holiday.

It's all too easy to fall in love with the beauty and allure of Italy and sign a contract without giving it sufficient thought. If you're uncertain, don't allow yourself to be rushed into making a hasty decision, e.g. by fears of an imminent price rise or because someone else is interested in a property. Although many people dream of buying a holiday or retirement home in Italy, it's vital to do your homework thoroughly and avoid the 'dream sellers' (often fellow countrymen) who will happily prey on your ignorance and tell you anything in order to sell you a home.

It's a lucky person who gets his choice absolutely right first time, which is why most experts recommend that you rent before buying unless you're absolutely sure of what you want, how much you wish to pay and where you want to live (see **Renting Before Buying** on page 99). Have a good look around in your chosen region(s) and obtain an accurate picture of the types of property available, their relative prices and what you can expect to get for your money. However, before doing this, you should make a comprehensive list of what you want (and don't want) from a home, so that you can narrow the field and save time on wild goose chases.

There's no shortage of properties for sale in Italy (although rural properties in Tuscany and Umbria are now in short supply) and whatever kind of property you're looking for, you're likely have an abundance to choose from. In most areas, properties for sale include derelict farmhouses, unmodernised village homes, modern apartments with all mod cons, and a wide choice of detached villas. Another option is to buy a plot and have a house built to your specifications.

> ☑ SURVIVAL TIP
>
> Wait until you find something you fall head over heels in love with and then think about it for a week or two before rushing headlong to the *notaio*.

One of the advantages of buying property in Italy is that there's often another 'dream' home around the next corner – and the second or third dream home is often even better than the first. What seems at first to be the opportunity of a lifetime can turn out to be an expensive pile of stones. Don't dally too long, however, as good properties at the right price don't remain on the market for long.

If you're looking for a holiday home, you may wish to investigate mobile homes or a scheme that restricts your occupancy of a property to a number of weeks each year. These include shared ownership, leaseback and time-sharing (*multiproprietà*). Don't rush into any of these schemes without fully researching the market and before you're absolutely clear about what you want and what you can realistically expect to get for your money.

RESEARCH

The secret of successfully buying a home in Italy (or anywhere) is research, research and more research. A successful purchase is much more likely if you thoroughly investigate the various regions, the types of property available, prices and relative values, and the procedure for buying property. The more research you do before committing yourself the better; this should (if possible) include advice from those who already own a home in Italy, from whom you can usually obtain invaluable information (often based on their own mistakes), as well as by reading publications and visiting property exhibitions.

There are a number of books especially written for those planning to live or work in Italy (like this one and our sister publication, *Living and Working in Italy*, edited by Graeme Chesters).

Property exhibitions are now commonplace in the UK and Ireland, and are increasingly popular with prospective buyers, who can get a good idea of what's available and make contact with estate agents and developers. **Appendix A** includes a list of the main exhibition organisers in the UK and Ireland. *World of Property* (🖥 www.worldofproperty.co.uk) organise property exhibitions throughout in the south and north of England. Property is also advertised in many newspapers and magazines in Italy and abroad (see **Appendix B**), and on the Internet.

> ☑ SURVIVAL TIP
>
> The cost of investing in a few books or magazines (and other research) is tiny compared with the expense of making a big mistake.

AVOIDING PROBLEMS

The problems associated with buying property abroad have been highlighted in the last few decades or so, during which the property market in some countries has gone from boom to bust and back again. From a legal point of view, Italy is a relatively safe country in which to buy a home, and buyers have a high degree of protection under Italian law. However, you should take the usual precautions regarding contracts, deposits and obtaining proper title.

Among the most common 'problems' experienced by buyers in Italy are:

● buying in the wrong area (rent first!);

● buying a home that's difficult to resell: a property with broad appeal in a popular area is usually easiest to sell, although it will need to be very special to sell quickly in some areas. A modest, reasonably-priced property is usually likely to be much more sellable than a large expensive home, particularly one requiring restoration or modernisation.

- buying a house and garden much larger than you need because they seem to offer such good value. Although buying a house with umpteen rooms and several acres of land may seem like a good investment, bear in mind that, should you wish to sell, buyers may be thin on the ground, particularly if the price has doubled or trebled after the cost of renovation (see below). You should think carefully about what you're going to do with a large house and garden. Both will require a lot of maintenance, and your heating costs will be high. After you've installed a swimming pool, tennis court and croquet lawn, you will still have a lot of change left out of even a couple of acres. Do you like gardening or are you prepared to live in a jungle? Can you afford to pay a gardener? Of course, you can always plant an orchard or vineyard, create a lake or take up farming!

  Don't, on the other hand, buy a property that's too small; when you have a home in Italy, you will inevitably discover that you have many more relatives and 'friends' than you realised!

- buying a property for renovation and grossly underestimating the restoration costs;

Don't buy a rural property that doesn't have a reliable water supply, which is common problem in the south and on the islands.

- not having a survey done on an old property;

- not taking legal advice (see below);

- not including the necessary conditional clauses in the contract;

- buying a property for business, e.g. to convert to self-catering accommodation,

and being too optimistic about the income.

- paying too much, often due to overcharging by vendors and agents, particularly when selling to foreigners;

- taking on too large a mortgage;

- buying a property without a legal title;

- buying a property that has been built or extended without planning permission (see **Illegal Building** on page 97);

- buying a property that's subject to embargoes or an undischarged mortgage, is part of assets of a company, has been sold illegally by a bankrupt builder or company, is subject to claims by relatives or has been sold to more than one buyer;

- buying from a builder who absconds with your money before completing a property.

If an Italian company or builder goes bankrupt (*fallito*) within two years of selling a property, the liquidator can issue a 'revocation' (*revocatoria*) of the sale and include the buyer as one of the company's creditors.

Always beware when a property is offered at a seemingly bargain price by a builder, developer or other businessman (*imprenditore*), in which case you should run a thorough credit check on the vendor and his business.

Legal Advice

It cannot be emphasised too strongly that anyone planning to buy property in Italy must take expert, independent legal advice. If you aren't prepared to do this, you shouldn't even think about buying in Italy! The vast majority of people who buy a home in Italy don't obtain independent legal advice, and most of those who experience problems take no precautions whatsoever. Of those who do take legal advice, many do so only after having paid a deposit and signed a contract or, more commonly, after they have run into problems.

⚠ Caution

Never sign anything, or pay any money, until you've sought legal advice in a language in which you're fluent, from a lawyer who's experienced in Italian property law.

You will find that the relatively small cost (in comparison to the cost of a home) of obtaining legal advice to be excellent value, if only for the peace of mind it affords. Trying to cut corners to save a few Euros on legal costs is foolhardy in the extreme when a large sum of money is at stake.

Your lawyer (*avvocato*) will carry out the necessary searches regarding such matters as ownership, debts and rights of way. Your lawyer should also check that the notary does his job correctly, thereby providing

an extra safeguard. It isn't wise to use the vendor's lawyer, even if this will save you money, as he's primarily concerned with protecting the interests of the vendor and not the buyer.

Enquiries must be made to ensure that the vendor has a registered title and that there are no debts against a property. It's also important to check that a property has the relevant building licences, conforms to local planning conditions and that any changes (alterations, additions or renovations) have been approved by the local town hall and have planning permission (*concessione edilizia*). If a property is owned by several members of a family, which is common in Italy, all owners must give their consent before it can be sold (see **Conveyancing** on page 192).

Before hiring a lawyer, compare the fees charged by a number of practices and obtain quotations in writing. Always check what's included in the fee and whether it's 'full and binding' or just an estimate (a low basic rate may be supplemented by much more expensive 'extras'). A lawyer's fees may be calculated as an hourly rate (e.g. €200 per hour) or as a percentage of the purchase price of a property, e.g. 1 to 2 per cent, with a minimum fee of €500 to €1,000. You could employ a lawyer just to check the preliminary contract (see below) before signing it to ensure that it's correct and includes everything necessary, particularly regarding conditional clauses.

You may be able to obtain a list of lawyers who speak your national language and are experienced in handling Italian property sales, either in Italy or in your home country, e.g. British buyers can obtain a list from the Law Society in Britain. Note, however, that if you use a lawyer in your home country, you may have to pay extra fees, as your lawyer will almost certainly also have to use the services of a lawyer in Italy.

However, be careful who you engage, as some lawyers are part of the problem rather than the solution (overcharging is also rife)! Don't pick a lawyer at random, but engage one who has been recommended by someone you can trust.

Galoppino

A *galoppino* is an official agent licensed by the Italian government as a middleman between you and the bureaucracy. It isn't compulsory to employ a *galoppino*, but without one you will usually need to speak fluent Italian (or have an interpreter), possess boundless patience and stamina, and have unlimited time to deal with the mountains of red tape and obstacles. A *galoppino*'s services aren't generally expensive.

The quality of service provided by *galoppini* varies and they cannot always be relied upon to do a professional job (some have been known to take money from clients and do absolutely nothing).

Professionals

There are professionals speaking English and other languages in most areas of Italy,

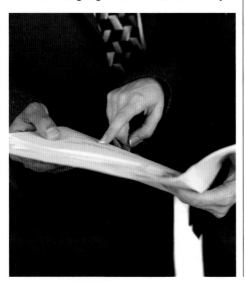

and many expatriate professionals (e.g. architects, builders and surveyors) also practise there. However, don't assume that because you're dealing with a fellow countryman he will offer you a better deal or do a better job than an Italian (the contrary may be true). It's wise to check the credentials of professionals you employ, whether Italian or foreign. It's important to deal only with a qualified and licensed estate agent (see page 117). A surveyor (*geometra*) may also be necessary, particularly if you're buying an old property or a property with a large plot (see **Inspections & Surveys** on page 153).

It's never wise to rely solely on advice proffered by those with a financial interest in selling you a property, such as a builder or estate agent, although their advice may be excellent and totally unbiased.

Illegal Building

Building illegally (called *abusivismo*) is a common practice in Italy, where it's estimated that around 150 houses a day are built illegally somewhere on the peninsula. Some 20,000 illegal homeowners in Italy have received demolition orders, although most aren't carried out. However, in one incident, the authorities demolished 72 villas that had been built illegally along a 3km stretch of the Salerno coastline and in recent years many *abusivi* villas on the outskirts of Rome have been bulldozed.

The Galasso law of the '70s declared that there were to be no new buildings within 250m (800ft) of the sea, but it has been ignored almost everywhere. In contrast, some inland regions have strict building regulations that have changed little in centuries. New development in many areas, including Emilia Romagna, Tuscany and Umbria, is prohibited and renovation is strictly regulated, e.g. existing buildings must be replaced with properties built in the same style and of the same size.

If you employ a lawyer, he should ensure that a property is legal, e.g. by checking that the building is registered at the Land Registry and that planning permission was obtained for it (see **Conveyancing** on page 161).

Subrogation

One Italian law that property buyers should be aware of is the law of subrogation, whereby property debts, including mortgages, local taxes, utility bills and community charges, remain with a property and are inherited by the buyer. This is an open invitation to dishonest sellers to 'cut and run'. It is, of course, possible to check whether there are any outstanding debts on a property, and this must be done by your legal advisor a few days before completion.

Finance

It's recommended to have your finances in place before you start looking for a property and, if you need a mortgage, to obtain a mortgage guarantee certificate from a bank that guarantees you a mortgage at a certain rate, which is usually subject to a valuation (see **Mortgages** on page

156). Under Italian law, you can withdraw from a contract and have your deposit returned if you're unable to obtain a mortgage. You will need to pay a deposit when signing a contract (see page 195), and must pay fees and taxes (see **Fees** on page 127) of between 10 and 20 per cent of the purchase price on completion, although resident, first-time buyers pay considerably less.

Declared Value: It's customary in Italy for buyers (and sellers) to under-declare the amount paid for a property, although this practice is illegal. If you under-declare the price, the authorities can re-value the property and demand that you pay the shortfall in tax plus interest and fines (see page 201).

Buying Off Plan

Many problems can arise when buying off plan (i.e. an unbuilt property) or a property on an unfinished development. Because of the problems associated with buying off plan, such as the difficulty in ensuring that you actually get what's stated in the contract and that the developer doesn't go broke, some experts have even advised buyers against buying an unfinished property. However, this isn't practical, because in a seller's market it's essential to buy off plan if you wish to buy a home in a popular development. Although there are many satisfied buyers of off plan property, the process is generally more time-consuming and stressful than buying a resale property.

An off plan property isn't finished until the building is complete in every detail (as confirmed by your own lawyer or architect), communal services have been installed, and all the infrastructure is in place, such as roads, parking areas, external lighting and landscaping. A builder is supposed to provide buyers who are purchasing off plan through stage payments with an insurance policy or banker's 'termination' guarantee, which protects them against the builder going broke before construction is completed. Note, however, that some builders fail to obtain insurance, and insurance certificates have even been found to be forged! See **Buying A New Home** on page 136

Buying Land

Before buying building land, ensure that it has planning permission (*concessione edilizia*) or that planning permission will be a formality. Don't take the vendor's word for this, but make it a condition of the purchase of a building plot. (see **Building Your Own Home** on page 142).

RENTING BEFORE BUYING

To reduce the chance of making an expensive error when buying in an unfamiliar region, it's often prudent to rent a house for a period, taking in the worst part of the year (weather-wise), especially if you're uncertain about exactly what sort of home you want and where you wish to live. This allows you to become familiar with the region and the weather, and gives you plenty of time to look around for a home at your leisure.

☑ SURVIVAL TIP

Renting before buying is even more important for those planning to live permanently or set up a business in Italy, when it isn't wise to buy a home until you're sure that the business will be a success.

If possible, you should rent a similar property to that which you're planning to buy, during the time of year when you intend to occupy it. Renting allows you to become familiar with not only the weather, but also the amenities and the local people, to meet other foreigners who have made their homes in Italy and share their experiences, and, not least, to discover the cost of living for yourself. Renting 'buys' you time to find your dream home at your leisure. You may even wish to consider renting a home in Italy long-term (or 'permanently'), as it saves tying up your capital and can be surprisingly inexpensive in many regions. Some people let their family homes and rent one in Italy for a period (you may even make a handsome profit!).

If you're looking for a rental property for three to six months, it's best not to rent unseen but to rent a holiday apartment for a week or two to allow yourself time to look around for a long-term rental. Properties for rent are advertised in Italian newspapers and magazines, including expatriate publications, and can also be found through property publications in many countries (see **Appendix B** for a list). Many estate agents offer short-term rentals, and builders and developers may rent properties to potential buyers.

Short-term rentals can be found through local tourist offices in Italy and Italian State Tourist Offices abroad, travel agents, the Internet and many overseas newspapers. The best newspapers in the UK are the *Sunday Times*, *Sunday Telegraph* and *Observer*, all of which contain holiday rental classifieds from British homeowners in Italy (although rents are usually astronomical). Most rental properties in Italy are let unfurnished (*non ammobiliato*), particularly for lets longer than a year; long-term furnished (*ammobiliato*) properties are difficult to find.

Long-Term Rentals

Italy has a strong, long-term rental market; there's considerable demand for property, particularly in Milan and Rome, although in recent years the number of Italian families renting has fallen significantly. It's possible to rent every kind of property, from a tiny studio apartment (*monolocale*) to a huge, rambling *castello*.

Long-term contracts (*patti in deroga*) are usually for four years with an automatic renewal for a second four-year period. Owners must give notice (*disdetta*) to tenants in writing six months prior to the expiration of a lease (three months for annual contracts) to terminate a contract. Luxury apartments (*di lusso*), public housing and tourist apartments are exempt from four-year contracts.

Rental costs vary considerably according to the size (number of bedrooms) and quality of a property, its age and the facilities provided. However, the most significant factor affecting rents is the region of Italy, the city and the neighbourhood. Italy recently had a fair rent (*equo canone*) law that limited rents to those set by the local authorities, rather than allowing them to find their own level according to demand. This resulted in a shortage of rental properties in some areas and owners are now permitted to set their own rents, which has encouraged more owners to rent their properties.

Most rents are negotiable and you should try to obtain a reduction. Sometimes an agent will even suggest offering a reduced rent and will even tell you what to offer. Italian landlords (*padroni*) often prefer renting to non-resident foreigners, who pay higher rents and are easier to evict! Note that rent is tax deductible for residents.

Long-term rents are roughly as follows:

Size Of Property	Monthly Rental (€)
Studio (bed-sitter)	350 – 950
1 bedroom	500 – 1,250
2 bedroom	700 – 1,650
3 bedroom	800 – 2,250

The above rents are for unfurnished, good quality, new or renovated properties in most rural and suburban areas. They don't include properties in major city centres and popular resort areas (such as the Alps, Italian lakes and coastal resorts), exclusive residential areas or furnished accommodation, which can cost **much** more.

You shouldn't rent a furnished property long-term without a written contract, which is important if you wish to have a deposit returned.

Short-Term Rentals

Italy has an abundance of self-catering accommodation for short-term rental (i.e. less than three months). You can choose from literally thousands of cottages, apartments, villas, bungalows, mobile homes, chalets, and even *castelli* and *palazzi*. Most property is available for holiday lets only, particularly during the peak summer season, and little furnished property is let for more than a few weeks. However, some foreign owners let their homes long-term, particularly outside the peak summer period.

Standards vary considerably, from dilapidated, ill-equipped cottages, to luxury villas with every modern convenience. A typical holiday rental is a small cottage or self-contained apartment with one or two bedrooms (sleeping two to four and usually including a sofa bed in the living-room), a large living-room/kitchen with an open fire or stove, and a toilet and bathroom. Always check whether a property is fully equipped (which should mean whatever you want it to mean!) and whether it has some sort of heating, preferably central heating, if you're planning to rent in winter.

For short-term lets, the cost is calculated on a weekly basis (Saturday to Saturday) and depends on the standard, location, number of beds and the facilities provided. For holiday rentals (except in ski resorts), the year is generally split into three rental periods: low (October to April), mid (May and September) and peak (July and August). A rural property sleeping two costs from around €350 per week in low season to €700 per week in peak season, while a property sleeping four costs from €525 per week in low season to €1,300 in high season. At the other end of the scale, you can easily pay €3,500 to €7,000 per week for a farmhouse with a swimming pool in Tuscany in summer.

There are *agriturismo* apartments in country areas sleeping four and costing as little as €350 per week in low season. If you rent for a short period from an agent, you should negotiate a lower commission than is usual (a month's rent), e.g. 10 per cent of the total rent payable. You can make agreements by fax or email when renting from abroad.

Rental laws and protection for tenants don't extend to holiday lettings, furnished lettings or sub-lettings. For holiday letting, parties are free to agree such terms as they see fit concerning the period, rent, deposit and the number of occupants permitted, and there's no legal obligation for the landlord to provide a written agreement.

HOTELS & HOSTELS

Hotels aren't a cost-effective solution for home hunters, although there's often little choice if you need accommodation for a short period only. Hotel rates in Italy vary according to the time of year, the location and the individual establishment, although you may be able to negotiate a lower rate outside the high season and for long stays. In most rural towns, a single room in a three-star hotel costs from around €60 and double rooms from €80 per night. You should expect to pay at least double or treble these rates in a major city, where cheap hotels are often used as permanent accommodation.

Bed and breakfast accommodation is also available, although it isn't usually budget accommodation. For budget accommodation you need to choose a hostel or residence, which is similar to a hotel but contains self-catering apartments or studios. There are also apartment hotels, listed in the yellow pages under *Residence e Appartamenti Ammobiliati*.

HOME EXCHANGE

An alternative to renting is to exchange your home abroad with one in Italy for a period. This way you can experience home living in Italy for a relatively small cost and may save yourself the expense of a long-term rental. Although there's an element of risk involved in exchanging your home with another family (depending on whether your swap is made in heaven or hell!), most agencies thoroughly vet clients and have a track record of successful swaps.

There are home exchange agencies in most countries, many of which are members of the International Home Exchange Association (IHEA). Home exchange companies in the USA include

HomeLink International, with over 12,500 members in around 50 countries (☎ 800-638 3841 or 954-566 2687, 💻 www. swapnow.com).

Two long-established home exchange companies in the UK are HomeLink International, 7 St. Nicholas Rise, Headbourne Worthy, Winchester S023 7SY (☎ 01962-886882, 💻 www.homelink. org.uk), which publishes a directory of homes and holiday homes for exchange, and Home Base Holidays, 7 Park Avenue, London N13 5PG, UK (☎ 020-8886 8752, 💻 www.homebase-hols.com). In Italy there's HomeLink International, Casa Vacanze, Viale Frassinette 84, 31046 Oderzo/TV (☎ 04-2281 5575, 💻 www. homelink.it) and Intervac International Home Exchange, Via Bottega 33, 40038 Vergato/BO (☎ 051-917 841, 💻 www. intervac-online.com).

HOUSE HUNTING

There are many ways of finding homes for sale in Italy, including the following:

- **Newspapers and magazines**, including the English-language publications listed in **Appendix B** and local property newspapers such as *Panorama Casa* (Tuscany), *La Pulce* (Florence), *Più Case* (Genoa, Milan, Piedmont, Rome and Turin), *Porta Portese Immobiliare* (Rome) and *Casa per Casa* (weekly and distributed free in Milan – city and province – and Rome), as well as magazines such as the monthly *Case e Country*, *Ville & Casali* and *Dimore* (mainly for up-market properties). Property is also advertised for sale in all major city newspapers, many of which contain property supplements on certain days.

- **Property tours**, which are organised by some companies, usually concentrating on a particular area in Italy over several days, during which you get a good idea of what's available. Some tours include visits to tourist attractions as well as the chance to sample local food and drink.

- **Property exhibitions** (see **Appendix A** for details);

- There are literally hundreds of websites dedicated to property in Italy. These can be found by typing in 'Italian property' in a search engine such as Google (💻 www.google.com). Most sites belong to (or are linked to) an estate agent.

- **Visiting an area**. Many property owners in Italy sell privately to avoid paying an agent's commission and put '*For Sale/ Vendesi*' signs outside a property. This is particularly common in rural areas, where properties may also be advertised in bars. You can also ask the locals if they know of any properties for sale.

Public Holidays	
Date	**Holiday**
1st January	New Year's Day (*Capodanno* or *Primo dell'Anno*)
6th January	Epiphany (*La Befana* or *Epifania*)
March or April	Easter Monday (*Lunedì di Pasqua*)
25th April	Liberation Day (*Festa della Liberazione*)
1st May	Labour Day (*Primo Maggio* or *Festa del Lavoro*)
First Sunday in June	Republic Day (*Festa della Repubblica*)
15th August	Feast of the Assumption (*Ferragosto*)
1st November	All Saints' Day (*Ognissanti or Tutti i Santi*)
First Sunday in November	Armistice Day (*Caduti di Tutti le Guerre*)
8th December	Immaculate Conception (*Immacolata Concezione*)
25th December	Christmas Day (*Natale*)
26th December	St Stephen's/Boxing Day (*Santo Stefano*)

● **Estate agents** (see below).

Public Holidays

If you're making a house-hunting trip to Italy, make sure you avoid public holidays (and, if a holiday falls on a Tuesday or a Thursday, the preceding Monday or following Friday respectively). Italian public holidays are shown above.

ESTATE AGENTS

Unlike some other countries, where almost all property sales are handled by estate agents (*agenzie immobiliari*) or other agents (*mediatore*), a large percentage of sales in Italy are private (directly between vendors and buyers) to avoid agents' fees. However, to buy privately you will need to speak good Italian or use an Italian intermediary who speaks English or your mother tongue. For this reason, foreign buyers often miss out on the best property buys, as well as some of the more interesting properties.

Most Italian agents are local and don't have a list of properties in other regions. This may mean that the seller is a friend or relative, in which case the agent won't have the buyer's best interests at heart (or anyone's but his own!). There are no national property listings, and most agents jealously guard their list of properties, although many work with overseas agents in areas popular with foreign buyers.

Nation-wide estate chains in Italy include Gabetti (🖥 www.gabetti.it), Grimaldi (🖥 www.grimaldi.net) and Tecnocasa (🖥 www. tecnocasa.it), all of which operate on a franchise basis with numerous agents around the country. If you wish to find an agent in a particular town or area, look under *Agenzie Immobiliari* in the local yellow pages, which are available at main libraries in many countries and via the internet (🖥 www.paginegialle.it). In Rome and Milan, there are property 'exchanges', where you can buy and sell properties through agents. Buyers can list their details (name and telephone number and the type of property they're looking for or selling), which are accessed by estate agents.

It's common for foreigners in many countries, particularly the UK, to use an agent in their own country, who works with one or more Italian agents, or a British agent (for example) in Italy. Italian agents aren't noted for their efficiency and you may receive a better service from a British or other foreign agent who speaks English, and is used to dealing with foreigners and their particular requirements (such as old rural properties requiring renovation).

On the other hand, you may pay higher fees when dealing with a foreign agent, as there may be more people involved and local property owners may inflate the price when they think a 'rich' foreigner (all foreigners are rich to Italian country folk) is interested in buying their home. In the past, owners and agents selling to the British have been known to increase prices by as much as 50 per cent. Go around with a local agent or, even better, get a local person to negotiate the price for you –but make sure you can trust them!

A number of Italian agents advertise abroad, particularly in the publications listed in **Appendix B**. Many of them speak English or have English-speaking staff, so don't be discouraged if you don't speak Italian. You can also find English-speaking agents through the *English Yellow Pages* (🖳 www.englishyellowpages.it).

⚠ Caution
Whoever you buy through, make sure that you know the local market value of property, as it's easy to pay over the odds in popular areas.

Qualifications

Italian estate agents are regulated by law and must be professionally qualified and

licensed, and hold indemnity insurance. They also hold deposits on behalf of buyers and sellers, thus ensuring that the seller won't abscond with your money. To work in his own right in Italy, an agent must be registered with the local chamber of commerce (*camera di commercio*) and have a certificate issued by the local *comune* as proof of registration. An agent should also be registered with the Italian association of estate agents (AICI, Via Nerino 5, 20123 Milan, ☎ 02-7201 0974, 🖳 www.aici-italia.it), federation of mediators and agents (FIMAA, Piazza G. Belli, 2, Rome, ☎ 06-586 6476, 🖳 www.fimaa.it) or federation of professional estate agents (FIAIP, Piazzale Flaminio 9, 00196 Rome, ☎ 06-452 3181, 🖳 www.fiaip.it).

There are a number of unlicensed agents operating in Italy, and you shouldn't view properties with anyone who isn't a professional agent registered with one of the above bodies (which should be mentioned in the *Elenco Iscritti* section of the agent's website).

Some British estate agents operating in Italy may be registered with the Federation of Overseas Property Developers, Agents and Consultants (FOPDAC, c/o NAEA, Arbon House, 6 Tournament Court, Edgehill Drive, Warwick CV34 6LG, ☎ 01926-496800, 🖳 www.fopdac.com), an organisation whose members are English-speaking agents, lawyers and other property specialists. There are strict criteria for membership and all members are bound by a code of ethics.

Agents vary enormously in their efficiency, enthusiasm and professionalism. If an agent shows little interest in finding out exactly what you want, you should look elsewhere.

Commission

Agents' commissions (*provvigione*) vary considerably (e.g. from 3 to 8 per cent) and are usually shared equally between the vendor and buyer. Some agents levy a fixed commission, e.g. €2,000 on properties costing up to €50,000 and a maximum of €12,000 on properties costing up to €300,000. The cheaper the property, the higher the fee as a percentage of the sale; on the most expensive properties fees may be negotiable. Check in advance how much commission you're required to pay in addition to the sale price (apart from the normal fees and taxes associated with buying a property in Italy – see **Fees** on page 111) and when they must be paid. Check also whether the agent charges extra for services such as additional viewings, checking the property on your behalf, and arranging for the connection of utilities.

An agent's fees may be payable at the time the preliminary sales contract is signed and not on completion, and you should ensure that they're refundable if the sale doesn't go through (see **Contracts** on page 163).

Many foreign agents work with Italian agents and share the standard commission, so buyers usually pay no more by using a foreign agent.

Viewing

If possible, you should decide where you want to live, what sort of property you want and your budget **before** visiting Italy. Obtain details of as many properties as possible in your chosen area and make a shortlist of those you wish to view (it's also wise to mark them on a map). Traditionally, the details provided by Italian estate agents are sparse. Often there's no photograph and even when there is, it usually doesn't do a property justice (or is flattering). However, the advent of the Internet has changed this somewhat, and most good agents have extensive websites providing details of properties they offer, although not all properties are included on them and you may need to register to view those that are.

Italian agents who advertise in foreign journals or who work closely with overseas agents may provide colour photographs and a full description, particularly for expensive properties. The best agents provide an abundance of information, although, in the case of old properties in need of renovation, there obviously isn't much information that can be provided except the land area and the number and size of buildings.

If you've made an appointment via a foreign agent to see particular properties, make a note of their reference numbers in case the Italian agent hasn't been informed (or has lost them). It isn't unusual for an Italian agent's reference numbers not to match those you're given by an agent abroad! Some agents, particularly outside Italy, don't update their records frequently and their lists may be considerably out of date.

If you're using a foreign agent, confirm (and reconfirm) that a particular property is still for sale and the price, before travelling to Italy to view it.

Some Italian agents expect customers to know where they want to buy within a 30 to 40km (20 to 25mi) radius and may even expect you to narrow your choice down to certain towns or villages. If you cannot define where and what you're looking for, tell the agent so that he will know that you're undecided. If you're 'just looking' (window shopping), say so. Most agents will still be pleased to show you properties, as they're well aware that many people fall in love with (and buy) a property on the spot, but some agents now charge a fee (e.g. €50 for an afternoon) for showing properties in order to discourage time wasters.

An Italian agent may ask you to sign a document before showing you any properties; this is simply to protect his commission should you obtain details from another source or try to do a deal directly with the owner. You're usually shown properties personally by agents and won't be given the keys (particularly to furnished properties) or be expected to deal with tenants or vendors directly. One reason is that many properties are almost impossible to find if you don't know the area and it isn't unknown even for agents to get lost when

looking for properties! Many rural properties have no numbers, and street names may not be marked. (If someone invites you to dinner in Italy, make sure you have a telephone number for when you get lost!)

You should make an appointment to see properties, as agents don't like people simply turning up and asking to view a property. If you make an appointment, you should keep it or call and cancel it. If you're on holiday, you can drop in unannounced to have a look at what's on offer, but don't expect an agent to show you any properties without an appointment. If you view properties during a holiday, it's wise to do so at the beginning so that you can return later to inspect any you particularly like a second or third time. Italian estate agents usually work on Saturdays and even on Sundays in some areas during the peak season.

You should try to view as many properties as possible during the time available, but allow enough time to view each property thoroughly, to travel and get lost between houses, and for breaks for sustenance (it's **mandatory** to have a good lunch in Italy). Although it's important to see sufficient properties to form an accurate opinion of price and quality, don't see too many in one day (between four and six is usually a manageable number), as it's easy to become confused as to the merits of each property. If you're shown properties that don't meet your requirements, tell the agent immediately. You can help the agent to narrow the field by telling him exactly what's wrong with the properties you reject.

It's wise to make notes of both the good **and** bad features, and take lots of photographs of the properties you like, so that you're able to compare them later at your leisure, but keep a record of which photos are of which house! It's also wise to mark each property on a map so that, should you wish to return, you can find them without getting lost (too often).

Legal Advice

Never allow yourself to be pressurised into a purchase and always take independent expert legal advice. Some agents pressurise clients into signing contracts and paying deposits quickly, alleging that there are queues of other clients waiting to buy the property (which may be true!). Some even claim that legal advice is unnecessary or that they provide it themselves, which is both illegal and unethical.

There are a large number of complaints concerning fraud and malpractice against estate agents in Italy, particularly from foreign buyers, and there's little consumer protection.

Your chance of solving any problems is greater if you take legal advice – registered lawyers have professional indemnity insurance. There are, however, many reputable estate agents in Italy, who provide an excellent and reliable service.

PROPERTY PRICES

Property prices in Italy rose considerably in the '80s in most areas, driven by the high demand for second homes from both foreigners and Italians. However, as the recession hit Italy in the late '80s and early '90s, prices fell as buyers disappeared, although Italy didn't experience the dramatic falls that many other European countries and North America experienced. During the recession, most Italians simply refused to accept the lower market prices and only sold if they were forced to do so. Prices were also maintained by the cautious lending policies of Italian banks, which led to fewer repossessions than in some other countries.

In 1998, however, a decade of property recession ended, helped by the weakness of the lira against the British pound and US dollar and the entry of foreign lenders into the mortgage market, which made home loans easier to obtain. Since 2002, the poor performance of stock markets world-wide has led to a marked increase in investment in Italian property (as in many other countries) and the property market is currently booming.

Between 2004 and mid-2007, prices rose on average by some 25 per cent country-wide, but throughout 2007, price increases have been slowing, although they're still well ahead of inflation (which was around 1.8 per cent in mid-2007). In rural areas, where there's no strong local demand, prices are unlikely to rise or fall dramatically.

Rural Areas

As in most countries, property is at its cheapest in rural areas, where the exodus in the last 30 years has left the countryside with a surfeit of empty properties and, with the exception of properties within commuting distance of a major city, the further south you go the cheaper rural property becomes. Except in the most popular areas (see **Tuscany** below, rural property generally costs between €550 and €2,500 per m2.

Although you can spend several million Euros on a luxurious *palazzo* or a large country estate, it's possible to buy a renovated village house or a one or two-bedroom apartment in a small town for as little as €75,000. In many areas, old village houses in need of complete restoration can be purchased for €50,000, although you can easily pay as much again (or more) in restoration costs (see **Renovation &**

Restoration on page 135). In many rural areas, €80,000 to €185,000 will buy a restored two-bedroom farmhouse with a bit of land. However, you can pay over €1m for a small farmhouse in a fashionable area of Tuscany or an apartment with a view on the Italian Riviera.

Among the most popular rural areas are the Italian lakes (where little property is available except for apartments), which is reflected in the above average prices, e.g. from €150,000 for a new or restored one-bedroom apartment on Lake Como or Maggiore, and from €180,000 for a two-bedroom apartment. If you dream of living in Venice, bear in mind that a studio on the Grand Canal will set you back around €400,000 – if you can find one! – and *palazzo* apartments go for millions. Homes on the Italian Riviera are also highly prized and expensive, but a good investment. Here a studio apartment will cost you €125,000 and a two-bedroom, sea-front apartment €375,000 or more. A short distance inland, however, traditional unrestored village houses can be bought for as little as €50,000.

Properties in ski resorts and on most islands are also expensive due to the shortage of building land and high demand, but are a good investment and have excellent rental potential. In a top ski resort, such as Cortina, you will pay from €120,000 for a studio, from €210,000 for a one-bedroom apartment and from €300,000 for a two-bedroom apartment. Two or three-bedroom villas cost up to €1.2m. For those with smaller bank balances, holiday apartments in many coastal resorts and Sicily start at around €125,000.

Tuscany

Tuscany is by far the most popular (and expensive) region for country homes among foreigners, particularly the so-called 'golden triangle' bounded by Florence, Sienna and Volterra, which is claimed to have the world's most expensive rural property. So many Britons have purchased homes in Tuscany that the Chianti region has been dubbed 'Chiantishire' by expatriate Brits ('a corner of Italy that's forever England'). Much of Tuscany is absurdly expensive, but in areas such as Lunigiana, Mugello, north of Lucca and around Arezzo, prices are around half those in the more expensive areas.

> ☑ **SURVIVAL TIP**
>
> If you're looking for a country property in an attractive area, you will find that in the Marche and Umbria prices are around 30 to 50 per cent lower than the most expensive areas of Tuscany and properties often come with much more land.

Cities

Prices in the major cities vary considerably with the suburb or zone, and properties may be sub-divided into *signorile* (refined or luxury), *medio* (average) and *economico* (economy). Italy's most expensive property is found in Milan and Rome, and, of course, Venice. Here a three-bedroom apartment can easily cost over €500,000. Prime properties can cost up to €10,000 per m2 (*al m²* or *al metro quadrato*) in central Milan, Rome and Venice, and €1,750 to €6,500 in other major cities and resort areas. However, property in most cities is typically from €850 per m2 for old unrenovated properties and up to €5,000 per m2 for new or renovated properties. In cities and towns, garages and external parking places are usually sold separately and may cost around €30,000 and €15,000 respectively.

Negotiating the Price

To get an idea of property prices in different regions of Italy, check the prices of properties advertised in English-language property magazines and Italian newspapers, magazines and property journals (see **Appendix B**). Property price indexes for various regions are published by some Italian property magazines (e.g. *Ville & Casali*), although these should be taken as a rough guide only.

There has been evidence of dual pricing in the past, and the practice of quoting higher prices to foreigners, although now rare, still occurs. Check the local prices and make sure that you aren't paying (too much) over the odds.

When buying a property in Italy it pays to haggle over the price, even if you think it's a bargain (don't show too much enthusiasm or the price is likely to increase suddenly!). Don't be put off by a high asking price, as most sellers are willing to negotiate. Many properties sell for a lot less than their original asking prices, particularly luxury properties priced at over €1m. Sellers generally presume that buyers will bargain and rarely expect to receive the asking price, although some vendors ask an unrealistic price and won't budge a Euro! In popular areas (e.g. the Italian Riviera and Tuscany), asking prices may be unrealistically high particularly to snare the unsuspecting and ignorant foreign buyer. It may be worthwhile obtaining an independent valuation (appraisal) to determine a property's 'true' value.

Italians drive a much harder bargain than most foreigners when buying a property, particularly an old property. They're often astonished at the prices foreign buyers are prepared to pay for nondescript homes in uninspiring areas, although they **never** complain about foreigners pushing up prices when they're selling! Many Italians think the British are particularly insane for buying up their tumbled down farmhouses and crumbling *palazzi*. (Few foreigners share the British passion for renovating old homes, although they have a grudging admiration for their painstaking and often sensitive restorations.)

If you're using an agent, you should ask him what to offer, although he may not tell you (and indeed shouldn't, if he's also acting for the seller). If you make an offer that's too low you can always raise it, but it's usually impossible to lower an offer once it has been accepted (if your first offer is accepted without discussion, you will never know how low you could have gone!). On the other hand, if you make a very low offer, an owner may feel insulted and refuse to do business with you! If an offer is rejected, it may be worth waiting a week or two before making a higher offer, depending on the market and how keen you are to buy a particular property.

If you make a low offer, it's wise to indicate to the owner a few points of weakness (without being too critical) that merit a reduction in price. If a property has been realistically priced, you shouldn't expect to obtain more than a 5 or 10 per cent reduction, although cash buyers in some areas may be able to negotiate a considerable reduction for a quick sale, depending on the state of the local property market and the urgency of the sale. An offer should be made in writing, as it's likely to be taken more seriously than a verbal offer. Always be prepared to walk away from a deal rather than pay too high a price.

If you simply want to buy a property at the best possible price as an investment, then shopping around and buying a 'distress sale' from an owner who simply must sell is likely to result in the best deal. Obviously you will be in a better position if you're a cash buyer and are able to close quickly. If you're seeking an investment property, it's best to buy in an area that's in high demand, preferably with both buyers and renters. For the best resale opportunities, it's usually best to buy in an area or community (and style) that's attractive to Italian buyers.

You should find out as much as possible about a property before making an offer, such as:

● when it was built;

● how long the owners have lived there;

● whether it's a permanent or holiday home;

● why they're selling (they may not tell you outright, but may offer clues);

● how keen they are to sell;

● how long it has been on the market;

● the condition of the property;

● what the neighbours and the neighbourhood are like;

● local property taxes and insurance rates;

● and not least, whether the asking price is realistic.

Timing is of the essence in the bargaining process and it's essential to find out how long a property has been on the market (generally the longer it has been for sale, the more likely a lower offer will be accepted) and how desperate the vendor is to sell. Some people will tell you outright

that they must sell by a certain date and that they will accept any reasonable offer. You may be able to find out from neighbours why someone is selling, which may help you to decide whether an offer would be accepted. If a property has been on the market for a long time, e.g. longer than six months in a popular area, it may be overpriced (unless it has obvious problems). If there are many desirable properties for sale in a particular area or development that have been on the market a long time, you should find out why.

For your part, you must ensure that you keep any 'sensitive' information from a seller and give the impression that you have all the time in the world (even if you're desperate to buy immediately!). All this 'cloak and dagger' stuff may seem unethical, but you can rest assured that if you were selling and a prospective buyer knew you were desperate and would accept a low offer, he certainly wouldn't be in a hurry to pay you any more!

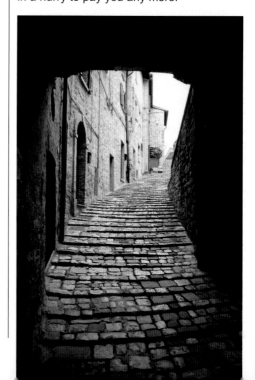

☑ SURVIVAL TIP

Before deciding on the price, make sure you know exactly what's included, as it isn't unusual for Italians to strip a house or apartment bare when selling, and remove the kitchen sink, toilets, light fittings and even light switches!

If applicable, have fixtures and fittings listed in the contract. It's also wise to take photographs if a property contains original architectural details, such as stone fireplaces, door and window lintels, and garden statuary, which may be removed or replaced by copies. See also **Final Checks** on page 167.

FEES

A variety of fees (also called closing or completion costs) are payable when you buy a property in Italy. These vary considerably according to the price, whether the property is new or old, whether you're buying via an agent or privately, and whether you have employed a lawyer or other professionals. Most property fees are based on the 'declared' value of a property, which is usually less than the actual purchase price or its 'market' value (see **Declared Value** on page 168).

The fees associated with buying a property in Italy are among the highest in Europe and may include registration tax, land registry tax, value added tax (VAT), a notary's and estate agent's fees, mortgage fees and legal fees, as detailed below. Fees are usually payable on the completion of a sale and range from around 9 to 15 per cent for a non-resident (the average is around 13 per cent), although they can be as high as 20 per cent for luxury properties. **Before signing a preliminary contract,** **check exactly what fees are payable and have them confirmed in writing.** If you're a resident, the fees associated with buying a property in Italy can be offset against income tax (see page 182).

Registration Tax

Registration tax (*imposta di registro*) is the main tax on property and is levied at between 0 and 10 per cent of the declared value or *rendita catastale*. The amount payable depends on whether it's your first and only home or a second home, whether it's a new home and whether you're a resident, as follows:

● Buyers of new properties don't pay registration tax, but must pay VAT (see below).

● On your first home, you're eligible for a reduced tax of 3 per cent. The property must be your principal home for residential use and be located in your present or future *comune* of residence (or in the *comune* where you have or plan to have your main place of business) and it mustn't be classified as a 'luxury' home. This concession is theoretically available once only, although this isn't always the case in practice.

● The registration tax for non-residents and those buying second homes is 7 per cent, so if you're planning to become a resident in Italy it will pay to do so before buying a home there.

● If you're buying an agricultural property, you must pay tax at 10 per cent, although it may be possible to have it 'de-ruralised' (*deruralizzato*) before the sale, thus reducing the tax payable from 10 to 7 per cent (or to 3 per cent if it's your main residence). Agricultural land, however, is always taxed at 10 per cent. When a property comprises both an urban building and agricultural land, tax

is calculated separately for the building and the land.

Registration tax is payable on completion (see page 168).

Land Registry Tax

Land registry tax (*imposta catastale*) is payable on all property purchases and, as with registration tax, the amount payable depends on whether it's your first and only home or a second home, whether it's a new home and whether you're a resident. First home resident buyers of new or resale properties pay a fixed fee of €129.11. Buyers of second homes and non-residents pay 1 per cent of the declared price.

Value Added Tax

Buyers of new properties must pay VAT (*IVA*), which is levied at 4 per cent if it's to be your main residence, at 10 per cent for second homes and non-resident buyers, and at 20 per cent on luxury homes (with a rating of A1 in the property register). VAT may be included in the price by the builder

or developer, but make sure you check this. If you build your own home, you pay VAT at 4 per cent; if you buy from a company, you must pay VAT at 20 per cent irrespective of the type of property. VAT at 20 per cent is also levied on all professionals' fees (see below).

Mortgage Fees

There are various fees associated with mortgages (*spese istruttoria*). All lenders charge an arrangement fee for establishing a loan, usually around 1 per cent of the loan amount. There's a mortgage tax (*imposta ipotecaria*) of €129.11 for resident first-home buyers and 1 per cent otherwise, and a fee of 0.25 per cent (*imposta sostitutiva*) is payable to the notary (*notaio*) for registering the charge against the property at the land registry (*catasto*). Most lenders also impose an 'administration' fee of around 1 per cent of the loan value, and it's compulsory to take out insurance cover with the lender against fire, lightning strikes and gas explosions. The insurance is usually a one-off payment of 0.21 per cent of the property's value and is valid for 20 years.

Notary's Fees

Notary's fees depend on the price of a property and are higher (as a percentage of the selling price) on cheaper properties. There's also a fee for each page and each copy of a contract, plus fees for extra services such as taxes (e.g. tax stamps), expenses, legal advice and any payments made on your behalf. Notary's fees for the completion vary, although there are maximum charges for each service. Typical fees are €1,400 for a property costing €50,000 and €3,000 for a property costing €500,000 plus fees for other services. Fees for a preliminary contract are around half these.

You can obtain an estimate in writing, although fees depend on the work involved and are subject to a surcharge known as the *rimborso delle spese generali di studio* for 'overheads', levied by all professionals in Italy. All fees are itemised in the notary's bill (*parcella*). If you buy a home through an agent, he may have an agreement (*notaio convenzionato*) with a notary (*notaio*) whereby all notary's expenses are incorporated into a 'standard' fee and agreed with the buyer. Check in advance.

Legal Fees

The fees for conveyancing, which is usually performed by a lawyer (*avvocato*), are usually from 1 to 2 per cent of the declared price of a property or a fixed fee, depending on the amount of work involved. Fees are subject to VAT at 20 per cent.

Estate Agent's Commission

Agents' commissions (*provvigione*) vary considerably, e.g. from 3 to 8 per cent, and are usually shared equally between the vendor and buyer (see **Commission** on page 104).

Utility Fees

If you buy a new property, you must usually pay for electricity, gas and water connections and the installation of meters. You should ask the builder or developer to provide the cost of connection to services in writing. If you buy a resale property, you must usually pay for the cost of new contracts, particularly water. See **Utilities** on page 240.

Other Fees

Other fees may include surveyor's or inspection fees (see **Inspections & Surveys** on page 130), architect's fees and the cost of moving house (see **Chapter 6**).

Running Costs

In addition to the fees associated with buying a home, you must also take into account the running costs. These include local property taxes (see page 187), building insurance (see page 198), contents insurance (see page 199), standing charges for utilities (see page 113); community fees for a community property (see page 124); refuse tax (*tassa communale dei rifiuti*), garden and pool maintenance costs, and a caretaker's or management fees if you leave a home empty or let it (see page 213). Annual running costs usually average around 2 to 4 per cent of the cost of a property.

TYPES OF PROPERTY

There's an overwhelming choice of property for sale in Italy, which is a buyers' market in most rural areas, with the exception of the saturated areas of Tuscany and Umbria. In most areas, properties range from derelict farmhouses, barns and village homes, to modern townhouses and apartments with all modern conveniences; from dilapidated *castelli* and mansions requiring complete restoration to luxury modern chalets and villas (see below).

> A myriad of civilisations have left their mark on Italian architecture, one of the world's richest and most colourful and, many would argue, among the best preserved.

Perhaps nowhere else in the world do so many towns and villages proudly display street after street of beautiful buildings, many of which are architectural gems – in Venice alone there are some 5,000 palaces built between the 15th and 19th centuries, some 1,500 of which are preserved (listed) buildings.

Each region has a typical type of property, which include elaborately decorated Tyrolean-style chalets in Trentino, stunning *palazzi* in pink Istrian stone in Venice, *trulli* (small white-washed houses with dark conical roofs) in Puglia, *sassi* (small cave houses built deep into the rocks) in Basilicata, and rustic stone farmhouses with terracotta roofs in Tuscany. The purchase and restoration of these typical homes, particularly those in the north and centre of Italy, is enormously popular among foreigners, especially those keen to establish small hotels or bed and breakfast businesses. If you would rather purchase a more modern property, there are many apartments, townhouses and villas purpose-built for the holiday-home market.

The main types of property available are detailed below. Note, however, that it's sometimes difficult to compare homes in different regions, as they often vary considerably and few houses are exactly comparable. The variety of homes in Italy is almost infinite and, with the exception of modern apartments, few are alike.

Modern Apartments

Like many of their southern European counterparts, the Italians like to live in apartments (*appartamenti*), which are ubiquitous in towns and cities, and common on the coast in resort areas. Most suburban apartments have been built since the '50s, but the quality varies considerably from poor (in the first rapidly constructed blocks) to excellent (in some of the more recent buildings). There are few brand new apartments, as building has practically ceased. Apartments in the centre of towns and cities tend to be older, and often form part of a larger building that has been restored and divided into several apartments. It's increasingly popular in the inner cities to convert non-residential buildings, e.g. factories or warehouses, into luxury apartments, where Italian design comes into its own. Older apartments tend to have high ceilings and small rooms (unless they once formed part of a palace or noble's home), all highly decorated, often with stucco.

Apartments are generally good value and, if they're in a popular tourist location, offer year-round rental potential. The advantages of apartment living include low maintenance (once you've carried out any necessary work), security (especially if the block has 24-hour security or a *concierge/ portiere*), and the use of communal gardens and pool (and possibly other facilities such as tennis courts). Apartments in towns have the added advantage of local facilities and amenities within walking distance. Disadvantages can include noisy neighbours, poorly-maintained communities, crowded complexes during holidays, little storage space (although many new apartments have fitted wardrobes), and antiquated electricity and plumbing which may require replacing. Bear in mind that Italian apartments generally have a maximum of three bedrooms.

> Under Italian law, all owners of apartments are members of the community of owners, and must abide by the community's rules and regulations and pay community fees (see Community Properties on page 140).

Modern Townhouses & Villas

Although most Italians live in apartments, among the younger generation it's becoming increasingly desirable to live in semi-detached houses (*casa bifamiliare* or *terratetto*) or detached houses (*villa unifamiliare* or *villette*) with small gardens or patios, which usually form part of a purpose-built residential area. Construction is generally of excellent quality – marble floors and top-of-the-range kitchens are the norm.

Resort developments, some of which are among the most exclusive in the world (e.g. the Costa Smeralda on Sardinia), often have communal gardens with a swimming pool and sports facilities such as tennis courts. There may also be 24-hour security. Both Milan and Rome have numerous villa and townhouse developments (the former Italian premier, Silvio Berlusconi, is reported to have made his first millions when he developed the first such complexes, Milano 2 and 3 in the early '70s), while coastal resorts usually contain purpose-built holiday villas in residential complexes, which are popular among Italians as second homes (most Italians wouldn't be seen dead restoring a Tuscan ruin!). Note, however, that these may not be suitable as permanent homes.

The advantages of a modern home on a residential complex include little upkeep (and no restoration work!), spacious living, use of communal gardens and pool without maintenance costs or work, and community living with fewer neighbours than in an apartment. Among the disadvantages are high community fees and a lack of historic architecture, although modern Italian architectural design features among the world's best.

As in the case of apartments, all owners of properties within a residential complex in Italy are members of the community of owners, and must abide by the community's rules and regulations and pay community fees (see **Community Properties** on page 121).

Country Properties

By far the most popular homes among foreigners in Italy are country properties, of which there are many, although in some regions (e.g. Marche, Tuscany and Umbria) there are now few country homes for sale. In other regions there are endless possibilities, ranging from humble shepherds' huts to vast estates (see below), particularly in areas where there's high rural unemployment and the population is migrating from the country to the cities, e.g. Campania and Abruzzo. Almost all country properties come with large plots and many include vineyards, fruit trees, olive groves or pasture land. Renovation is almost always necessary, unless you pay a premium for a property that has already been modernised.

Advantages of country properties include lower prices (except in Tuscany), peace and quiet, low local taxes and the opportunity to live in the 'real' Italy.

On the other hand, rural properties usually involve extensive maintenance as well as restoration work, utilities may be poor or non-existent, amenities and facilities are often some distance away, and you don't have the advantage of a ready-made community. The good news is that Italian village communities are generally among the friendliest and most welcoming in the world. In some rural areas of Tuscany, there are well-established expatriate communities, particularly English or German-speaking, if you don't want to take the plunge into the 'real' Italy.

The Italian countryside is littered with farmhouses (*casali*), which are probably the most popular purchase among foreigners, particularly the British. Farmhouses,

most of which date from the 16th to 18th centuries, generally have thick stone walls (to retain the heat in winter and keep it out in summer) with terracotta roofs, and often an exterior bread oven (*forno a legna*). Traditionally the family lived on the first floor and the livestock was kept on the ground floor. Farmhouses are generally large and are sold with a considerable amount of land. Bear in mind that you cannot restore a farmhouse unless the property has been registered as 'urban' (see **Restoration & Renovation** on page 135).

Village homes are becoming increasingly popular with foreign buyers, keen to experience the 'real' Italy without the isolation of the countryside. Properties vary greatly in size, age (expect to find medieval houses as well as modern) and state of restoration, although many older properties are now sold already restored. In the regions of Marche, Tuscany and Umbria, you're more likely to find a home in one of the many villages than a property in the countryside.

Castles, Monasteries, Estates & Villages

Castles (*castelli*) and monasteries (*conventi*) are available for sale around Italy and often include unique architectural features such as frescos or a medieval chapel, although more often than not this sort of property has been abandoned for years and requires extensive restoration, which can cost at least as much as the property itself if not more (see Restoration & Renovation on page 135). Some restored castles and monasteries have been converted into successful hotel businesses.

Those with deep pockets might consider buying a country estate (known simply as a *villa*), which are found throughout the country, usually within easy reach of a large town or city. Estates, once summer residences for Italy's nobility, generally

consist of a large house, often in Baroque or Renaissance style, set in extensive gardens and grounds, which may include vineyards (*vigneti*). Estates with vineyards producing *DOC* wines attract a premium, and the running of a wine estate is not for the faint-hearted, particularly if you wish to make it a successful business venture.

Emigration from the countryside to the cities has left entire villages abandoned, particularly in the south, although some can also be found in the north and centre. Some villages are for sale in their entirety, although as with a castle or monastery, they usually require extensive restoration and are generally found in isolated and disadvantaged areas (which is why their inhabitants left in the first place!), so that it would be difficult to make a business venture (e.g. holiday accommodation) of the project.

ITALIAN HOMES

Italian homes and living standards used to be basic, particularly in rural areas, where many homes had no bathroom or toilet. However, with the huge rise in the standard (and cost) of living in the last few decades,

Italian homes have been transformed and today's average Italian is better housed than many other Europeans.

☑ **SURVIVAL TIP**

Whether their homes are old or new, Italians take great pride in them, and no expense is spared to make them comfortable and beautiful.

Homes in Italy are as varied as the climate and people, but one thing they all have in common is sturdy building materials. The exterior may be made of wood, stone, brick or other (usually fire resistant) materials. Interior walls are usually white *stucco* plaster (*intonaco*), which may be painted in pastel colours and makes a perfect backdrop for paintings and tapestries, while bedroom walls are often covered with wallpaper. Wood floors (*parquet*) are common in northern Italian homes, but are considered a luxury in the rest of Italy and therefore generally reserved for the master bedroom. Marble or travertine (*travertino*) is often used in entrance halls (*ingressi*), corridors (*corridoi*) and living rooms (*saloni*), while kitchens (*cucine*) and baths (*bagni*) are generally enhanced by beautiful ceramic tiles (for which Italy is famous).

Bathrooms are usually fitted with a toilet, washbasin (*lavandino*), bidet and shower (*doccia*) or bath (*vasca*), or perhaps a bath with a shower attachment. Luxury homes often have a Jacuzzi (*idromassaggio*). When there's no separate utility or laundry room (*lavanderia*), the water heater (*scaldabagno*) and washing machine (*lavatrice*) are usually stored in the main (*servizio*) bathroom.

Italian homes are completely empty when purchased, except perhaps for the bathroom porcelain and the kitchen sink.

All furnishings and appliances must be chosen and installed by the new owner, who can have the kitchen fitted by a local carpenter-artisan or buy factory-produced kitchen cabinets. Ovens may be electric or mains gas (which is available in most urban areas – see page 245), and country properties may have an exterior pizza/ bread oven (*forno a legna*) and a *tinello* or *taverna*, which is used as a family room or a summer kitchen/dining room. Very few Italians use clothes dryers (the sun and wind suffice), but washing machines are common. If you live in a rural area you may find a public washhouse (*lavatoio*), which is good for washing voluminous things such as curtains, in addition to being a good place to catch up on local gossip and for summer swimming for children.

Unrestored country properties rarely have central heating ('What you don't spend in wood, you spend in wool' is an old Italian saying), but numerous fireplaces. The thick stone walls (which in old buildings may measure over a metre) keep out the cold in winter, thus reducing heating (*riscaldamento*) costs, while in summer they act as insulation against the heat. In northern Italy and mountainous areas, however, double-glazing is necessary. Heating systems may consist of an oil-fired furnace, mains gas or gas bottles (*bombolone*) in rural areas (see **Heating** on page 218). In apartments, hot water and heating are centralised and paid for along with other community services (see **Community Fees** on page 124).

In old rural homes, the fireplace (*camino*) plays an important role, being used for heating and cooking as well as for atmosphere. (Most city dwellers dream of having a fireplace, while many country homeowners would like to have central heating!) Sometimes the fireplace surround is missing, as old buildings are often 'stripped' of architectural detail, although replacements can be bought from architectural salvage dealers. However, an old fireplace surround in marble or *peperino* costs between €1,500 and €5,500, although a local artisan can make a new one to order for much less. If you suspect that a room once had a fireplace, you can 'sound' the walls to find the flue, which can then be reopened.

Windows are usually protected with shutters, which can be closed to keep heat in (or out) and prying eyes out. In city apartments, rolling shutters (*tapparelle* or *avvolgibili*) are made of metal, wood or plastic slats, and are raised and lowered manually with cords (that break frequently) or with an electric motor.

BUYING A NEW HOME

Italy's wealth of stunning historic architecture sadly isn't reflected in many of its modern buildings, particularly apartment blocks, although at its best Italy's modern home design is among the most beautiful and innovative in the world. Although new properties may lack the charm and character of older buildings, they offer attractive financial and other advantages. There are no costs or problems associated with renovation or modernisation, and they're cheaper to heat and maintain due to the modern building methods and materials employed. It's often cheaper to buy a new home than restore a derelict property, as the price is fixed, unlike the cost of renovation, which can soar way beyond original estimates – as many people have discovered to their cost! If required, a new property can usually be let immediately, and modern homes have good resale potential and are considered a good investment by Italian buyers. On the other hand, new homes are usually smaller than old properties and rarely come with a large plot of land.

The standard of new buildings in Italy is strictly regulated (with the exception of illegally built homes!) and is generally higher than that of old houses. New homes usually have central heating, and must use low maintenance materials and have good insulation and ventilation (including double glazing, cavity and under-floor insulation, and a dehumidifying system), providing lower heating bills in winter and keeping homes cooler in summer. New properties are covered by a 10-year warranty (*responsabilità della ditta*) against structural defects, and systems and equipment are also guaranteed for a period.

A huge variety of new properties are available in Italy, including coastal and city apartments, sports developments (e.g. skiing or golf), and a wide range of individually designed detached houses. Many new properties are part of purpose-built developments, often located near the coast or in the mountains, and offer a range of sports facilities, which may include a golf course, swimming pool, tennis and squash courts, a gymnasium or fitness club, and a restaurant. Many purpose-built developments are planned as holiday homes and may not be attractive as permanent homes (they're also generally expensive).

If you're buying an apartment or a house that's part of a development, check whether your neighbours will be mainly Italians or other foreigners. Some people don't wish to live in a *comune* of their fellow countrymen and this will also deter Italian buyers when you want to sell.

Most new properties are sold by property developers (*costruttore*) or builders, although they're also marketed by estate agents.

☑ **SURVIVAL TIP**

Bear in mind that Italian developers and builders aren't required to be underwritten by a bank, so it's possible for buyers to lose their money or end up with an unfinished property.

It's possible to check a developer's or builder's financial status, although your best insurance is their reputation. Ask for details of their previous developments and, if possible, visit them and ask owners whether they're satisfied with their homes. New developments have a sales office and may have a show house or apartment.

Buying Off Plan

When buying a new property in a development, you're usually obliged to buy it 'off plan' (*acquistare su carta*), i.e. before it's built. In fact, if a development is built and largely unsold, particularly a quality development in a popular area, it usually means that there's something wrong with it! The contract contains the timetable for the property's completion, payment dates, the completion date and penalties for non-completion, guarantees for building work, and a copy of the plans and drawings. The floor plan and technical specifications are signed by both parties to ensure that the standard and size of construction is adhered to.

Payments are spread over 12 to 18 months, although the payment schedule can vary considerably. A typical payment schedule may consist of a 5 per cent reservation fee (*prenotazione*), 15 per cent on signing the preliminary contract (*compromesso*), 30 per cent during construction (*stato avanzamento lavori*) and 50 per cent on completion (*consegna*). If a property is already partly built, the builder will ask for a higher initial payment, depending on its stage of completion. You may be able to persuade a builder to agree to your withholding 5 or 10 per cent of the final payment for a period (e.g. six months) as an insurance against defects.

If you're buying a property off plan, you can usually choose your bathroom suite, kitchen, fireplace, wallpaper and paint, wall and floor tiles, and carpet in bedrooms, some of which may be included in the

price. You may also be able to alter the interior room layout, although this will increase the price. New homes in Italy don't usually contain a high level of 'luxury' features, such as are common in many other countries. Some developers will negotiate over the price or include extras free of charge (such as a fitted kitchen, if it isn't included in the price), particularly if a development isn't selling well.

You should make any changes or additions to a property, such as including a chimney or additional shower room, during the design stage, as they will cost much more to make later.

BUYING A RESALE HOME

The vast majority of homes for sale in Italy are 'resale' homes, i.e. any property which has been previously owned and occupied. There are many advantages to buying a modern resale home, compared with a brand new home, which may include the following:

● An established development with a range of local services and facilities in operation;

● More individual design and style;

- No 'teething troubles';

- Savings on the cost of installing water and electricity meters and telephone lines, or the cost of extending these services to the property;

- Furniture and other extras included in the price;

- A mature garden and trees;

- A larger plot.

With a resale property you can see exactly what you will get for your money, and the previous owners may have made improvements or added extras such as a swimming pool, which may not be fully reflected in the asking price.

Resale properties often represent good value, particularly in resort areas, where many apartments and townhouses are sold fully furnished, although the quality of furnishings varies considerably (from luxurious to junk) and may not be to your taste. (Luxury properties and villas, e.g. costing upwards of around €300,000, are rarely sold furnished.)

When buying a resale property in a development, it's wise to ask the neighbours about any problems, community fees, planned developments, and anything else that may affect your enjoyment of the property (see **Community Properties** on page 121). Most residents are usually happy to tell you, unless of course they're trying to sell you their own property!

You should consider having a survey done on a resale property, as major problems can even be found in properties less than five years old (see **Inspections & Surveys** on page 130).

BUYING AN OLD HOME

In Italy, the term 'old home' usually refers to a building that's pre-WWII and possibly hundreds of years old, which either is in need of restoration and modernisation or has already been restored. If you want a property with abundant charm and character, a building for renovation or conversion, outbuildings or a large plot, you must usually buy an old property.

Italy has a wealth of beautiful historic buildings, particularly from the 17th to 19th centuries, covering the whole spectrum from tiny village houses to *castelli* and *palazzi*. Note, however, that if an old building is listed (preserved) there may be limitations on its use and any changes you may wish to make to it (see **Conveyancing** on page 161). If a building is listed, this should be stated in its registration at the land registry.

In many rural areas it's still possible to buy old properties for as little as €50,000, although you will need to carry out major renovation work, which will double or treble the price. Because the purchase price is often low, many foreign buyers believe they're getting a wonderful bargain, without fully investigating the renovation costs. Renovation and modernisation costs will invariably be higher than you imagined or planned, and taking on too large a task in terms of restoration is a common mistake among foreign buyers in all price brackets.

Although rural properties are cheaper in Italy than in many other western European countries, most require complete renovation and modernisation. Some even lack basic services such as electricity, a reliable water supply and sanitation. Unless you're into do-it-yourself in a big way, you may be better off buying a new or recently built property. This often works out cheaper in the long term, as the cost of restoration (to say nothing of the sweat and toil) is rarely fully reflected in the sale price.

☑ **SURVIVAL TIP**

If you're planning to buy a property that needs restoration or renovation and you won't be doing the work yourself, obtain an accurate estimate of the costs before signing a purchase contract.

If a property is off the beaten track, you may need to include the cost of building or at least resurfacing a road so that heavy vehicles can reach the building work. The cost of building the most basic road is at least €50 per metre.

It isn't usually cheaper to buy and restore an old building than buy a new one, and it can be much more expensive. If you buy and restore a property with the intention of selling it for a profit, you must take into account not only the initial price and the restoration costs, but also the fees and taxes included in the purchase, plus possibly capital gains tax if it's a second home (see page 188). It's often difficult to sell an old renovated property at a higher than average market price, irrespective of its added value. The Italians have little interest in old restored properties, which is an important point if you need to sell an old home quickly in an area that isn't popular with foreign buyers. If you're buying for investment, you're usually better off buying a new home.

Nevertheless, old properties may provide better value than new homes, although you must check their quality and condition carefully. As with most things in life, you generally get what you pay for, so you shouldn't expect a fully restored property for €50,000. At the other end of the scale, for those who can afford them there's a wealth of beautiful *castelli*, *palazzi* and mansions, many costing no more than an average four-bedroom house in other countries. However, if you aspire to live the life of the landed gentry in your own *castello*, bear in mind that the reason prices are so low is that the cost of restoration and maintenance is **astronomical**. This is the reason many larger buildings, such as *palazzi* and large farmhouses, have been converted into apartments.

Don't buy a derelict property unless you have the courage, determination and money to overcome the many problems you will certainly face. Unless you're prepared to wait until you can occupy it or are willing to live in a caravan for a long time while you work on it, it's better to spend a bit more and buy something habitable but untidy, rather than buy a property that needs gutting before you can occupy it.

Although many old rural properties are described as *abitabile* (habitable), this word should immediately set the alarm bells ringing. In Italy, habitable can mean anything from 'derelict' to 'in need of redecoration'. When a property is described as habitable, you should be prepared to ask a lot of questions and ensure that it means exactly what you need it to mean. See also **Renovation & Restoration** on page 135.

COMMUNITY PROPERTIES

In Italy, properties with common elements (whether a building, amenities or land) shared with other properties are owned through a system of part-ownership, in a similar way to condominiums in the USA. A community property (*condominio*) may be an apartment, townhouse or detached (single-family) home on a private estate with

Capri, Campania

communal areas and facilities. Over half of all Italians live in apartments, which are common in cities and resorts (and anywhere building land is limited). Community properties include most properties that are part of a development. In general, the only homes that aren't community properties are detached houses built on individual plots in public streets or on rural land.

Owners of community properties not only own their homes, but they also own a share of the common elements of a building or development, including foyers, hallways, passages, lifts, patios, gardens, roads, and leisure and sports facilities. When you buy a community property, you automatically become a member of the community of owners.

Many community developments are located near coastal or mountain resorts and may offer a wide range of sports and leisure facilities, including a golf course, swimming pools, tennis courts, a gymnasium or fitness club, and a restaurant. Most have landscaped gardens, high security and a full-time caretaker (*custode*), and some even have their own 'village' and shops. At the other extreme, some developments consist of numerous cramped studio apartments. Bear in mind that community developments planned as holiday homes may not be practical as permanent homes.

Advantages & Disadvantages

The advantages of owning a community property include:

● increased security;

● lower property taxes than detached homes;

● a range of community sports and leisure facilities;

● community living with lots of social contacts and the companionship of close neighbours;

● no garden, lawn or pool maintenance;

● properties are often situated in locations where owning a detached home would be prohibitively expensive, e.g. a beach-front or town centre.

The disadvantages of community properties may include:

- excessively high fees (owners may have no control over increases);
- restrictive rules and regulations;
- a confining living and social environment and possible lack of privacy;
- noisy neighbours (a BIG problem in Italy);
- limited living and storage space;
- expensive covered or secure parking (or insufficient off-road parking);
- acrimonious owners' meetings, where management and factions may try to push through unpopular proposals (sometimes using proxy votes).

You should check whether there are any restrictions regarding short or long-term rentals, or leaving a property unoccupied for any length of time.

In a large development, communal facilities may be inundated during peak periods: a large swimming pool won't look so big when 100 people are using it, and getting a game of tennis or using a fitness room may be difficult.

If you're planning to live permanently in a community property, you should avoid buying in a development with a high percentage of rental units, i.e. units that aren't owner-occupied, as they may be filled with rowdy holidaymakers and the owners may be unconcerned with the smooth running of the resort.

Checks

Before buying a community property, you should ask current owners about the community. For example:

- Do they like living there?
- What are the fees and restrictions (see below)?
- How noisy are other residents?
- Are the recreational facilities frequently available?

- Is the community well managed?
- Would they buy there again (why or why not)?

You may also wish to check on your prospective neighbours and, if you're planning to buy an apartment above the ground floor, whether a building has a lift. Bear in mind that upper floor apartments are both colder in winter and warmer in summer, and may incur extra charges for the use of lifts. On the other hand, they offer more security than ground floor apartments. An apartment that has other apartments above and below it will generally be more noisy than a ground or top floor apartment. Under-roof apartments may also have temperature control problems (hot in summer, cold in winter), although they enjoy better views.

Heating in new properties is usually independent and controlled by owners, but in older properties it's usually controlled by the *condominio* and switched on in October and off in the spring (irrespective of the outside temperature), which may result in higher heating bills, especially if you occupy an apartment for only part of the year. If you're buying a holiday apartment that will be vacant for long periods (particularly in winter), don't buy in an apartment block where heating and/or hot water charges are shared, or you will be paying towards your neighbours' heating and hot water bills.

Cost

Prices vary considerably depending on the location: for example, from around €75,000 for a studio or one-bedroom apartment in an average location to over €1m for a luxury apartment or townhouse in a prime location. Generally, the higher the floor the more expensive an apartment is (unless it's number 17, considered by many Italians to be an unlucky number), as it will have more light, less road noise, better views and will be more secure. Garages and parking spaces must often be purchased separately in developments, a lock-up garage usually costing €30,000 or more and a parking space around €15,000.

If you're buying a resale property, check the price paid for similar properties in the same area or development in recent months, but bear in mind that the price you pay may have more to do with the seller's circumstances than the price fetched by other properties. Find out how many properties are for sale in a particular development; if there are many on offer you should investigate why, as there could be management or structural problems. If you're still keen to buy, you can use any negative aspects to drive a hard bargain.

Community Fees

Owners must pay community fees (*spese del condominio*) for the upkeep of communal areas and for communal services. Charges are calculated according to each owner's share of the development (and not whether they're temporary or permanent residents), the size of apartments and the number of balconies. The proportion (*unità immobiliare*) of the common elements (*l'ente condominiale*) assigned to each apartment owner also depends on the number in the block. It's expressed in fractions of thousandths (*millesimi*), e.g. ten apartments of the same size in a block would each own 100/1,000ths of the common elements. Ground floor owners don't usually pay for lifts, and other owners pay more or less according to the floor they're on (those on the top floor pay the most because they use the lifts most – unless they're fitness fanatics or claustrophobic).

General charges are levied for services such as a caretaker, upkeep of the garden and surroundings, swimming pool maintenance and refuse collection. In addition to general charges, there may be special charges for services and equipment such as lifts, central heating and hot water, which may be divided according to the share of the utility allocated to each apartment. An apartment block in a city with a resident concierge (*portiere*) will have much higher community fees than one without (nevertheless, it's preferable to buy in a block with a concierge). Always check the level of general and special charges before buying an apartment.

Fees vary considerably: from around €500 per year for a two-bedroom apartment in a modest development up to €5,000 or more for similar accommodation in a luxury development with a range of services and amenities such as a clubhouse, porter, swimming pool and tennis courts. However, high fees aren't necessarily a negative

point, assuming you can afford them, as the value of a community property depends to a large extent on how well it's maintained and managed. Some community expenses are tax deductible if you're a resident.

Service charges are usually billed quarterly or half-yearly in advance (but can also be in arrears) and the amount paid is adjusted at the end of the year (which can be a nasty shock) when the annual accounts have been approved. If you're buying a resale apartment, ask to see a copy of the accounts and bills for previous years and the minutes of the last annual general meeting, as owners may be 'economical with the truth' when stating service charges, particularly if they're high.

Maintenance & Repairs

If necessary, owners can be assessed an amount in addition to their community fees to make up any shortfall of funds for maintenance or repairs. You should check the condition of the common areas (including all amenities) in an old development and whether any major maintenance or capital expense is planned, for which you could be assessed. Beware of 'bargain' apartments in buildings requiring a lot of maintenance work or refurbishment. Under Italian law, however, disclosure of impending expenditure must be made to prospective buyers before they sign a contract. Owners' meetings can become rather heated when finances are discussed, particularly when assessments are being made to finance capital expenditure.

Management

The ownership and management of community properties are regulated by Italian law, and the rules and regulations (*regolamento di condominio*) for each development are contained in a document produced by the community, a copy of which you should receive. If you don't understand it, you should have it explained or translated.

A block containing five or more apartments must employ an administrator (*amministratore del condominio*), who's elected by the owners to manage the property on their behalf. He's responsible for the efficient daily running of the block and the apportioning of charges (*spese*) relating to the building, e.g. insurance, repairs and maintenance. The administrator bills individual owners for service charges and management fees.

A residents' meeting (*riunione di condominio* or *assemblea condominiale*) must be held at least once a year to approve the budget and discuss other matters of importance, such as capital expenditure and, if necessary, to appoint a new administrator. Owners must be given at least seven days' notice of a meeting and all decisions are made by a majority vote. If you're unable to attend, you should give someone a proxy to vote for you. Non-residents can give someone in Italy (such as a *commercialista*) a 'permanent' proxy and have communications sent to him.

 Caution

Community property management disputes are frequent, and Italian courts are inundated with cases that cannot be resolved among owners.

Restrictions

Community property owners are normally bound by certain restrictions on their use of a property and their behaviour. These usually apply to:

- noise levels;
- the keeping of pets (usually permitted);
- renting;
- exterior decoration and plants (e.g. the placement of shrubs);
- refuse disposal;

- the use of swimming pools and other recreational facilities;
- parking;
- business or professional use;
- the hanging of laundry.

Check the regulations and discuss any restrictions with residents.

RETIREMENT HOMES

There's a steady demand in Italy for retirement and second homes, from both Italians and foreigners, although there are few purpose-built holiday-home developments in Italy, such as are common in France and Spain. Retirement homes are generally purpose-built communities (or sheltered housing) and are becoming more common, particularly in resort areas, although they're still fairly rare. Most retirement developments are developed by foreign companies for foreigners, as the Italians prefer to live among their family and friends in their 'twilight' years. Many sheltered housing developments attract elderly people, e.g. aged 70 plus, with limited mobility. Developments usually consist of one and two-bedroom apartments or a combination of apartments, townhouses and villas, which can be purchased freehold or leasehold, i.e. a lifetime occupancy.

Properties usually have central heating, air-conditioning, fully-fitted kitchens and satellite TV. A wide range of communal facilities and services are provided, including medical and dental clinics (possibly with a resident doctor and dentist), nursing, lounges, laundry, housekeeping, sauna, Jacuzzi, restaurant, bar, meal delivery, handyman, mini-supermarket, post office and banking services, guest apartments, free local transport, 24-hour security with closed-circuit television (CCTV), intercom, personal emergency alarm system and a 24-hour multi-lingual reception. Sports and leisure facilities may include a swimming pool, tennis courts, lawn bowling, a gymnasium, video room, library and social club.

Most sheltered housing developments levy monthly service charges, e.g. between €250 and €1,000, which may include a number of weeks' nursing care for illness each year. Charges usually include heating and air-conditioning, hot and cold water, satellite TV, and all the other services listed above.

GARAGES & PARKING

The cost of parking is an important consideration when buying in a town or resort in Italy, particularly if you have a number of cars. A garage or private parking space isn't usually included in the price when you buy a new apartment or townhouse in Italy, although secure parking may be available at an additional cost, possibly in an underground garage. Modern detached homes usually have a garage or a basement that can be used as a garage. Smaller homes normally have a single garage, while larger properties may have garaging for up to four cars. Parking isn't usually a problem when buying an old home in a rural area, although there may not be a purpose-built garage.

A lock-up garage usually costs around €30,000 and a reserved parking space can cost €15,000 or more. It may be possible to rent a garage or parking space, although this can be prohibitively expensive in cities.

☑ SURVIVAL TIP

The cost of a garage or parking space isn't always recouped when selling, although it makes a property more attractive and may clinch a sale.

Without a private garage or parking space, parking can be a nightmare, particularly in cities and during the summer in busy resorts or developments. Free on-street parking can be difficult or impossible to find in cities and large towns, and in any case may be inadvisable for anything but a wreck. A lock-up garage is important in areas with a high incidence of car theft and theft from cars, and is also useful to protect your car from inclement weather such as ice, snow and extreme heat.

If you're buying in a large development, bear in mind that the nearest parking area may be some distance from your home. This may be an important factor, particularly if you aren't up to carrying heavy shopping hundreds of metres and possibly up several flights of stairs.

TIMESHARE & PART-OWNERSHIP SCHEMES

If you're seeking a holiday home, you may wish to investigate a scheme that provides sole occupancy of a property for a number of weeks each year. Schemes include part-ownership, leaseback and timesharing.

Don't rush into any of these schemes without fully researching the market and before you're absolutely clear what you want and what you can realistically expect to get for your money.

Part-Ownership

Part-ownership includes schemes such as a consortium of buyers owning shares in a property-owning company and co-ownership among family, friends or even strangers. Part-ownership allows you to recoup your investment in savings on holiday costs and still retain your equity in a property. A common deal is a 'four-owner' scheme (many consider four to be the optimum number of co-owners), where you buy a quarter of a property and can occupy it for up to three months a year. However,

there's no reason why there cannot be as many as 12 co-owners with a month's occupancy each per year (usually shared between high, medium and low seasons).

Part-ownership provides access to a size and quality of property that would otherwise be unimaginable, and it's even possible to have a share in a substantial *castello* or *palazzo*, where a number of families could live together simultaneously and hardly ever see each other if they didn't want to. Part-ownership can be a good choice for a family seeking a holiday home for a few weeks or months a year and has the added advantage that (because of the lower cost) a mortgage may be unnecessary.

It's usually cheaper to buy a property privately with friends than through a developer, when you may pay well above the market price for a share of a property (check the market value of a property to establish whether it's good value), although some developers offer a 'turnkey' deal, whereby a home is sold fully furnished and equipped. Part-ownership is much better value than a timeshare and needn't cost a lot more.

A water-tight contract must be drawn up by an experienced lawyer to protect co-owners' interests.

One of the best ways to get into part-ownership (if you can afford it) is to buy a house yourself and offer shares to others. This overcomes the problem of getting together a consortium of would-be owners and trying to agree on a purchase in advance, which is difficult unless it's just a few friends or family members.

Many people form an Italian company to buy and manage the property, which can in turn be owned by a company in the co-owners' home country, thereby allowing disputes to be dealt with under local law. Each co-owner receives a number of shares according to how much he has paid, entitling him to so many weeks' occupancy a year. Owners don't need to have equal shares and can all be made direct title holders. If a co-owner wishes to sell his shares, he must usually give first refusal to other co-owners. However, if they don't wish to buy them and a new co-owner cannot be found, the property must be sold.

Leaseback

Leaseback (or sale-and-leaseback) schemes are designed for those seeking a holiday home for a limited number of weeks each year. Properties sold under a leaseback scheme are located in popular resort areas, e.g. golf, ski or coastal resorts, where self-catering accommodation is in high demand. Buying a property through a leaseback scheme allows a purchaser to buy a new property at less than its true cost, e.g. 30 per cent below than the list price. In return for the discount, the property must be leased back to the developer, normally for around ten years, so that he can let it as self-catering holiday accommodation.

The buyer owns the freehold of the property and the full price is shown in the title deed. He's also given the right to occupy the property for a period each year, e.g. two to eight weeks, spread over high, medium and low seasons. These weeks can usually be let to provide income or possibly even exchanged with accommodation in another resort (as with a timeshare scheme). The developer furnishes and manages the property, and pays the maintenance and bills (e.g. for utilities) during the term of the lease, even when the owner is in occupation.

☑ **SURVIVAL TIP**

It's important to have a contract checked by your lawyer to ensure that you receive vacant possession at the end of the leaseback period without having to pay an indemnity charge, or you could end up paying more than a property is worth.

Timesharing

Timesharing (*multiproprietà*), where you purchase the right to occupy a property at designated times, isn't as popular in Italy as in some other countries, notably Spain and the US. The best timeshare developments are on a par with luxury hotels and offer a wide range of facilities, including bars, restaurants, entertainment, shops, swimming pools, tennis courts, health clubs, and other leisure and sports facilities.

If you don't wish to take a holiday in the same place each year, you can choose a timeshare development that's a member of an international organisation such as Resort Condominium International (RCI, ☎ UK 0870-609 0141, 🖳 www.rci.com), Interval International (☎ UK 0870-744 4222, 🖳 www.intervalworld.com) or Marriott (☎ 0800-1927 1927, 🖳 www.marriott.co.uk), which allow you (usually for an additional fee) to exchange your timeshare with one in another area or country.

Timesharing (also called 'holiday ownership', 'vacation ownership' and 'holidays for life') has earned a poor reputation in the last few decades, although things are slowly improving. In recent years, the Organisation for Timeshare in Europe (OTE) has been trying to restore respectability to timesharing, and its members (which include Italy) are bound by a strict code of ethics. Buyers must have secure occupancy rights and their money be properly protected before the completion of a new property.

Since April 1997, an EU Directive has required timeshare companies to disclose information about the vendor and the property and allow prospective buyers a 'cooling off period' (normally ten days), during which they may cancel a sales agreement without penalty. However, although the directive technically binds timeshare companies, if they flout it you must seek redress in a court of law, which may not be something you want (or can afford) to do!

Italy isn't plagued by the timeshare touts common is some other countries. However, you may be invited to a 'presentation' (i.e. sales pitch) in a popular resort and should know what to expect. If you're tempted to attend a sales pitch (usually lasting at least two hours), you may be subjected to some of the most persuasive, high-pressure sales methods employed anywhere on earth, and many people are simply unable to resist. If you do attend, don't take any cash, credit cards or cheque books with you so that you won't be pressured into paying a deposit without thinking it over.

It isn't difficult to understand why there are so many timeshare companies and why salespersons often employ such intimidating, hard-sell methods. A week's timeshare in an apartment worth €200,000 can be sold for €20,000 or more, making a total income of some €1m for the timeshare company if they sell 50 weeks (five times

the market value of the property!), plus management and other fees.

Although it's illegal for a timeshare company to accept a deposit during the cooling-off period, many companies will try to get you to pay one. If you pay a deposit, your chance of getting it back is slim (unless you pay by credit card); if it is repaid, it's likely to take a long time. Of those who agree to buy a timeshare, around half cancel within the cooling-off period.

A personal guarantee must be provided by a timeshare company that the property is as advertised and, where applicable, the contract must be in the language of the EU country where the buyer is resident or the language of the buyer's choice (you cannot sign away your rights, irrespective of what's written in the contract). If you're an EU citizen and get into a dispute, you can take legal action in your home country for a sale made in Italy.

Most experts believe that there's little or no advantage in a timeshare over a normal holiday rental and that it's simply an expensive way to pay for your holidays in advance.

Top-quality timeshares usually cost at least €20,000 for one week in a one or two-bedroom apartment in a top-rated resort at a peak period, to which must be added annual management fees, e.g. €250 to €1,000 or more for each week, plus 'miscellaneous' charges and hefty levies, which can run into hundreds of Euros per owner.

Most financial advisers believe that you're better off putting your money into a long-term investment, where you retain your capital and may even earn sufficient interest to pay for a few weeks' holiday each year. If you wish to buy a timeshare, it's best to buy a resale privately from an existing owner or a timeshare resale broker, which may sell for a fraction of their original cost. When buying privately, you can usually drive a hard bargain and may even get a timeshare 'free' simply by assuming the current owner's maintenance contract.

Often timeshares are difficult or impossible to sell at any price and 'pledges' from timeshare companies to sell them for you or buy them back at the market price are usually just a sales ploy, as timeshare companies aren't interested once they've made a sale. The resale market for timeshares is almost non-existent and, if you need to sell, you're highly unlikely to get your money back.

Further information about timesharing can be obtained from the Timeshare Consumers Association (TCA, Nornay, Blyth, Notts, S81 8HG, UK, ☎ 01909-591100, 🖵 www.timeshare.org.uk), who publish several useful booklets with advice on timesharing.

There are timeshare properties in many areas of Italy, including most of the major resorts (e.g. the islands, Tuscany and Venice).

INSPECTIONS & SURVEYS

When you've found a property that you like, you should make a close inspection of its condition. Obviously, the nature of the inspection will depend on whether it's a ruin in need of complete restoration, a property that has been partly or totally modernised, or a modern home.

An old property may show signs of damage and decay, such as bulging or cracked walls, rising damp, missing roof tiles and rotten woodwork. Some areas are susceptible to flooding, storms and subsidence, and it's wise to check an old property after a heavy rainfall, when any leaks should come to light.

In the case of a property that has been restored, it's important to ascertain how well the job has been done, particularly if the owner did it himself. Although a vendor must certify that a property is free from 'hidden defects', this provides little assurance as he can usually just plead ignorance and it's usually difficult or expensive to prove otherwise.

The most important thing is to ensure that a property is structurally sound. Although building standards in Italy are generally high, you should never assume that a building is sound, as even relatively new buildings can have serious faults (although rare). After the collapse of several apartment blocks built in the '60s, properties in Rome and other major cities have had to have a *libretto* testifying to their sound structure.

The cost of an inspection is a small price to pay for the peace of mind it affords. Some lenders insist on a 'survey' (*perizia*) before approving a loan, although this usually consists of a perfunctory valuation (*stima*) to confirm that a property is worth the purchase price. A master builder will be able to tell you whether the price is too high, given any work that needs to be done.

☑ SURVIVAL TIP

An Italian wouldn't make an offer on a property before, at the very least, having it checked by a builder.

If a property is pre-1945, a builder or engineer (*ingegnere*) can be employed to check it for soundness, which an architect (*architetto*) is usually better qualified to check a modern house (unless he designed it himself!). Alternatively, you can employ a professional valuer or *geometra* (see **Geometra** on page 135).

You can also have a full structural survey carried out, although this is rare in Italy. However, if you would have a survey carried out if you were buying the same property in your home country, you should have one done in Italy. You will usually need to pay at least €350 for a 'rough' appraisal (*valutazione*) and around €1,000 (depending on the work involved) for a 'full' structural survey (*perizia strutturale*).

You may be able to make a satisfactory survey a condition of the preliminary contract, allowing you to withdraw from the purchase and have your deposit returned if serious faults are revealed. However, this isn't usual in Italy and a vendor may refuse or insist that you carry out a survey **before** signing the contract. You may, however, be able to negotiate a satisfactory compromise with the vendor.

If a property needs work doing on it to make it habitable, don't accept what you're told regarding the likely cost of repairs or restoration unless you have a binding quotation in writing from a local builder. One of the most common mistakes foreigners make when buying old properties in Italy is to underestimate the cost of restoration and modernisation (it bears repeating over and over again!). You should obtain accurate estimates for renovation and modernisation costs before signing a contract.

You may prefer to employ a foreign (e.g. British) surveyor practising in Italy, who will write a report in English, although an Italian surveyor (or other local expert) usually has an intimate knowledge of local properties and building methods. If you employ a foreign surveyor, you must ensure that he's experienced in the idiosyncrasies of Italian properties and that he has professional indemnity insurance covering Italy, which means that you can happily sue him if he does a bad job!

Checks

Always discuss with a surveyor exactly what will be included in a survey and, most importantly, what will be excluded (you may need to pay extra to include certain checks and tests). A general inspection should include the structural condition of buildings (particularly the foundations, roofs, walls and woodwork), plumbing, electricity and heating systems, and anything else you want inspected, such as a swimming pool and its equipment, e.g. filter system or heating.

You should receive a written report on the structural condition of a property, including anything that could become a problem in the future. Some surveyors will allow you to accompany them and may even produce a video of their findings

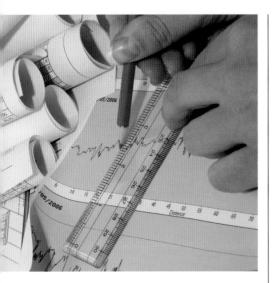

Additions or alterations to a property may require new registration for the entire property. If so, enquire whether the current owner will register the change before you buy, or pay the costs if they're obtained on completion.

Exterior

- Check for cracks and damp patches on walls.

- On older properties, check that the walls are vertical and not bulging;

- Check that all the roof tiles are in place and that there's no sagging. Plants growing on a roof are an indication that it isn't well maintained.

Interior

- Check for damp patches throughout a property, including inside cupboards and wardrobes.

- Check for cracks in walls.

- Check that the floor is level and that tiles are in good condition.

- Check the condition of doors and windows and whether they close properly.

- Check the woodwork for rot and signs of wood-boring insects, such as woodworm and termites (termites are difficult to detect unless damage is extensive).

Furniture & Fittings

- Check what is included in the sale (see **Conveyancing** on page 161).

- Check that any appliances included in the sale are in good working order.

Utilities

- Check that the water/electricity/gas supplies are functional, particularly the hot water supply and central heating

in addition to a written report. A home inspection can be limited to a few items or even a single system only, such as the wiring or plumbing in an old house. You may also wish to have a property checked for termites and other pests, which are found in many areas, and to have a radon test on a building or land in an area where radon levels are high (see page 76).

Below is a list of items you should check or have checked by an expert when inspecting a property. See also **Checks** on page 123.

Description

- Make sure that the property corresponds with the description in the title deeds.

- Check the number of rooms and the area of the property, terraces and the plot.

- If there are added rooms (e.g. an extension), terraces, a garage or a swimming pool that aren't mentioned in the property description, the owner should provide proof that planning permission was obtained.

system. Don't take someone's word that these are in good order, but check them yourself.

- Enquire about the annual cost of heating and air-conditioning systems.

- Check the reliability of the electricity supply.

- If a property doesn't have electricity or mains water, check the nearest connection point and the cost of extending the service to the property, as it can be **very** expensive in remote rural areas. If there's no mains electricity supply, find out whether you can install alternative means (e.g. solar panels).

- In the case of a waterside property, you should ensure that it has been designed with floods in mind, e.g. with electrical installations above flood level and solid tiled floors. You should be particularly wary of purchasing a waterside property with a ground floor in Venice, where high tides (*acqua alta*) are common in autumn and winter (the incidence of flooding has increased in recent years). High tides can also cause havoc with the plumbing. Avoid a ground floor property unless you're certain it isn't affected by flooding – check for yourself or ask neighbours in the area (but take their information with a pinch of salt, as almost all Venetians have a good flood story to tell!).

- Check the water supply. If a property's water supply is provided by wells, make sure that there's sufficient for your needs.

- If a property has a well or septic tank, have it tested. If it doesn't have one, check whether one can be installed and how much it will cost (see **Septic Tanks** below.

Septic Tanks

The absence of a septic tank (*fossa settica*) or other waste water system isn't usually a problem, provided that the land size and elevation allows for its installation. If there's a stream running through a property, it may mean that an expensive system needs to be installed to cope with the effluent, which costs three or four times that of a septic tank.

> ☑ **SURVIVAL TIP**
>
> If a property already has a septic tank, check that it's in good condition. An old-style septic tank takes bathroom waste only, while new all-purpose septic tanks on a soak-away system can cope with a wide range of waste products.

Make sure that a septic tank is large enough for the property in question, e.g. 2,500 litres for two bedrooms and up to 4,000 litres for five bedrooms. Note that you mustn't use cleaning agents such as ammonia in a septic tank, as this will damage or even destroy it. Specially formulated cleaners are available, including products that will extend the life of the tank.

Pool & Equipment

- Check that the pool and equipment (especially the pump) is in good working order.

- Look for cracks in the pool structure and check the condition of paving around the pool.

- Enquire how much the pool costs to maintain and how much it will cost to refill it, e.g. if it's emptied in winter.

- If a property doesn't have a swimming pool, check that there's room to build one, that the terrain is suitable and that planning permission can be obtained if necessary.

For information about installing, maintaining and cleaning a pool, see **Swimming Pools** below.

Land

Before buying a home with a garden or a plot of land, you should walk the boundaries and look for fences, trees and the eaves of buildings that may be encroaching upon the property. If you're uncertain about the boundaries (e.g. of an unfenced rural property), you should have the property surveyed by a land surveyor (*perito agronomo*), which is wise in any case when buying a property with a large plot. If the plot isn't enclosed, check the local regulations regarding the height and type of boundary permitted.

When buying a rural property in Italy, you may be able to negotiate the amount of land you want to be included in the purchase. If a property is part of a larger plot owned by the vendor or the boundaries must be redrawn, you will need to hire a surveyor to measure the land and draw up a new cadastral plan. You should also check the local land registry to find out what the land can be used for, whether there are any streams or underground springs, whether any neighbours have rights to water on your land, and whether there are any rights of access (*diritto di passaggio*) across it or hunting rights on it. You or your lawyer should also ensure that there are no disputes over boundaries and that any buildings on your plot don't encroach on to neighbouring plots (see **Conveyancing** on page 161).

On rural land, find out whether the trees require maintenance, e.g. olive and fruit trees, and investigate what you can do with the crop after the harvest. If land is classed as agricultural, check your right of access to a water supply and whether it's sufficient for your needs.

If you're unable to maintain the garden yourself, check how much a gardener will cost. If you aren't prepared to pay for a gardener, find out what it will cost to turn the garden into a low-maintenance one.

Swimming Pools

It's common for foreign buyers to install a swimming pool at a home in Italy, which will greatly increase your rental prospects and the rent you can charge if you wish to let the property. Many self-catering holiday companies won't take on properties without a pool. However, before adding a pool you need to check whether there's sufficient water supply in the area and how it will affect your taxes, as the presence of a pool automatically places a home in the luxury (A1) category (see page 181).

You need planning permission to install a pool and this may be refused in areas with acute water shortages. Pools in some areas can only be rectangular in shape and must be finished in natural materials, e.g. marble or stone so that they blend into the landscape.

There are many swimming pool installation companies in Italy or you can buy and install one yourself. Above-ground pools are the cheapest but are unsightly. Expect to pay around €3,000 for an 8m x 4m (26ft x 13ft) above-ground pool. A better option is a liner pool, which can be installed by anyone with basic DIY skills, costing around €12,000 to €17,500. A conventional pool measuring 8m x 4m (with a simple but effective step/filter unit) can be purchased for around €20,000, including installation. A saline water option costs a bit more but gives a better quality of water and provides lower maintenance costs. A concrete, fully tiled 8m x 4m pool installed by professionals costs from around €25,000, including filtration and heating, and can be almost any shape (provided this is permitted).

Pools require regular maintenance and cleaning. If you have a holiday home in Italy or let a property, you will need to employ someone to maintain your pool (you may be able to get a local family to look after it in return for using it).

If you have a swimming pool you should take certain safety precautions such as building non-slip steps in the pool, a non-slip surface around it, and erecting a safety fence around it, which is particularly important if you have young children or any are likely to visit the property. You will also need third-party insurance for the pool, costing from €150 a year, as part of your house insurance policy (see **Household Insurance** on page 198).

RENOVATION & RESTORATION

Many old properties purchased by foreigners in Italy are in need of restoration, renovation and modernisation. The most common examples are the many farmhouses that have been almost totally neglected since they were built in the 18th and 19th centuries and were often abandoned decades ago. In general, the Italian attitude to old buildings is one of almost total neglect and many are literally in danger of falling down, when complete rebuilding is often necessary. A building sold as requiring renovation (*da restaurare* or *ristrutturare*) in Italy is usually

in need of **substantial** work (rebuilding may be a more accurate description). Partly renovated (*restaurato/rinnovato parzialmente*) usually means that part of a building is habitable, i.e. it at least has sanitation, but the rest is in need of restoration (*da ricostruire*). The most dilapidated 'buildings' are ruins (*ruderi*) consisting of just a few walls without a roof.

Before buying a property that needs renovation or restoration, it's vital to obtain accurate estimates of the work involved from one or more reliable local builders. You should budget for costs to be up to 100 per cent higher than quoted, as it isn't unusual for costs to escalate wildly from original estimates.

Before buying a property requiring restoration or modernisation, you should consider the alternatives. An extra €25,000 to €50,000 spent on a purchase may represent better value than spending a similar amount on building work. It's often cheaper to buy a restored or partly restored property than a ruin in need of total restoration, unless you're going to do most of the work yourself. See also **Buying An Old Home** on page 120.

The price of most restored properties doesn't reflect the cost and amount of work that went into them, and many people who have restored a ruin would never do it again and advise others against it.

Geometra

If your property requires major restoration, your first step should be to find a reputable *geometra*, a professional (probably unique to Italy) whose job is a combination of those of an architect, engineer and surveyor. *Geometri* are listed in the yellow pages (🖳 www.paginegialle.it) under *Certificati Agenzie*. A *geometra's* main tasks are dealing with the paperwork involved in planning applications (a local *geometra* may know the 'right people' in the 'right places'), drawing up the plans and specifications for the restoration, and overseeing the restoration work. His help is vital if you're a foreigner and don't speak Italian fluently – even if you do, you can save considerable time and stress if you employ one.

Ask around locally for recommendations (e.g. from an estate agent) and inspect restoration work overseen by a recommended *geometra*.

☑ **SURVIVAL TIP**

The *geometra* will be your right-hand man in practically the entire restoration process and you should choose someone who's highly recommended and who you can trust, particularly if you cannot be on site to supervise restoration work yourself.

A *geometra* usually visits the site every month or two or when stage payments are made. A good *geometra* will provide detailed information and progress reports after visits, e.g. via e-mail using digital photography. Fees vary, but are usually from 5 to 10 per cent of the value of the restoration work depending on the amount of work the *geometra* has to do.

Checks

It's important to ensure that a property has sound walls. Properties that have walls with serious defects are best avoided, as it's usually cheaper to erect a new building! Almost any other problem can be fixed or overcome at a price. A sound roof that doesn't leak is desirable and making a building waterproof is the most important priority if funds are scarce. Don't believe a vendor or agent who tells you that a roof or anything else can be repaired or patched up, but obtain expert advice from a local builder. Sound roof timbers are also desirable, as they can be expensive

to replace. Old buildings may also need a damp-proof course, timber treatment, new windows and doors, a modern kitchen and bathroom, re-wiring and central heating. You should also check a building for leaks (e.g. after a rainstorm) before investing in expensive decoration.

In earthquake-susceptible areas, structural restorations can be done using a 'minimal intervention unit' (*Unità Minima d'Intervento/UMI*), by which the walls and adjoining structures of buildings in historic centres are reinforced, providing major resistance against seismic movements in old buildings. In some areas, e.g. Tuscany, these reinforcements are compulsory in any restoration work. *UMI* reinforcement involves a 15 to 25 per cent increase in renovation costs.

See also **Checks** on page 123.

Planning Permission & Building Permits

If modernisation of an old building involves making external alterations, such as building an extension or installing larger windows or new doorways, you will need planning permission (*permessi comunali* or *concessione edilizia*) from your local town hall and a building licence (*licenza*). Planning regulations may be decided by a commune, province or region. It may be difficult to obtain planning permission if a property is situated in a historic town or village or an area of great natural beauty. Restoration must usually be carried out with local materials and in the traditional style.

In some regions, such as Emilia Romagna, the Marche, Tuscany and Umbria, planning regulations are rigorously enforced to maintain the beauty of the countryside, and restorations must maintain the character of a building; wholesale alterations are likely to be refused planning permission. You may need to obtain permission from the Ministry of Culture

(*Belli Arti*) to restore a building of historical importance.

In most areas, there are restrictions on renovation; for example, you may not be able to change the windows, doors, colour of exterior walls, entrances, staircases or build garden walls. Italian law requires a ceiling height of 2.75 metres for living space (except for property located in villages, which are exempt) and you may need to raise the roof or lower the floor when converting a building. When applying for planning permission, bear in mind possible future extensions and the likelihood of their being granted.

It's important to find out **exactly** what you can and can't do before buying a property for restoration.

The only way to be sure of obtaining planning permission is to apply for and obtain it **before** buying a property. If this isn't possible or practical, you should include a conditional clause in the preliminary contract (*compromesso di vendita*) stating that the purchase is contingent on obtaining planning permission. Sometimes a property already has planning permission, although you should check the period of validity (which

should be at least two years) and whether it can be changed or extended, if necessary.

If you buy property classed as 'rural' (*rurale*) in the Land Registry, such as a barn, outbuilding or stables, and wish to convert it into a dwelling, e.g. convert a barn into an apartment or a stable into a kitchen, you cannot do so until the property's usage is changed from rural to urban (*urbana*). The change should be requested of the local authority (*comune*) and accompanied by detailed plans of all proposed changes. If the *comune* grants permission, the change is registered with the Land Registry and only then may building work start.

A building contract must also be dependent on the necessary licences being issued. Never start any building work before you have official permission, which usually takes at least three weeks for a simple job and a minimum of two months (often as much as six) for anything complex. It's also wise to obtain permission from your local town hall before demolishing buildings on your land, irrespective of how dilapidated they are. You may be able to sell the building materials or get a builder to demolish

them free of charge in exchange for the materials.

Most people hire a *geometra* (see page 135) to draw up plans and make a planning application. Obtaining planning permission usually costs at least €500 for the simplest job and can cost €2,500 or more when renovating a house.

Italians often resort to bribery (which is a way of life in some parts of Italy) when dealing with planning officials, rather than go through the tortuous planning procedures. If this fails, many Italians simply build illegally (called *abusivo*) and wait to be fined. The government frequently has amnesties (*condono*) for people who have built or altered their homes illegally, which allows them to pay a fee rather than pay a much larger fine or even face demolition. However, a foreigner would be extremely unwise to follow their example and may not be treated so leniently. In recent years, many properties that have been built illegally or have been extended or renovated without permission, have been demolished by order of the local authorities!

After restoration, a certificate is required to confirm that building work has been carried out according to the planning application. You will also need a professional valuation of your home for insurance purposes.

DIY or Builders?

One of the first decisions you need to make regarding restoration or modernisation is whether to do all or most of the work yourself or have it done by professional builders or artisans. A working knowledge of Italian is essential for DIY (*fai da te*), particularly the words associated with building materials and measurements – renovating a house will also greatly improve your ability to swear in Italian! If you're doing a lot of DIY or simply wish to confirm the cost of building materials, you can obtain catalogues for each branch of the building trade from DEI Tipografia del

Genio Civile, Via Nomentana 16/20, 00161 Rome (☎ 06-441 6371, 🖳 www.build.it – in Italian only).

You shouldn't tackle jobs by yourself or with friends unless you're sure you're doing it right (such as cleaning or restoring marble floors or tiles, which is a specialist job). It's important to have a sensitive approach to restoration and, in general, you should aim to retain as many of a property's original features as possible and stick to local building materials (wood, stone and tiles), reflecting the style of the property. In fact, this may be required by law. When renovations and 'improvements' have been botched, there's often little that can be done except to start again from scratch. It's important not to over-modernise an old property, in case too much of its natural rustic charm and attraction are lost.

Before starting work and while work progresses, most people keep a photographic record of their accomplishments, if only to justify the expense. Also keep all bills (labour and materials) for restoration work, both for legal reasons and to prove to a prospective buyer that the work that has been done and how much it cost.

> There are many useful sources of information about restoring Italian property, including the sumptuous, *Restoring a Home in Italy*, by Elizabeth Helman Minchilli (Artisan), featuring the tales of some 22 homeowners who have bought and restored properties in Italy (be warned: this book can seriously damage your wealth!).

DIY & Building Supplies

If you decide to go it alone, there's a wide range of DIY equipment, tools and building supplies in Italy, although there's less choice than in some other European countries (e.g. the UK) and prices are

do excellent work. There are no jobbing builders or 'jacks of all trades' in Italy, where all artisans are specialists: bricklayers, stonemasons, joiners, roofers, plasterers, plumbers or electricians. If you employ local builders, you can virtually guarantee that the result will be authentic and it could also save you money. Italian builders' quotations are binding and their prices are usually reasonable.

It's usually better to use a local building consortium or contractor rather than a number of independent tradesmen, particularly if you won't be around to supervise them (although it will cost you a bit more). On the other hand, if you supervise the work yourself using local hand-picked craftsmen, you can save money and learn a great deal into the bargain.

Foreign builders may do an excellent job, but bringing in foreign labour won't endear you to the local populace and may even create friction. Never employ 'black' labour (Italian or foreign); apart from the risks of having no insurance, there are stiff penalties.

generally higher. There are many DIY hypermarkets and superstores, which in addition to stocking most DIY materials, have a wide range of tools and machinery for hire. Most DIY stores stock a large selection of goods (and keep most items in stock), accept credit cards and have helpful staff. Always look out for special promotions; even if nothing appears to be on offer, it's worth asking, as offers aren't always advertised.

Most towns have a hardware store that's handy for tools and small items, and there are building yards that are good for plumbing parts, porcelain, fireplaces and doors. Ask your neighbours about where to buy fittings and materials, as they usually know the best places locally. It's also possible to buy reclaimed materials such as porcelain, tiles, doors and fireplaces from architectural salvage dealers.

Italian or Foreign Builders?

When it's a choice between Italian and foreign builders, most experts recommend using local labour for a number of excellent reasons. Italian artisans understand the materials and the traditional style of building, are familiar with local planning and building regulations, and usually

Finding a Builder

When looking for a builder (*muratore*) it's wise to obtain recommendations from local people you can trust, e.g. an estate agent, *geometra*, *notaio*, mayor or neighbours. However, estate agents or other professionals aren't always the best people to ask, as they may receive a commission. Always obtain references from previous customers.

Any tradesmen you employ should be registered at the local chamber of commerce in the requisite category and in the official list of artisans (*albo degli artigiani*) for his trade.

Quotations

You should obtain a written quotation (*preventivo*) from at least two builders before employing anyone. It's sensible to obtain a few quotations and offer to pay a fee for a quotation for a large job, which should be reimbursed by the builder who gets the job. Builders usually provide an estimate per square metre (*al m²* or *al metro quadrato*), which includes both labour and materials, although where it's difficult or impossible to provide an estimate, jobs are done at an hourly (*a ore*) or daily rate. **However, you should be extremely wary of doing this, as costs can escalate wildly.**

For quotations to be accurate, you must detail exactly the work required; for example, for electrical work this would include the number of lights, points and switches, and the quality of materials to be used. If you have only a vague idea of what you want, you will receive an unreliable quotation.

Make sure that a quotation includes everything you want done and that you fully understand it (if you don't, get it translated). Look out for any terms allowing for the price to be increased for inflation or a general rise in prices, and check whether the quote is definitive or provisional, i.e. dependent on further exploratory work. You should fix

a date for completion and, if you can get a builder to agree to it, include a penalty for failing to meet it. It's difficult to get Italian builders to agree to this, but it's worth persevering. A major building contract also needs a strict penalty clause, or it can drag on for months (or years) or be left half-finished. Always ask for start and finish dates in a quotation. After signing a contract, it's usual to pay a deposit, e.g. 10 to 25 per cent, depending on the size of the job.

Supervision

If you aren't on the spot and able to supervise work, you should hire a 'clerk of works' (*direttore dei lavori*) such an architect (*architetto*) or *geometra* (see page 135) to do so on your behalf. He can be employed to oversee an entire project or just one or two aspects of it. The fee is usually a percentage of the total cost, e.g. 10 per cent, and is usually worth every Euro. Shop around and compare rates, but beware of expatriate project managers, who have been known to rip off their compatriots.

Some Italian estate agents will organise renovations and restoration and oversee a project for around 10 per cent of the total cost. Some specialist companies offer a complete restoration service, although the disadvantage of such services is that they may offer little choice regarding how they restore a property and you will have to trust them completely. Always obtain references from previous customers.

If you don't speak Italian, it's even more important to employ someone to oversee building works. Progressing on sign language and a few words of Italian is a recipe for disaster!

Italian artisans never like to turn down work so tend to take on much more than they can handle and work a day here and a day there, thus annoying all their customers. Many unsupervised Italian workmen are about as disciplined as Italian drivers, and it isn't uncommon for artisans to work for a few days and then disappear for a few weeks or months!

Be extremely careful who you employ if you have work done in your absence and ensure that your instructions are accurate in every detail. Always make sure that you understand exactly what has been agreed and if necessary get it in writing (with drawings). It isn't unusual for foreign owners to receive huge bills for work done in their absence that shouldn't have been done at all!

Cost

All building work, including electrical installations, masonry and plumbing is priced by the square metre (m^2) or metre. The cost of total restoration by professional builders varies according to the type of work involved, the quality of materials used and the region. You should expect to pay a minimum of €900 per m2 to bring a ruin to a habitable condition and up to €1,750 per m2 for a top quality job, e.g. insulated roofs, double glazing, full central heating, marble or expensive tiles in kitchens and bathrooms, fully fitted kitchens and elaborate fireplaces.

As a rough guide, you should expect the cost of fully renovating an old 'habitable' building to be at least equal to its purchase price and possibly much more. The cost must include VAT at 20 per cent, although a project may be eligible for a reduction of VAT (*l'abbattimento dell'IVA*) to 4 per cent on materials and labour for properties in historic centres (check with the local town hall).

How much you spend on restoring a property will depend on your purpose and the depth of your pockets. If you're restoring a property as an investment, it's easy to spend much more than you could ever hope to recoup when you sell it. One of the reasons there are so many derelict buildings for sale in some parts of Italy is that restoration costs are far higher than potential resale costs. Many foreigners spend a fortune on renovations, only to find it impossible to sell and recoup their investment. It isn't

unusual for buyers to embark on a grandiose renovation scheme, only to run out of money before it's completed and be forced to sell at a huge loss. On the other hand, if you're restoring a property as a holiday or permanent home, you can spend as much as you can afford.

☑ SURVIVAL TIP

Always keep an eye on your budget (which will inevitably be at least 25 per cent **below** the actual cost!) and don't be in too much of a hurry. Some people take many years to restore an Italian holiday home, particularly when they're doing most of the work themselves.

It's possible to obtain a mortgage that includes the cost of renovation work, but you must obtain detailed written quotations for a lender. It's also possible to obtain a grant to restore a historic property in some regions.

It's important to ensure that you pay for work on time; if you get a reputation as a late payer (or for not paying at all) you will soon find that you cannot get anyone local to work for you. However, you should make sure that a job's completely finished (including repairing any damage done by workmen) and passed by your architect or surveyor, before paying bills. Never pay a builder in advance (apart from a deposit), particularly a large sum, as it's possible that he will disappear with your money (particularly if he's a foreign, non-registered builder). It's best to pay a month in arrears, which most builders will agree to.

On the other hand, if you want a job done while you're away you will need to pay a builder a sum in advance or get someone local to supervise his work and pay him regularly, otherwise he's unlikely to finish the job. Cash deals are often negotiated

without VAT, although you should bear in mind that, if you don't have a legitimate bill, you won't be able to offset the cost of work against rental income and won't have a guarantee.

BUILDING YOUR OWN HOME

If you want to be far from the madd(en) ing crowd, you can buy a plot (see **Buying Land** below) and have a house built to your own design or to a standard design provided by a builder. Although Italian builders have a range of standard designs, they will accommodate almost any interior or exterior variation (for a price), provided they're permitted by local building regulations.

If you decide to build your own home, you must ensure that the proposed size and style of house is legal by checking with the local town hall. Don't rely on the builder or developer to do it for you, but check yourself or have your architect or surveyor do it. If a mistake is made, a building may need to be demolished! See **Planning Permission & Building Permits** on page 136.

After building a new house, you must obtain a certificate that building work has been carried out according to the planning application. You will also need a professional valuation of your home for insurance purposes.

Buying Land

There are numerous opportunities to purchase land in the Italian countryside – from a few hectares to several hundred, usually consisting of olive groves or orchards. The land may include a hut or barn, or more frequently, a ruin. Note, however, that permission to restore such a building may be difficult to obtain, particularly if it isn't classed as a dwelling (see **Planning Permission & Building Permits** on page 136).

You must take the same care when buying land as you would when buying a home. The most important point is to ensure that land has been approved for building and that the plot is large enough and suitable for the house you plan to build. When a plot has planning permission, the maximum size of building (in square metres) that can be built is usually stated and depends on the density permitted by the local commune and possibly also the province or region. If you buy land from an agent, it will usually already have planning permission but, if it doesn't, this should be made a condition of purchase. Always obtain confirmation in writing from the local town hall that land can be built on and has been approved for road access.

Some plots are unsuitable for building, as they're too steep or require prohibitively expensive foundations. Also check that there aren't any high-tension electricity lines, water pipes or rights of way that may restrict building. A plot should have mains electricity and (preferably) a reliable water supply; the cost of providing services to a property in a remote rural area may be prohibitively expensive.

Builders may have a selection of building plots for sale. Most builders offer package deals, which include the land and the cost of building your home. However, it isn't always wise to buy the building plot from the builder who's going to build your home, and you should shop around and compare separate land and building costs.

☑ **SURVIVAL TIP**

If you decide to buy a package deal from a builder, you must insist on separate contracts for the land and the building, and obtain the title deed for the land before signing a building contract.

Obtain a receipt showing that the plot is correctly presented in the local property register and check for yourself that the correct planning permission has been obtained (don't simply leave it to the builder). If planning permission is flawed, you may need to pay extra to improve the local infrastructure or the property may have to be demolished! See also **Planning Permission & Building Permits** on page 136.

SELLING YOUR HOME

Although this book is primarily concerned with buying a home in Italy, you may wish to sell your home at some time in the future. Before offering your home for sale, it's wise to investigate the state of the property market. For example, unless you're forced to sell, it definitely isn't wise to try to do so during a property slump. It may be better to let your home long-term and wait until the market has recovered. It's also unwise to sell in the early years after purchase, when you will probably make a loss unless it was an absolute bargain.

Having decided to sell, your first decision will be whether to try to sell it yourself or use the services of an estate agent. Although the majority of properties in Italy are sold through estate agents, a large number of owners sell their own homes.

If you need to sell a property before buying a new one, this must be included as a conditional clause (see page 165) in the purchase contract for a new home.

Price

It's important to bear in mind that (like everything) property has a market price and the best way of ensuring a quick sale (or any sale) is to ask a realistic price. In a buyers' market, some properties remain unsold for ages largely because owners ask absurd prices. If your home is fairly standard for the area, you can find out its value by comparing the prices of other homes on the market or those that have recently been sold. Most agents will provide a free appraisal of a home's value in the hope that you will sell it through them. However, don't believe everything they tell you, as they may over-price it simply to encourage you. You can also hire a professional appraiser to determine the market value.

You should be prepared to drop the price slightly (e.g. 5 or 10 per cent) and should set it accordingly, but shouldn't grossly over-price a home, as this will deter buyers. Don't reject an offer out of hand unless it's ridiculously low, as a prospective buyer may raise his offer.

You may wish to include furnishings and major appliances in the sale, particularly when selling a relatively inexpensive property with modest furnishings. You should add an appropriate amount to the price to cover the value of the furnishings; alternatively, you can use them as an inducement to a prospective buyer who is undecided (although this isn't usual in Italy).

When selling a home in Italy, you may need to wait a number of weeks after completion before you receive payment.

Presentation

The secret to selling a home quickly lies in its presentation, assuming that it's competitively priced. First impressions (both exterior and interior) are vital when marketing your home, and it's essential to make every effort to present it in its best light and make it as attractive as possible to potential buyers. It may even pay to invest in new interior decoration, new carpets, exterior paint and landscaping. A few plants and flowers can work wonders. However, when decorating a home for resale, it's important to be conservative and not to do anything radical (such as install a red or black bathroom suite); white is a good neutral colour for walls, woodwork and porcelain.

It may also pay you to do some modernisation such as installing a new kitchen or bathroom, as these are of vital importance (particularly kitchens) when selling a home.

Note, however, that although modernisation may be necessary to sell an old home, you shouldn't overdo it, as it's easy to spend more than you could ever hope to recoup on its sale. If you're using an agent, you can ask him what you should do (or need to do) to help sell your home.

If your home is in poor repair, this must be reflected in the asking price and, if major work is needed that you cannot afford, you should obtain a quotation (or two) to show prospective buyers. You have a duty under Italian law to inform a prospective buyer of any defects that aren't readily apparent and which materially affect the value of a property. There are also special disclosure requirements for apartments and other community properties (see page 121).

SELLING YOUR HOME YOURSELF

While certainly not for everyone, selling your own home is a viable option for many people and is particularly recommended when you're selling an attractive home at a realistic price in a favourable market. It may allow you to offer it at a more appealing price, which could be an important factor if you're seeking a quick sale. How you market your home will depend on the type of home, the price, and the country or area from which you expect your buyer to come. For example, if your property isn't of a style or in an area desirable to Italians, it's usually a waste of time advertising it in the local press.

Advertising is the key to selling your home. The first step is to get a professional looking 'For Sale' (*vendesi*) sign made showing your telephone number and display it in the garden or a window. These are available in bright colours from tobacconists (*tabacchi*) and stationery (*cartoleria*) shops, and sellers usually put them up in many places, not just on the building for sale.

Do some market research into the best newspapers and magazines for advertising your property, and place an advertisement in those that look most promising. You could also have a leaflet printed (with pictures) extolling the virtues of your property, which you could drop into local letter boxes or have distributed with a local newspaper (many people buy a new home in the vicinity of their present home).

You may also need to have a printed 'fact sheet' if your home's vital statistics aren't included in the leaflet mentioned above, and could offer a finder's fee (e.g. €1,000) to anyone finding you a buyer. Don't forget to market your home around local companies, schools and other organisations, particularly if they have many itinerant or foreign employees.

Finally, it may help to provide information about local financing sources for potential buyers. With a bit of effort and practice you may even make a better job of marketing your home than an agent! When selling a home yourself, you will need to obtain legal advice regarding contracts and engage a *notaio* to complete the sale. Unless you're in a hurry to sell, set yourself a realistic time limit for success, after which you can try an agent.

As when buying a home, you must be very, very careful who you deal with when selling a home. Never agree to accept part of the sale price 'under the table' (which is illegal in any case); if the buyer refuses to pay, there's nothing you can do about it (legally!) – see also **Avoiding Problems** on page 94. When the buyer has a mortgage, you must usually wait a few weeks after completion to receive payment.

Using an Agent

Most vendors prefer to use the services of an agent, either in Italy or in their home country, particularly when selling a second home. If you purchased the property through an agent, it's often wise to use the same agent when selling, as he will already be familiar with it and may still have the details on file. You should take particular care when selecting an agent, as they vary considerably in their professionalism, expertise and experience (the best way to investigate agents is by posing as a buyer). Many agents cover a relatively small area, so you should take care to choose one who regularly sells properties in your area and price range.

> ☑ **SURVIVAL TIP**
>
> If you own a property in an area popular with foreign buyers, it may be worthwhile using an overseas agent or advertising in foreign newspapers and magazines, such as the English-language publications listed in **Appendix B**.

Agents' Contracts

Before offering a property for sale, an Italian agent must have a signed authorisation from the owner or his representative. There are generally two types of agreement: an ordinary or non-exclusive agreement, which means that you reserve the right to deal with other agents and to negotiate directly with private individuals, and an exclusive agreement. An exclusive agreement gives a single agent the right to sell a property, although you can reserve the right to find a private buyer.

If you sign a contract without reserving the right to find your own buyer, you must still pay the agent's commission even if you sell your home yourself.

You must also pay an agent's fee if you sell to someone introduced by him within a certain period (e.g. one year) of the expiry of an agreement. There are no multiple listings in Italy, so if you don't have an exclusive agreement you must contact a number of agents individually. An agent's fees are usually lower with an exclusive agreement than with a non-exclusive agreement (see below). Make sure that you don't sign two or more exclusive agreements to sell your home!

Check the contract and make sure that you understand what you're signing. Contracts state the agent's commission, what it includes, and most importantly, who must pay it (see below).

Agents' Commission

Agents' commissions vary considerably, e.g. from 3 to 8 per cent, depending on the agent and area and on whether you have an exclusive or non-exclusive agreement (see above). The agent's commission is usually included in the purchase price but it's customary in Italy for the vendor to pay half the commission. For example, if you want to obtain €100,000 for your property and the agent's commission is 5 per cent,

you must sell it for around €102,500. Generally, you shouldn't pay any agent's fees unless you require extra services and you should never pay commission before a sale is completed. Foreign agents who work with Italian agents share the standard commission, so you should pay no more by using a foreign agent.

☑ **SURVIVAL TIP**

Capital Gains Tax

Capital gains tax has been abolished for property owners in Italy. However, you may be liable for CGT or income tax in another country (see page 229). When CGT is payable, a percentage may be withheld from the proceeds of a sale by the notary.

Todi, Umbria

4.
MONEY MATTERS

O ne of the most important aspects of buying a home in Italy and living there (even for relatively brief periods) is finance, which includes everything from transferring and changing money to mortgages and taxes. Italy is one of the highest taxed countries in the European Union (EU), when both direct and indirect taxes (including social security) are taken into consideration.

If you're planning to invest in a property or business in Italy financed with imported funds, it's important to consider both the present and possible future exchange rates. On the other hand, if you live and work in Italy and are paid in Euros, this may affect your financial commitments abroad. If your income is received in a currency other than Euros, it can be exposed to risks beyond your control when you live in Italy, particularly regarding inflation and exchange rate fluctuations.

If you own a home in Italy, you can employ an Italian accountant or tax adviser to look after your financial affairs there and declare and pay your local taxes. You can also have a representative receive your bank statements, ensure that your bank is paying your standing orders (e.g. for utilities) and that you have sufficient funds to pay them. If you let a home in Italy through an Italian company, they may perform the above tasks as part of their services.

If you plan to live in Italy for long periods, you must ensure that your income is (and will remain) sufficient to live on, bearing in mind devaluations, rises in the cost of living, and unforeseen expenses such as medical bills or anything else that may reduce your income.

Foreigners, particularly retirees, often under-estimate the cost of living in Italy and some are forced to return to their home countries after a few years.

Although the Italians prefer to pay cash (which cannot be traced by the taxman!), rather than use credit or charge cards, it's wise to have at least one credit card when visiting or living in Italy. Even if you don't like credit cards and shun any form of credit, they have their uses, e.g. no-deposit car rentals, no pre-paying hotel bills (plus guaranteed bookings), obtaining cash 24 hours a day, simple telephone and mail-order payments, greater safety and security than cash and, above all, convenience. However, not all Italian businesses accept credit cards, particularly small businesses, and you should check in advance.

ITALIAN CURRENCY

The Italian unit of currency is the Euro, which is also the currency of the Republic of San Marino and the Vatican City (although you will no longer be a millionaire with the demise of the lira, you will at least be able to manage the numbers!). Euro notes and coins became legal tender on 1st January 2002, replacing the lira. The Euro

(€) is divided into 100 cents (*centesimi*), and coins (*monete*) are minted in values of 1, 2, 5, 10, 20, 50 cents, €1 and €2. The 1, 2 and 5 cent coins are copper-coloured and the 10, 20 and 50 cent brass-coloured. The €1 coin is silver-coloured in the centre with a brass-coloured rim, and the €2 coin has a brass-coloured centre and silver-coloured rim. The reverse ('tail' showing the value) of Euro coins is the same in all Euro-zone countries, but the obverse ('head') is different in each country.

Italian coins carry eight designs, all depicting masterpieces by artists (e.g. Leonardo Da Vinci's drawing of the ideal body proportions on the €1 and Botticelli's *Birth of Venus* on the 10 cent coin) and the date of minting. All Euro coins can, of course, be used in all Euro-zone countries (although minute differences in weight occasionally cause problems in cash machines, e.g. at motorway tolls!).

Euro banknotes (*banconote*) are identical throughout the Euro-zone and depict a map of Europe and stylised designs of buildings. Notes are printed in denominations of €5, €10, €20, €50, €100, €200 and €500 (worth over £300), the size increasing with their value. Euro notes have been produced using all the latest anti-counterfeiting devices; nevertheless,

you should be especially wary of €200 and €500 notes. The Euro symbol may appear before the amount (as in this book), after it (commonly used by the Italians, e.g. 24€) or even between the Euros and cents, e.g. 16€50. When writing figures (for example on cheques), a full stop/period (.) is used to separate units of millions, thousands and hundreds, and a comma to denote fractions, e.g. €2.500,50.

If possible, it's wise to obtain some Euro coins and banknotes before arriving in Italy and to familiarise yourself with them. Bringing some Euros with you (e.g. €50 to €100 in small notes) will save you having to change money on arrival at an Italian airport (where exchange rates are poor). It's sensible not to carry a lot of cash and ideally you should avoid high value notes (above €50), which aren't widely accepted, particularly for small purchases or on public transport. Beware of short-changing, which is common in some areas (always check your change, particularly when tendering a large note).

More than a year after the change-over, most Italians continue to think and talk in their old currency (in common with all other Euro-zone nationals!), so it may be helpful to know that there were 1,936.27 lire to the Euro (e.g. '1 million lire' is roughly €500).

IMPORTING & EXPORTING MONEY

There are no exchange controls in Italy and no restrictions on the import or export of funds. An Italian resident is permitted to open a bank account in any country and to export unlimited funds. You may import or export up to €12,500 in any combination of foreign currency, Italian currency, travellers' cheques and securities without formality. Amounts over €12,500 (e.g. to buy a home) must be declared to the Italian Exchange Controls Office (Ufficio Italiano dei Cambi) to prevent money laundering and provide statistical data for the Banca d'Italia.

International Bank Transfers

When transferring or sending money to (or from) Italy you should be aware of the alternatives, which include the following:

- **Bank Draft** – A bank draft (*assegno circolare*) should be sent by registered post. However, in the (albeit unlikely) event that it's lost or stolen, it's impossible to stop payment and you must wait six months before a new draft can be issued. Bank drafts aren't treated as cash in Italy and must be cleared, as with personal cheques.

- **Bank Transfer** – A normal bank transfer (*trasferimento bancario*) should take three to seven days, but in reality can take much longer and an international bank transfer between non-affiliated banks can take weeks! Italian banks are among the slowest in Europe to process bank transfers and you should expect them to take at least twice as long as a bank says it will. It isn't unusual for transfers to and from Italy to get 'stuck' in the pipeline, which allows the Italian bank to use your money for a period interest free. Except for the fastest (and most expensive) methods, transfers between international banks are a joke in the age of electronic banking, when powerful financiers can switch funds almost instantaneously.

- **SWIFT Transfer** – One of the safest and fastest methods of transferring money is via the Society of Worldwide Interbank Financial Telecommunications (SWIFT) system. A SWIFT transfer should be completed in a few hours, funds being available within 24 hours, although even SWIFT transfers can take five working days, especially from small branches that are unused to dealing with foreign transfers. Australian and UK members of the SWIFT system are listed on the Society's website (💻 www.swift.com). The cost of transfers varies considerably – not only commission and exchange rates, but also transfer charges – but is usually between around €30 and €50.

Always check charges and exchange rates in advance and agree them with your bank (you may be able to negotiate a lower charge or a better exchange rate). Shop around a number of banks and compare fees. Banks are often willing to negotiate on fees and exchange rates when you're transferring a large amount of money. Some foreign banks levy a flat-fee for electronic transfers, irrespective of the amount. British banks charge between £10 and £60 for transfers taking from one to five days or longer.

When you have money transferred to a bank in Italy, make sure that you give the account holder's name, the account number, the branch number and the bank code. If money is 'lost' while being transferred to or from an Italian bank account, it can take weeks to locate it.

☑ **SURVIVAL TIP**

If you plan to send a large amount of money to Italy or abroad for a business transaction such as buying property, you should ensure that you receive the commercial rate of exchange rather than the tourist rate.

There are many companies who specialise in foreign exchange, particularly large sums of money, such as Currencies Direct (☎ UK 0845-389 3000, 💻 www.currenciesdirect.com), HiFX (☎ UK 01753-859159, 💻 www.hifx.co.uk) and Moneycorp (☎ UK 020-7589 3000, 💻 www.moneycorp.com).

Obtaining Cash

There are various methods of obtaining smaller amounts of money for everyday use. These include the following:

● **Bureaux De Change** – Most banks in major cities have foreign exchange windows, where you can buy and sell foreign currencies, buy and cash travellers' cheques, and obtain a cash advance on credit and charge cards. Banks tend to offer the best exchange rates and the post office the lowest charges. The post office charges a flat rate of around €0.50 per transaction (irrespective of the amount), while banks charge €3 or more.

There are many private exchange bureaux at airports, main railway stations and in major cities with longer business hours than banks, particularly at weekends. Most offer competitive exchange rates and low or no commission (but always check). They're easier to deal with than banks and, if you're changing a lot of money, you can usually negotiate a better exchange rate. At airports and in tourist areas in major cities, there are automatic change machines accepting up to 15 currencies, including US$, £sterling and Swiss francs. **However, airport bureaux de change and change machines usually offer the worst exchange rates and charge the highest fees (e.g. handling charges).** Never use unofficial money changers, who are likely to short change you. The exchange rate (*tasso di cambio*) against the Euro for most European and major international currencies is listed in banks and daily newspapers.

● **Cards** – If you need instant cash, you can draw on debit, credit or charge cards (but there's usually a daily limit). Many foreigners living in Italy (particularly retirees) keep the bulk of their money in a foreign account (perhaps in an offshore bank) and draw on it with a cash or credit card. This is an ideal solution for holidaymakers and holiday homeowners (although homeowners will still need a Italian bank account to pay their bills). Exchange rates are better when obtaining cash with a credit or debit card as you're given the wholesale rate, although there's a 1.5 per cent charge on cash advances and ATM transactions in foreign currencies. Some ATMs may reject foreign cards – if this happens try again or try another ATM.

● **Eurogiro** – Giro postcheques (Eurogiros) issued by European post offices can be cashed (with a postcheque guarantee card) at main post offices in Italy. The maximum value per cheque depends on the country where issued, e.g. €250 if issued in the UK. There's a standard charge for each cheque of €3.80 plus 0.7 per cent of the amount. You can also send money to Italy via the Girobank Eurogiro system from post offices in 15 European countries and the USA to some Italian banks.

● **Telegraphic Transfer** – One of the quickest (it takes around ten minutes) and safest methods of transferring cash is via a telegraphic transfer, e.g. Moneygram (🖳 www.moneygram.com) or Western Union (🖳 www.westernunion.com), but it's also one of the most expensive, e.g. commission of 7 to 10 per cent of the amount sent! Western Union transfers can be picked up from a post office in Italy (and 100 other countries) just 15 minutes after being paid into an office abroad. Money can be sent via American Express offices by Amex cardholders.

BANKS

There are some 900 banks (*banche*) in Italy, around 200 of which are large, some 50 of which are branches of foreign banks (mostly in Rome and Milan). The remaining 700 or so are primarily local banks with few branches, of which over 500 are co-operative credit banks. The number of banks in Italy is continually decreasing as banks merge or are taken over.

There are three kinds of bank in Italy: ordinary commercial or credit banks (*banche commerciali*), co-operative banks (*banche popolari cooperative*) and co-operative credit banks (*banche di credito cooperativo*). As in other countries, co-operative banks were established to provide loans (particularly home loans) to their customers. Co-operative credit banks are rural and artisan savings banks, funded and owned by farmers and craftsmen. They comprise the largest number of banks in Italy, but because their average size is very small, they account for just a tiny percentage of total deposits. The Banca d'Italia is owned by the public sector banks and is the only bank permitted to issue notes in Italy.

The Banca Nazionale del Lavoro, Cassa di Risparmio, Banca Commerciale Italiana, Banca di Roma, Banco di Napoli and Banco di Sicilia all have nation-wide branch networks. The post office serves as a savings bank for many Italians and foreigners with a fiscal code.

Bank opening hours vary with the bank and town, but are generally from 8 or 8.30am until 1pm or 1.30pm and from 2.30 or 3pm until 4 or 4.30pm, Mondays to Fridays. Some branches in major cities

open from 9am to noon on Saturdays. Banks usually open only in the morning on the day before a public holiday. Offices at major airports and railway stations have longer opening hours for changing money and cashing travellers' cheques, and there are also *bureaux de change* in major cities and resorts with extended opening hours.

Italian banks have traditionally levied some of the highest charges in the world, although they've come down in recent years. However, interest rates charged by many Italian banks are still exorbitant, particularly for business and consumer loans, and credit cards. However, lenders are now required to publish the highest rates they charge and the market average, so that borrowers can make comparisons. Shop around and compare rates before signing any contracts or taking out a loan (banks must also publish their conditions).

Italy has traditionally had one of the least efficient banking services in Europe; even the simplest operation was inordinately complicated and time-consuming. Electronic banking has improved efficiency somewhat, but northern Europeans may find customer service and the range of products available more limited than they're used to. On the other hand, Italian banks are quite safe and most deposits are covered by a Bank Deposit Insurance Fund (*Fondo Interbancario di Garanzia dei Depositi*).

Branches of EU banks operating in Italy can join an Italian deposit guarantee plan and increase the amount of financial protection they offer clients above and beyond the protection provided by their home country's guarantee plan. If a bank from a non-EU country is licensed to operate in Italy, the Italian branch must be part of the Italian deposit guarantee plan, unless it's a member of an equivalent foreign plan. The maximum amount reimbursed to each depositor is limited to the very precise figure of €103,291.38. Bear in mind that foreign banks in Italy operate in the same way as other Italian banks, and you shouldn't expect a branch of Barclays, for example, to function as if it were in the UK.

Opening an Account

You can open a bank account in Italy whether you're a resident or a non-resident. It's best to open an Italian bank account in person, rather than from abroad. Ask your friends, neighbours or colleagues for their recommendations and just go along to the bank of your choice and introduce yourself. You must be at least 18 and provide proof of identity, e.g. a passport, and your address in Italy (a utility bill usually suffices). Before choosing a bank, it's wise to compare the fees charged for international money transfers and other services, which can be high.

If you wish to open an account with an Italian bank while abroad, you must obtain an application form from a branch of an Italian bank (either in Italy or your home country) and choose a branch from the list provided. If you open an account by correspondence, you must provide a reference from your bank, including a certificate of signature or a signature witnessed by a solicitor or lawyer. You also need a photocopy of the relevant pages of your passport and a Euro draft to open the account.

All banks provide credit cards and debit cards (called *Bancomat* cards) to obtain cash throughout Italy and also abroad, usually via the CIRRUS and NYCE networks. However, it's unwise to rely solely on ATMs (also referred to as *Bancomats* in Italy) to obtain cash, as they often run out of money or are out of operation. Bear in mind that daily withdrawals with a *Bancomat* card are generally limited to €300.

Non-Residents

If you're a non-resident, you're entitled to open a non-resident account (*conto estero*) only. Only foreign currency or imported Euros can be paid into a non-resident account, which pays higher interest than resident accounts. There's no withholding tax on interest earned on deposits, as there is for resident Euro accounts (when withholding tax is deducted at source),

but bank charges are higher for non-resident accounts. If you're a non-resident, it's possible to survive without an Italian account by using girocheques, travellers' cheques and credit cards, although this isn't wise and is an expensive option. If you have a second home in Italy, you can have all documentation (e.g. cheque books, statements, etc.) sent to an address abroad, and some Italian banks provide written communications in English.

Residents

You're considered to be a resident of Italy (*residenti valutari*) if you have your main centre of interest there, i.e. you live or work there more or less permanently. To open a resident account you must usually have a residence permit (*certificato di residenza*) or evidence that you have a job in Italy, although some banks waive this requirement.

It isn't wise to close your bank accounts abroad when you're living permanently in Italy, unless you're certain that you won't need them in the future. Even when you're resident in Italy, it's cheaper to keep some money in local currency in an account in a country that you visit regularly, e.g. your home country, rather than pay commission to convert Euros (if applicable). Many foreigners living in Italy maintain at least two accounts; a foreign account (possibly offshore) for international transactions and a local account with an Italian bank for day-to-day business.

Offshore Banking

If you have a sum of money to invest or wish to protect your inheritance from the tax man, it may be worthwhile looking into the accounts and services (such as pensions and trusts) provided by offshore banking centres in tax havens such as the Channel Islands (Guernsey and Jersey), Gibraltar and the Isle of Man (around 50 locations world-wide are officially classified as tax havens). The big attraction of offshore banking is that money can be deposited in a wide range of currencies, customers are usually guaranteed a degree of anonymity, there are no double-taxation agreements, no withholding tax is payable, and interest is paid tax-free. Many offshore banks also offer telephone (usually seven days a week) and internet banking.

A large number of American, British and other European banks and financial institutions provide offshore banking facilities in one or more locations. Most institutions offer high-interest deposit accounts for long-term savings and investment portfolios, in which funds can be deposited in any major currency. Many people living abroad keep a local account for everyday business and maintain an offshore account for international transactions and investment purposes.

☑ **SURVIVAL TIP**

Most financial experts advise investors never to rush into the expatriate life and invest their life savings in an offshore tax haven until they know what their long-term plans are.

Accounts have minimum deposits levels which usually range from £500 to £10,000 ($750 to $15,000), with some as high as £100,000 ($150,000). In addition to large minimum balances, accounts may also have stringent terms and conditions, such as restrictions on withdrawals or high early withdrawal penalties. You can deposit funds on call (instant access) or for a fixed period, e.g. from 90 days to one year (usually for larger sums). Interest is paid monthly, quarterly or annually. Monthly interest payments are slightly lower than annual payments, although they have the advantage of providing a regular income.

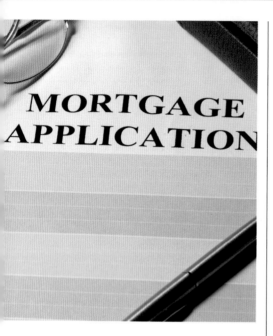

MORTGAGE APPLICATION

international bank or financial organisation with Moody's Investor Service. You should be wary of institutions offering higher than average interest rates, as if it looks too good to be true it probably will be – like the Bank of International Commerce and Credit (BICC), which went bust in 1992.

MORTGAGES

Mortgages or home loans (*mutuo ipotecario*) are available from all major Italian banks and many foreign banks. Mortgages from Italian banks may take some time to be approved (although it's now much faster than it was) and you may be able to obtain better terms and a larger loan from a foreign lender. Italian mortgages are repaid using the capital and interest method (repayment), and endowment and pension-linked mortgages aren't offered. Italian loans can have a fixed or variable interest rate (*tasso*). When comparing rates, the fixed rate (*tasso fisso*) is higher than the variable rate (*tasso variabile*), to reflect the increased risk to the lender. The advantage of a fixed rate is that you know exactly how much you must pay over the whole term. It's also possible to assume the mortgage (*accollo del mutuo*) of a vendor.

Among the foreign banks offering mortgages are the British banks, Abbey National (🖳 www.abbeynational.it) and Woolwich (🖳 www.bancawoolwich.it, now part of Barclays), the first banks to offer low rate home loans, and Deutschebank (🖳 www.deutsche-bank.it). All three have branches throughout the country. Loans are available from telephone mortgage lenders such as Banca Manager, who offer a fast response and lower fees than most traditional banks. When looking for a mortgage, shop around for the best deal. Mortgage quotes are available online from 🖳 www.mutuionline.it (in Italian only).

There are usually no charges, provided a specified minimum balance is maintained. Many accounts offer a debit card, e.g. Mastercard or Visa, which can be used to obtain cash via ATMs throughout the world.

When selecting a financial institution and offshore banking centre, your first priority should be for the safety of your money. In some offshore banking centres, all bank deposits are guaranteed up to a certain amount under a deposit protection scheme, whereby a maximum sum is guaranteed should a financial institution go bust (the Isle of Man, Guernsey and Jersey all have such schemes). Unless you're planning to bank with a major international bank (which is only likely to fold the day after the end of the world!), you should check the credit rating of a financial institution before depositing any money, particularly if it doesn't provide deposit insurance.

All banks have a credit rating (the highest is 'AAA') and a bank with a high rating will be happy to tell you (but get it in writing). You can also check the rating of an

Interest rates in Italy used to be high, although they've dropped considerably since the introduction of the Euro, and Italian lenders' margins and fees are among the highest in Europe (mortgages may also contain restrictive clauses). The European Central Bank interest rate was 4 per cent in autumn 2007, with Italian mortgage rates generally around 1 to 2 per cent higher. Those seeking a first mortgage are usually offered the best deals. Many lenders offer low-start mortgages, which are fixed for an initial period (*tasso/rata d'ingresso*), e.g. two or three years, after which they may change to a variable rate. Some banks offer lower interest rates to attract buyers in certain areas.

You can have a clause in your mortgage whereby you aren't required to accept an increase in your payments of over 10 per cent or more than the standard of living index (i.e. inflation). Any additional amount owed is added to your loan or the loan period is extended.

Most banks don't have a maximum limit for mortgages, although some limit the minimum loan to between €50,000 and €100,000. Mortgages repayments are generally limited to a maximum of around 30 per cent of your net income. Some foreign lenders apply stricter rules than Italian lenders regarding income, employment and the type of property on which they will lend, although some are willing to lend more than Italian financial institutions.

Up to the mid-'90s, Italian banks rarely lent more than 50 per cent of the value of a property, although this has now risen to around 80 per cent for buyers of a principal home (*mutuo prima casa*). However, this applies only to residents with their principal home in Italy (see **Mortgages For Second Homes** below). Mortgages of 95 or 100 per cent aren't available, although it may be possible to obtain a larger (e.g. 90 per cent) mortgage for a

property requiring restoration (*mutuo per ristrutturazione*). Loans are usually repaid over a short period (*durata*) in Italy (e.g. 10 or 15 years), although some Italian banks offer mortgages for up to 30 years. It's customary in Italy for a property to be held as security for a loan taken out on it, i.e. the lender takes a first charge on the property.

> ## ▲ Caution
>
> It's unwise to over-stretch your finances when taking out a mortgage, as there will inevitably be added costs that you haven't bargained for. If you default on your mortgage repayments, your property can be repossessed and sold at auction, although most lenders are willing to negotiate and arrange lower repayments if borrowers get into financial difficulties.

If you're buying a new property off plan, where payments are made in stages, a bank will provide a 'staggered' loan, where the loan amount is advanced in instalments as required by the contract. During the period before completion, interest is payable on a monthly basis on the amount advanced by the bank (plus life insurance). When the final payment has been made and the loan is fully drawn, the mortgage enters its amortisation period (*periodo di ammortamento/durata del mutuo*).

When buying a property in Italy, the deposit paid when signing the preliminary contract (*compromesso di vendita*) is automatically protected under Italian law should you fail to obtain a mortgage. It's possible to obtain a mortgage guarantee from most lenders, valid for two to four months, during which period you're guaranteed a mortgage for a specified sum, subject to an acceptable property valuation.

It isn't usual to have a survey in Italy, where an Italian lender may value a property or simply accept the fiscal value, although foreign lenders usually insist on a valuation before they will grant a loan.

Procedure & Fees

To obtain a mortgage from an Italian bank, you must provide proof of your monthly income and out-goings, such as existing mortgage payments, rent and other loans or commitments. Proof of income usually includes three month's pay slips for employees, confirmation of income from your employer and tax returns. If you're self-employed, you require an audited copy of your balance sheets and trading accounts for the past three years, plus your last tax return. If you want an Italian mortgage to buy a property for commercial purposes, you must provide a detailed business plan (in Italian).

There are various fees (*spese istruttoria*) associated with mortgages. All lenders charge an application or arrangement fee for establishing a loan, usually 0.5 to 1 per cent of the loan amount. There's a mortgage tax (*imposta ipotecaria*) of €168 and a mortgage registration tax (*imposta sostitutiva*) of 0.25 per cent for residents and first-time buyers or 2 per cent for second homes (e.g. no-residents). Most lenders also impose an 'administration' fee of around 1 per cent of the loan value, and it's compulsory to take out insurance cover with the lender against fire, lightning strikes and gas explosions. The insurance is usually a one-off payment of 0.21 per cent of the property's value and valid for 20 years.

If you're an Italian taxpayer and the property is your principal residence, you can claim a deduction for your Italian mortgage against your tax liabilities.

Mortgages for Second Homes

It's more difficult for non-residents than for residents to obtain a mortgage for a home in Italy and usually only 50 or 60 per cent of its value can be borrowed, although some foreign banks offer non-residents loans of up to 80 per cent over 25 years. Interest rates for non-residents are also usually higher than for residents. It's generally difficult for non-residents to obtain a mortgage with an Italian bank to purchase a ruin, and many non-residents find it quicker and easier to buy without a mortgage and then apply for one to cover restoration costs.

If you have spare equity in an existing property (either in Italy or abroad), it may be more cost effective to re-mortgage (or take out a second mortgage) on that property than to take out a new mortgage for a second home; it involves less paperwork and therefore lower legal fees. Depending on the equity in your existing property and the cost of your Italian property, this may enable you to pay cash for a second home.

It's also possible to obtain a foreign currency mortgage, e.g. sterling, Swiss francs or $US. However, you should be wary of taking out a foreign currency mortgage, as interest rate gains can be wiped out overnight by currency swings and devaluations.

> ☑ **SURVIVAL TIP**
>
> It's generally recognised that you should take out a loan in the currency in which you're paid or in the currency of the country where a home is situated.

When choosing between a Euro loan and a loan in another currency, be sure to take into account all charges, fees, interest rates and possible currency fluctuations. However you finance the purchase of a second home in Italy, you should obtain professional advice from your bank manager and accountant.

If you have a foreign currency mortgage, you must usually pay commission charges each time you make a transfer to pay your mortgage or remit money to Italy. However, some lenders will transfer mortgage payments to Italy each month free of charge or for a nominal amount. If you let a second home, you may be able to offset the interest on your mortgage against rental income, but pro rata only. For example, if you let an Italian property for three months of the year, you may be able to offset a quarter of your annual mortgage interest against your rental income.

Three Pinnacles, Dolmomites

Pienza, Tuscany

5.
THE PURCHASE PROCEDURE

This chapter details the purchase procedure for buying a home in Italy. It's wise to employ a lawyer before paying any money and, if necessary, have him check anything you're concerned about regarding a property you're planning to buy. See also Avoiding Problems on page 94.

CONVEYANCING

Conveyancing (*pratica*), or more correctly 'conveyance', is the legal term for processing the paperwork involved in buying and selling real property and transferring the deeds of ownership. Conveyancing is strictly governed by Italian law and can be carried out only by a public notary (*notaio*), who's a qualified legal professional and a representative of the state. A notary is responsible to the provincial authorities for the registration of land and property transfers at the local land registry (*catasto*). He (they're usually men) must follow a strict code of conduct and have personal insurance covering his professional responsibility and guaranteeing clients against any errors he may make.

A notary represents neither the seller nor the buyer, but the Italian government, and one of his main tasks is to ensure that all taxes are paid to the Ministry of Finance on completion of a sale. A notary usually acts for both the vendor and buyer, and must remain strictly impartial, although a buyer can insist on choosing the notary, as he usually pays his fee. Notaries' fees vary, so you should check them in advance (see Fees on page 111). A notary won't necessarily protect or act in your interests, and you should engage your own lawyer to ensure that everything is carried out to your satisfaction.

There are two main stages when a notary usually becomes involved in a property purchase. The first is the signing of the preliminary contract (*compromesso di vendit* or *contratto preliminare di vendita*), when the presence of a notary isn't mandatory, and the second is completion, i.e. the signing of the deed of sale (*rogito*), which must be done in the presence of a notary. The notary is responsible for ensuring that the deed of sale is drawn up correctly and that the purchase price is paid to the vendor. He also witnesses the signing of the deed, arranges for its registration (in the name of the new owner) at the land registry (*catasto*), and collects any fees and taxes due. The notary doesn't verify or guarantee the accuracy of statements made in a contract or protect you against fraud.

Don't expect a notary to speak English (few do) or any language other than Italian, or to explain the intricacies of Italian property law. A notary will rarely point out possible pitfalls in a contract, proffer advice or volunteer any information.

The notary should check the following (this **isn't** intended to be a definitive list):

- Verifying that a property belongs to the vendor, as shown in the deed (*rogito*) and listed at the land registry (*catasto*) or that he has the legal authority to sell it. The owner should produce a certified copy of the deed. The descriptions of the property at the land registry and on the deed should be identical.

- Obtaining a certificate that an old property is fit for habitation (*certificato di abitabilità*);

- Obtain certificates of inspection for all electrical and gas systems and appliances, which must be inspected annually. These must be attached to the deed of sale (*rogito*).

If you're buying a 'listed' building (*beni culturali*), of which there are thousands in Italy, the notary should check whether the state wishes to exercise its right to pre-empt the sale (*diritto di prelazione*). He should apply for the right to proceed with a sale after the signing of the preliminary contract and the state has 60 days in which to pre-empt it. If so, the contract becomes void and the seller is obliged to return your deposit. The notary should also check whether there are any restrictions over the use and possible future sale of the property. You should ask your lawyer to check that both these things have been done.

> ⚠ **Caution**
>
> If any restoration work has been carried out or any alterations have been made to a listed building illegally, it can be confiscated by the state.

You or your lawyer should do the following:

- Check that there are no pre-emption rights over a property and that there are no plans to construct anything (e.g. roads, railway lines, airports, shops, factories, etc.) that would adversely affect the value, enjoyment or use of the property. Check whether there's a zoning policy (*piano regolatore*) in the town or area that may affect a property you're planning to buy.

- Check whether the property is subject to a compulsory purchase order. If you buy a rural property (*casa rurale*), it could be subject to compulsory purchase by a neighbouring farmer under a farmer's rights (*diritto del coltivatore*) law. This law allows farmers who earn over 70 per cent of their income from agriculture or agro-tourism, to increase the size of their property by giving them the right to buy adjacent buildings or land **for up to two years after it has been sold**. To avoid this, you can have your lawyer draw up a document asking the farmer to confirm within 30 days whether he intends to exercise his right of purchase. If the farmer doesn't declare his intention to buy the land within this period, he automatically waives any right to buy it in future.

- Check rights of access (*servitù di passaggio*). Land may have a mandatory right of way (*servitù di necessità*) for a neighbour whose only access is via your land; this may be permanent or renewable.

- Ensure that building permits and planning permissions are in order, and that a property was built in accordance with plans and permits (see **Planning Permission & Building Permits** on page 136). Any modifications, renovations, extensions or additions (such as a swimming pool) must be included on the plans and be authorised. Plans must be checked against the cadastral plan at the land registry.

- In cases where a property has been inherited, check whether each inheritor has agreed to the sale. Heirs who haven't been contacted have up to five years to contest the will.

- If a property was previously owned by a bankrupt company, ensure that the liquidator won't reverse the sale and claim it for the creditors;

- Check that there are no encumbrances, e.g. mortgages or loans, against a property or outstanding debts (see box).

☑ **SURVIVAL TIP**

All unpaid debts on a property in Italy are inherited by the buyer. If you buy a property on which there's an outstanding loan or taxes, the lender or local authority has first claim on the property and has the right to take possession and sell it to repay the debt. Any debts against a property must therefore be cleared before you sign the deed of sale (*rogito*) – see also Completion on page 167.

- Enquire at the town hall whether there are any unpaid taxes such as property tax (see page 187) or other charges outstanding against a property.

- Check that there are no outstanding community (*condominio*) charges for the last five years (it may be possible for a vendor to pay the last year and ignore previous bills), and obtain copies of the co-ownership rules and the latest accounts of the community of owners (which should state whether there are any impending levies for repairs for which you would be liable);

- Check that all bills for electricity, water, telephone and gas have been paid for the last few years. Receipts should be provided by the vendor for all taxes and services.

- Before buying land, obtain a certificate from the local town hall stating what can be built on it and what the property and the land can be used for. It's important to check the size of dwelling that can be built on a plot or how far an existing building can be extended.

- If the property is a listed building, check that the notary has made the necessary enquiries concerning state pre-emption rights and restrictions on use or resale (see above).

CONTRACTS

In some transactions, the first stage in buying a home is the signing of a 'purchase proposal' (*promessa d'acquisto* or *prenotazione* or *promessa di vendita*), which is usually drawn up by the estate agent and presented to the seller on the buyer's behalf. A purchase proposal usually includes little more than the offer made by the seller for the property and is binding only on the seller; you're free to accept or reject the offer, usually within a time limit of up to 15 days. If you reject the proposal, your deposit (see page 165) is returned to the buyer. If you accept the purchase proposal, both parties then sign a preliminary contract (see below). Purchase proposals are rare and, if an estate agent insists that you sign a purchase proposal and pay a deposit before signing a preliminary contract, you should make sure the money is deposited in a safe (escrow) account.

The first stage in buying a home in Italy is usually the signing of a preliminary contract (*compromesso di vendita*, also referred to as a *contratto preliminare di vendita* but normally called simply the *promessa*), which may be drawn up by the vendor, estate agent, notary or a lawyer. The *compromesso* may be hand-written or a standard printed document available from stationery stores. On signing the preliminary contract, both parties are bound to the transaction and the *compromesso* must be registered at the tax office (*Agenzie delle Entrate*) within 20 days of the date of signing. The preliminary contract must be drawn up in four original copies, and signed by the seller and buyer; one copy for each of the parties, two for the registration.

Registration is in two stages (sometimes carried out by the estate agent), involving a visit to any bank and to an office of the *Agenzia delle Entrate*. A fixed registration fee (*imposta di registro*) of €168 is payable at the bank and a further charge is payable if a deposit is paid. If the deposit is also an initial payment, this charge is 3 per cent of the deposit amount. This 3 per cent is refunded when the final deed is signed at the notary. If the deposit is only a guarantee deposit, the charge is 0.5 per cent of the deposit (which is also refunded when the final deed is signed). Form F23 – which has been stamped by the bank – is taken to the *Agenzia delle Entrate*, along with the original preliminary contract. Official stamps (*bolli*) of a value of €14.62 each must be attached as follows: one stamp per every four pages

of the contract and an additional stamp for every 100 lines over and above an original 100. The *Agenzie* issues a receipt, which must be presented to the notary.

The *compromesso* contains the essential terms of the sale, including full details of the property, details of the vendor and buyer, the purchase price, how it is to be financed, the closing date, and any other conditions (see **Conditional Clauses** on page 165) that must be fulfilled before completion. Some agents provide an English translation of a contract, although translations are often so bad as to be misleading or meaningless. You should ensure that you understand **every** clause in the preliminary contract. A sale must be completed within the period stipulated in the *compromesso*, usually six to eight weeks (although it can be from two weeks to three or four months).

You should obtain a fiscal number (*codice fiscale*) as soon as possible after signing the *compromesso*, as this is necessary for the completion (see page 181).

Legal Advice

The preliminary contract is binding on both parties and therefore it's important to obtain

legal advice before signing it. Although it isn't necessary to employ a lawyer (or a notary) when signing a preliminary contract, it's often wise.

Most experts consider that you should have a preliminary contract checked by a lawyer before signing it.

One of the main reasons to engage a lawyer (*avvocato*) is to safeguard your interests through the inclusion of any necessary conditional clauses in the contract. If an estate agent's commission is payable when the *compromesso* is signed, you must ensure that it's refundable if the sale doesn't go through (get it in writing). There are various other reasons to employ a lawyer: for example, the best way to buy a property in Italy is sometimes through an Italian company or you may wish to make special provisions regarding inheritance (see **Inheritance Taxes** on page 189).

The method of buying Italian property has important consequences, particularly regarding Italian inheritance laws, and it can be difficult or expensive to correct any errors later.

Deposit

Some estate agents may ask the buyer to pay a reservation fee or deposit (*acconto anticipo caparra* or *deposito*) in order to secure a property and take it off the market, although in practice the property isn't secured for the buyer until a purchase contract is signed. Beware of paying large amounts of money as a reservation fee to an estate agent; from €250 to €1,000 is generally sufficient.

It's possible to pay a nominal sum as a holding deposit (*anticipo di pagamento*) before the *compromesso* is signed, as a gesture of good faith, but a deposit (*caparra* or *deposito*) of between 10 and 30 per cent must be paid to the vendor at the time of signing the preliminary contract and is forfeited if you don't go

through with the purchase (except under certain circumstances – see below); if the vendor reneges, he must pay you double the amount of the deposit. A deposit isn't usually paid to a third party, such as an agent or notary in Italy, although an agent may hold it if the seller is absent. It's preferable that the deposit is described as *caparra penitenziale* and not as *caparra confermatoria*. With the former, the buyer 'simply' loses his deposit if he withdraws from a sale, while with the latter the vendor can take legal action to force a buyer to go through with a purchase.

A deposit is refundable under strict conditions only, notably relating to any conditional clauses, such as the failure to obtain a mortgage, although it can be forfeited if you don't complete the transaction within the period specified in the contract. If you withdraw from a sale after all the conditions have been met, you won't just lose your deposit, but must also pay the estate agent's commission.

> ☑ SURVIVAL TIP
>
> **Always make sure that you know exactly what the conditions are regarding the return or forfeiture of a deposit.**

Conditional Clauses

A preliminary contract, whether for an old or new property, may contain a number of conditional clauses (*clausola condizionale/ resolutiva*) that must be met to ensure the validity of the contract. Conditions usually apply to events outside the control of the vendor or buyer, although almost anything the buyer agrees with the vendor can be included. If any of the conditions aren't met, the contract can be suspended or declared null and void and the deposit returned. However, if you attempt to withdraw from a purchase and aren't covered by a clause in the contract, you will forfeit your deposit or could be forced to go through with the purchase.

If any accessories such as carpets, curtains or appliances are included in the purchase price, you should have them listed and attached as an addendum to the contract. Any fixtures and fittings present in a property when you view it (and agree to buy it) should also be included in the contract (see also **Completion** on page 167).

There are many possible conditional clauses concerning a range of subjects, including the following:

- Being able to obtain a mortgage (see **Mortgage Clause** below);

- Obtaining planning permission and building permits, e.g. for a swimming pool or extension;

- Discovering that there are plans to construct anything (e.g. roads,

railways) that would adversely affect the enjoyment or use of the property;

- Obtaining confirmation that land is sold with a property;

- Pre-emption rights or restrictive covenants over a property (such as rights of access);

- Completion of the sale of another property;

- Obtaining a satisfactory building survey or inspection.

You may wish to convert a property that is classified as 'rural' (*casa rurale*) into an 'urban' property (*casa urbana*), for example when buying an agricultural property that you wish to convert into a holiday home (although this isn't always possible). If done before completion, conversion will reduce your registration tax (see **Registration Tax** on page 111). The cost of conversion varies with the province, e.g. from €100 to €300.

Mortgage Clause

The most common conditional clause states that a buyer is released from the contract should he be unable to obtain a mortgage. Even if you have no intention of obtaining a mortgage (you don't have to obtain a mortgage, even if you state that you're going to), it's recommended not to give up your right to do so; if you give up your right and later find that you need a mortgage but fail to obtain it, you will lose your deposit. The clause should state the amount, term and interest rate expected or already agreed with a lender, plus the lender's name (if known). If you cannot obtain a mortgage for the agreed amount and terms, you won't lose your deposit. You must make an application for the loan within a certain period after signing the contract and have a specified period in which to secure it.

Buying through a Company

Buying a property in Italy through an Italian company can be beneficial, particularly when two or more people or families are buying between them, or when you wish to avoid Italian inheritance laws. When a number of foreigners are buying a property together, the Italian company can in turn be owned by a company abroad, thus allowing legal disputes to be dealt with under local law. The principal advantage of buying a property through a company is that, when it's sold or bequeathed, its shares can be transferred to the new owner. On the death of an owner, shares in the company are treated as movable assets and can be bequeathed in accordance with the owner's domicile.

Owning Italian property through a company is of little or no benefit to residents, as most of the advantages don't apply. If you plan to own a property through a company, the company should be set up before you sign a contract, as it will be more expensive to do it later.

☑ **SURVIVAL TIP**

Before buying a property through a company, it's essential to obtain expert legal advice and carefully consider the advantages and disadvantages.

COMPLETION

Completion (closing or exchange of contracts), called *atto* in Italian, is the name for the signing of the final deed (*rogito, atto di compravendita* or *scrittura privata*), which is drawn up by a notary. The date of completion is usually six to eight weeks after signing the preliminary contract, as stated in the contract, although it may be moveable. Completion involves the signing of the deed of sale, transferring legal ownership of the property, and paying the balance of the purchase price, plus any other payments due, such as the notary's fees, taxes and duties.

When the necessary documents concerning a purchase have been returned to the notary, he will contact you and request the balance of the purchase price (i.e. less the deposit) and, if applicable, the amount of a mortgage. He will also give you a bill for his fees and state taxes, which must be paid on completion (see **Fees** on page 111).

Final Checks

Property is sold subject to the condition that it's accepted in the state it's in at the time of completion, so you should be aware of anything that occurs between signing the preliminary contract and completion. Before signing the deed of sale, it's **imperative** to check that the property hasn't fallen down or been damaged in any way, e.g. by a storm or the previous owners. If you've employed a lawyer or are buying through an agent, he should accompany you on this visit. You should also take an inventory immediately before completion (the previous owner should have already vacated the property) to ensure that the vendor hasn't absconded with anything that was included in the price or purchased separately, e.g. carpets, light fittings, curtains or kitchen appliances, and that they're in good working order where applicable.

You should also ensure that expensive or valuable items (such as kitchen apparatus or antique fittings) haven't been substituted by inferior (possibly second-hand) items. Any garden ornaments, plants and shrubs present in a garden when you viewed it should still be there when you take possession, unless otherwise stated in the contract. Some vendors will go to amazing extremes, for example removing not just light bulbs, but bulb-holders, wiring (flex) and even ceiling roses as well as bulbs, plants, shrubs and trees from the garden!

If you find that anything is missing, damaged or isn't in working order, you should make a note and insist on immediate restitution, such as an appropriate reduction in the amount to be paid. In such cases it's normal for the notary to withhold an appropriate amount in escrow from the vendor's proceeds to pay for repairs or replacements.

Although you or your lawyer should already have checked that there are no encumbrances, e.g. mortgages or loans, against a property or outstanding debts (see **Conveyancing** on page 161), it's important for you or your lawyer to go to the land registry and check ALL entries up to the day of the completion (this could be done a few days earlier and then you need only examine entries since the last check on the day of completion).

☑ SURVIVAL TIP

You should refuse to go through with the completion if you aren't completely satisfied, as it will be very difficult or impossible to obtain redress later.

If it isn't possible to complete the sale, you should consult your lawyer about your rights, and the return of your deposit and any other funds already paid.

Declared Value

The deed of sale includes a declaration of the price paid by the buyer. In Italy, it's customary for the declared price to be less that the actual price paid, in order that the buyer pays lower fees and taxes, although this is illegal. If you're tempted make an under-declaration (*sottodichiarazione*) and the buyer agrees to it (most will), make sure that it isn't less than the property's value recorded at the local land registry (*catasto*).

The declared price is usually between 10 and 20 per cent below the actual purchase price in cities, where property values are

well documented, but in rural areas prices are often under-declared by 50 per cent or more. However, the authorities have been revising property values in recent years and fiscal values are now closer to actual values in many areas. If you under-declare the value too much, the tax authorities may make their own valuation and tax the parties accordingly, which may also result in a fine. Take advice from your estate agent and/or lawyer when declaring the value on the deed of sale.

Signing

The final act of buying is the signing of the deed of sale (*rogito*), which takes place in the notary's office. Before the deed is signed, the notary checks that all the conditions contained in the preliminary contract have been fulfilled. It's normal for both parties to be present when the deed is read, signed and witnessed by the notary, although either party can give a representative power of attorney (*procura*). If you're married, you must produce your marriage certificate so that it can be noted whether the property is to be owned jointly by both spouses (*comunione dei beni*) or by one only.

If you don't understand Italian, an officially accredited interpreter must be present or a power of attorney must be given to your agent or lawyer. This can be drawn up by your agent or lawyer or a notary in Italy or by a foreign agent or notary, and authenticated by an Italian consulate in your home country, although the latter procedure is more complicated and expensive.

Payment

The balance of the price after the deposit and any mortgages have been subtracted is usually paid by banker's draft (*assegno circolare*) or bank transfer. The money can be transferred directly to the seller's bank account or you can pay by banker's draft (see **International Bank Transfers** on page 151), which is the better method, as you will have it in your possession (a bank cannot lose it!) and the notary can confirm payment immediately. It also allows you to withhold payment if there's a last minute problem that cannot be resolved (see **Final Checks** above).

If you and the buyer are of the same nationality, you can agree that the balance is paid in a currency other than Euros, although the notary must also agree to this. In this case, the money should be held by a lawyer or solicitor in the vendor's or buyer's home country.

After paying the balance due and receiving a receipt you're given the keys, but you aren't the legal owner until the property has been registered (see below).

Registration

There are no title deeds as in the UK, for example, and proof of ownership is provided and guaranteed by registration of the property at the land registry (*catasto*). The land registry's stamp is placed on the deed of sale, a certified copy of which is available from the notary around two to three months after completion. If you have a mortgage, it's also recorded at the land registry. The original deed is retained indefinitely by the notary.

Registration is of paramount importance; until a property is registered, you aren't the legal owner. It's also important to check your copy of the deed of sale after registration to ensure that it's correct in every detail.

Formal notification of the purchase must be given to the local police authorities (questura) via a form, usually provided by the notary.

Michelangelo's David

6.
MOVING HOUSE

Moving into your new Italian home may be the culmination of your dreams, but it can also be a highly stressful experience. However, it's possible to limit the strain on your mental and physical health by careful planning and preparation. This chapter contains checklists that should help to ensure that you don't forget anything important.

SHIPPING YOUR BELONGINGS

It usually takes just a few weeks to have your belongings shipped from within continental Europe. From anywhere else it varies considerably, e.g. around four weeks from the east coast of America, six weeks from the USA west coast and the Far East, and around eight weeks from Australasia. Customs clearance is no longer necessary when shipping your household effects from one European Union (EU) country to another. However, when shipping your effects from a non-EU country to Italy, certain formalities must be observed.

If you're moving to Italy from a non-EU country, you must present an inventory (in English and Italian) of the items that you're planning to import to your local Italian consulate, which must be officially stamped. You will also need a permit to stay (*permesso di soggiorno*) from the local police station (*questura*) in Italy. If you fail to follow the correct procedure, you can encounter delays, and may be charged duty or fined. The relevant forms to be completed by non-EU citizens depend on whether your Italian home will be your main residence or a second home. Removal companies usually take care of

the paperwork and ensure that the correct documents are provided and properly completed (see **Customs** on page 175).

It's usually wise to use a major shipping company with a good reputation. For international moves it's best to use a company that's a member of the International Federation of Furniture Removers (FIDI, 🖥 www.fidi,com) or the Overseas Moving Network International (OMNI, 🖥 www.omnimoving.com), with experience in Italy. Members of FIDI and OMNI usually subscribe to an advance payment scheme providing a guarantee: if a member company fails to fulfil its commitments, the removal is completed at the agreed cost by another company or your money is refunded. Some removal companies have subsidiaries or affiliates in Italy, which may be more convenient if you encounter problems or need to make an insurance claim.

You should obtain at least three written quotations before choosing a company, as costs vary considerably. Moving companies should send a representative to provide a detailed quotation. Most companies will pack your belongings and provide packing cases and special containers, although this is naturally more expensive than packing them yourself. Ask a company how they pack fragile and valuable items, and whether the cost of packing cases, materials and insurance (see below), is included in a quotation. If you're doing your own packing, most shipping companies will provide packing crates and boxes.

Shipments are charged by volume, e.g. the cubic metre in Europe and the cubic foot in the US. You should expect to pay from €3,500 to €7,500 to move the contents of a three to four-bedroom house within western Europe, e.g. from London to Italy. If you're flexible about the delivery date, shipping companies will quote a lower fee based on a 'part load', where the cost is shared with other deliveries. This can result in savings of 50 per cent or more compared with an individual delivery.

☑ **SURVIVAL TIP**

Whether you have an individual or shared delivery, obtain the maximum transit period in writing, or you may be made to wait months for delivery!

It's advisable to fully insure your belongings during removal with a well established insurance company. Don't insure with a shipping company that carries its own insurance, as it may fight every Euro of a claim. Insurance premiums are usually 1 to 2 per cent of the declared value of your goods, depending on the type of cover chosen. It's prudent to make a photographic or video record of valuables for insurance purposes. Most insurance policies cover for 'all risks' on a replacement value basis. Note that china, glass and other breakables can usually only be included in an all risks policy when they're packed by the removal company. Insurance usually covers total loss or loss of a particular crate only, rather than individual items (unless they were packed by the shipping company).

If there are any breakages or damaged items, they should be noted and listed before you sign the delivery bill; it's obviously impractical to check everything on delivery, but most (reputable) companies allow damage to be reported up to 48 hours after delivery. If you need to make a claim, be sure to read the small print, as some companies require clients to make a claim within a few days, although seven is usual. Send a claim by registered post. Some insurance companies apply an excess (deductible) of around 1 per cent of the total shipment value when assessing claims. This means that, if your shipment is valued at €50,000 and you make a claim for less than €500, you won't receive anything.

If you're unable to ship your belongings directly to Italy, most shipping companies will put them into storage and some allow a limited free storage period prior to shipment, e.g. 14 days.

If you need to put your household effects into storage, it's wise to have them fully insured, as warehouses have been known to burn down!

Make a complete list of everything to be moved and give a copy to the removal company. Don't include anything illegal (see **Prohibited & Restricted Goods** on page 176) with your belongings, as customs checks can be rigorous and penalties severe. Provide the shipping company with **detailed** instructions how to find your Italian home from the nearest motorway or main road and a telephone number where you can be contacted. If your Italian home has poor or impossible access for a large truck you must inform the shipping company (the ground must also be firm enough to support a heavy vehicle). In these cases, or where furniture needs to be taken in through an upstairs window, you may need to pay extra.

After considering the costs, you may decide to ship only selected items of furniture and personal effects, and buy new furniture in Italy. If you're importing household goods from another European country, it's possible to rent a self-drive van or truck. However, if you rent a vehicle outside Italy you will need to return it to the country where it was hired. If you plan to transport your belongings to Italy personally, check the customs requirements in the countries you must pass through.

Most people find it isn't a good idea to do their own move unless it's a simple job, e.g. a few items of furniture and personal effects only. It's no fun heaving beds and wardrobes up stairs and squeezing them into impossible spaces. If you're taking pets with you, you may need to ask your vet to tranquillise them, as many pets are frightened (even more than people) by the chaos and stress of moving house.

Bear in mind when moving home that everything that can go wrong often does, so allow plenty of time and try not to arrange your move from your old home on the same day as the new owner is moving in. That's just asking for fate to intervene! See also **Customs** on page 175.

PRE-DEPARTURE HEALTH CHECK

If you're planning to take up residence in Italy, even for part of the year only, it's wise to have a health check before your arrival, particularly if you have a record of poor health or are elderly. If you're already taking regular medication, you should ask your doctor for the generic name, as the brand names of medicines vary from country to country. If you wish to match medication prescribed abroad, you will need a current prescription with the medication's trade name, the manufacturer's name, the chemical name and the dosage. Most medicines have an equivalent in other countries, although particular brands may be difficult or impossible to obtain in Italy.

It's possible to have medication sent from abroad, when no import duty or value added tax is usually payable. If you're visiting a holiday home in Italy for a short period, you should take sufficient medication to cover your stay. In an emergency, a local doctor will write a prescription that can be filled at a local chemist's, or a hospital may refill a prescription from its own pharmacy. It's also wise to take some of your favourite non-prescription medicines (e.g. aspirins, cold and flu remedies and lotions), as they may be difficult or impossible to obtain in Italy or may be much more expensive. If applicable, take a spare pair of spectacles, contact lenses, dentures or a hearing aid with you. See also **Health** on page 33.

IMMIGRATION

On arrival in Italy your first task is to negotiate immigration. Fortunately this presents few problems for most people, particularly European Union (EU) nationals after the establishment of 'open' EU borders on 1st January 1993. However, with the exception of EU nationals and visitors from a number of other countries, all others planning to enter Italy require a visa (see page 27).

Italy is a signatory to the Schengen agreement (named after a Luxembourg village on the Moselle River where it was signed), which came into effect on 26th March 1995 and introduced an open-border policy between member countries. Other Schengen members include Austria, Belgium, Denmark, Finland, France, Germany, Greece, Iceland, Luxembourg, the Netherlands, Norway, Portugal, Spain and Sweden. Under the agreement, immigration checks and passport controls take place when you first arrive in a member country, after which you can travel freely between other Schengen countries (see also **Visitors** on page 25). Italy has some 300 frontier crossing points, although entry for non-EU nationals with a visa is restricted to certain road/rail crossings and major airports only (as stated in a visa). A list is available from Italian consulates and embassies.

When you arrive in Italy from a country that's a signatory to the Schengen agreement (see above), there are usually no immigration checks or passport controls, which take place when you first arrive in

a Schengen member country. Officially, Italian immigration officials should check the passports of EU arrivals from non-Schengen countries, although this doesn't always happen. If you're a non-EU national and arrive in Italy by air or sea from outside the EU, you must go through immigration (*immigrazione*) for non-EU citizens. If you have a single-entry visa it will be cancelled by the immigration official – if you require a visa to enter Italy and attempt to enter without one, you will be refused entry. Some people may wish to get a stamp in their passport as confirmation of their date of entry into Italy.

If you're a non-EU national coming to Italy to work, study or live, you may be asked to show documentary evidence. Immigration officials may ask non-EU visitors to produce a return ticket, proof of accommodation, health insurance and financial resources, e.g. cash, travellers' cheques and credit cards. The onus is on visitors to prove that they're genuine and won't violate Italy's immigration laws. Immigration officials aren't required to prove that you will break the law and can refuse you entry on the grounds of suspicion only.

Italian immigration officials are usually polite and efficient, although they're occasionally a little over-zealous in their attempts to exclude illegal immigrants, and certain nationalities or racial groups (e.g.

Africans and Albanians) may experience harassment or persecution.

All foreigners planning to remain in the country for longer than 90 days must apply for a permit to stay (see page 28) within eight days of their arrival in Italy.

CUSTOMS

The Single European Act, which came into effect on 1st January 1993, created a single trading market and changed the rules regarding customs (*dogana*) for EU nationals. The shipment of personal (household) effects to Italy from another EU country is no longer subject to customs formalities, although an inventory must be provided.

All those arriving in Italy from outside the EU (including EU citizens) are subject to duty-free customs' checks and limitations.

You may import or export up to €12,500 in any combination of foreign or Italian currency and travellers' cheques without formality. Amounts over €12,500 (e.g. to buy a home) must be declared in order to prevent money laundering and provide statistical data for the Bank of Italy (*Banca d'Italia*). Information about importing pets can be found on page 42.

Visitors

Your belongings aren't subject to duty or valued added tax (VAT) when you visit Italy for up to six months (183 days). This applies to the import of private cars, camping vehicles (including trailers or caravans), motorcycles, aircraft, boats and personal effects. Goods may be imported without formality, provided their nature and quantity doesn't imply any commercial aim (there may be limits on some items for non-EU nationals). All means of transport and personal effects imported duty-free mustn't be sold or given away in Italy, and must be exported when you leave the country.

If you enter Italy by road, you may drive through a border post without stopping (most are now unmanned anyway). However, any goods and pets that you're carrying mustn't be subject to any prohibitions or restrictions. Customs' officials can still stop anyone for a spot check, e.g. to check for drugs or illegal immigrants, anywhere in Italy.

If you arrive at a seaport by private boat, there are no particular customs' formalities, although you must show the boat's registration papers on request. A vessel registered outside the EU can remain in Italy for a maximum of six months in any calendar year, after which it must be exported or imported (when duty and tax must be paid). Foreign-registered vehicles and boats mustn't be lent or rented to anyone while in Italy.

Non-EU Residents

> ☑ SURVIVAL TIP
>
> If you're a non-EU resident planning to take up permanent or temporary residence in Italy, you're permitted to import your furniture and personal effects free of duty.

These include vehicles, mobile homes, pleasure boats and aircraft. However, to qualify for duty-free importation, articles must have been owned and used for at least six months. VAT (*IVA*) must be paid on all items owned for less than six months that weren't purchased within the EU. If goods were purchased within the EU, a VAT receipt must be produced.

All belongings should be imported within six months of the date of your change of residence, although they may be imported in a number of consignments (but it's best to have only one). A complete inventory (in English and Italian) of all items to be

for prescribed drugs and medicines), firearms and ammunition, certain goods and technologies with a dual civil/military purpose, and works of art and collectors' items. If you're unsure whether any goods that you're planning to import fall into the above categories, you should check with Italian customs. Visitors arriving in Italy from 'exotic' regions, e.g. Africa, South America, and the Middle and Far East, may find themselves and their baggage under close scrutiny from customs' and security officials looking for drugs.

EMBASSY REGISTRATION

Nationals of some countries are required to register with their local embassy or consulate after taking up residence in Italy. Registration isn't usually mandatory, although most embassies like to keep a record of their country's citizens resident in Italy (it helps to justify their existence). It makes it easier for them to find you in an emergency, for example, when someone is urgently trying to contact you. For a list of embassies, see **Appendix A**.

FINDING HELP

One of the most important tasks facing new arrivals in Italy is how and where to obtain help with essential everyday tasks, such as buying a car, obtaining medical help and insurance requirements. How successful you are at finding local help depends on your employer (if applicable), the town or area where you live (those who live in major cities are usually better served than those who inhabit small towns), your nationality, Italian proficiency and sex (women are usually better served than men, through numerous women's clubs). Some companies may have a department or staff whose job is to help new arrivals settle in, or they may contract this task out to a relocation company.

imported must be approved by your local Italian consulate abroad (it will be stamped and a copy returned to you), together with proof of residence in your former country and proof of settlement in Italy (i.e. a permit to stay – see page 28).

If there's more than one shipment, subsequent consignments should be cleared through the same customs office. If you fail to follow the correct procedure, you may encounter problems and delays. If you use a removal company to transport your belongings to Italy, they will usually provide all the necessary forms and take care of the paperwork. Always keep a copy of all forms and communications with customs officials, both with Italian customs officials and officials in your previous country of residence. You should have an official record of the export of valuables from any country in case you wish to re-import them later.

Prohibited & Restricted Goods

Certain goods are subject to special regulations and in some cases their import and export is prohibited or restricted. This applies in particular to animal products, plants, wild fauna and flora, and products derived from them, live animals, medicines and medical products (except

Unfortunately, many employers in Italy seem totally unaware of (or uninterested in) the problems and difficulties faced by their foreign employees.

You may find that your friends and colleagues can help, as they can often offer advice based on their own experiences and mistakes. **But take care!** Although they mean well, you're likely to receive as much false and conflicting information as accurate (it may not necessarily be wrong, but may be invalid for your particular situation). Your local community is usually an excellent source of reliable information, but you need to speak Italian to benefit from it.

If a woman lives in or near a major town, she is able to turn to many English-speaking women's clubs and organisations for help. The single foreign male must usually fend for himself, although there are men's expatriate clubs in the major cities and mixed social clubs throughout the country. Among the best sources of information and help for women are the American Women's Clubs (AWC) located in major cities. AWC provide comprehensive information in English about both local matters and topics of more general interest, and many provide data sheets, booklets and orientation programmes for newcomers to the area. Membership of the organisations is sometimes limited to Americans or those with active links to the US, e.g. through study, work or a spouse who works for a US company or the US government, but most publications and orientation programmes are available to other nationalities for a small fee. AWC are part of the Federation of American Women's Clubs Overseas (FAWCO), who can be contacted through their website (🖳 www.fawco.org).

In addition to the above, there are many social clubs and expatriate organisations for foreigners in Italy, whose members can help you find your way around. They may, however, be difficult to locate, as most clubs are run by volunteers and operate out of the president's or secretary's house, and they rarely bother to advertise or take out a phone listing. If you ask around among your neighbours or colleagues, it's possible to find various Anglo-Italian 'friendship' clubs or English-speaking organisations. Finally, don't neglect to check the Internet, where local newspapers, government offices, clubs and organisations usually have their own websites. Contacts can also be found through expatriate magazines and newspapers such as *Wanted in Rome* and *The Informer* (Milan), an Internet magazine (see **Appendix A** for a list).

Many businesses (particularly large multi-national companies) produce booklets and leaflets containing useful information about clubs or activities in the area. Bookshops may have some interesting publications about the local region, and tourist and information offices are also useful sources of information. Most embassies (see page 252) and consulates in Italy also provide their nationals with local information, including the names of lawyers, interpreters, doctors, dentists, schools, and social and expatriate organisations.

MOVING IN

One of the most important tasks to perform after moving into a new home is to make an inventory of the fixtures and fittings and, if applicable, the furniture and furnishings. When moving into a long-term rental property, it's necessary to complete an inventory (inventario) of its contents and a report on its condition. This includes the condition of fixtures and fittings, the state of furniture and furnishings, the cleanliness and state of the decoration, and anything that's damaged, missing or in need of repair.

An inventory should be provided by your landlord or agent and may include every single item in a furnished property, down to the number of teaspoons. The inventory check should be carried out in your presence, both when taking over and when terminating a rental agreement. If an inventory isn't provided, you should insist on one being prepared and annexed to the lease. If you find a serious fault after signing the inventory, send a registered letter to your landlord and ask for it to be attached to the inventory.

If the inventory made when you moved in doesn't correspond with the one made when you move out, you must make good any damages or deficiencies or the landlord can do so and deduct the cost from your deposit. Although Italian landlords are generally no worse than those in most other countries, some will do almost anything to avoid repaying a deposit.

Note the reading on your utility meters (e.g. electricity, gas and water) and check that you aren't overcharged on your first bill. The meters should be read by utility companies before you move in, although you may need to organise it yourself.

It's wise to obtain written instructions from the previous owner concerning the operation of appliances and heating and air-conditioning systems, maintenance of grounds, gardens and lawns, care of special surfaces such as wooden, marble or tiled floors, and the names of reliable local maintenance men who know a property and are familiar with its quirks.

Check with your local town hall regarding local regulations about such things as rubbish collection, recycling and on-road parking.

CHECKLISTS

Before Arrival

The following checklist contains a summary of the tasks that should (if possible) be completed before your arrival in Italy:

● Check that you and your family's passports are valid!

● Obtain a visa, if necessary, for all your family members (see **Chapter 1**). Obviously this **must** be done **before** your arrival in Italy.

● If possible, visit Italy prior to your move to compare communities and schools, and arrange for schooling for your children.

● Arrange temporary accommodation and buy a car, as necessary. If you purchase a car in Italy, you need to register it and arrange insurance.

● Arrange the shipment of your personal effects to Italy (see page 171).

> ☑ SURVIVAL TIP
>
> Arrange health (and travel) insurance for your family. This is essential if you aren't already covered by a private insurance policy and won't be covered by the Italian national health service (see Chapter 8).

● Open a bank account in Italy and transfer funds (see **Chapter 4**). You may also find it more convenient to obtain some Euros before you arrive, which will save you having to change money immediately on arrival.

- Obtain an international driving permit, if necessary.

- Obtain an international credit or charge card, which will prove invaluable during your first few months in Italy.

- Obtain as many credit references as possible, for example, from banks, mortgage companies, credit card companies, credit agencies, companies with which you've had accounts, and references from professionals such as lawyers and accountants. These will help you establish a credit rating in Italy.

If you're planning to become a permanent resident, you should also take all your family's official documents with you. These may include birth certificates, driving licences, marriage certificate, divorce papers or death certificate (if a, divorcee, widow or widower), educational diplomas and professional certificates, employment references and curricula vitae, school records and student ID cards, medical and dental records, bank account and credit card details, insurance policies (plus records of no-claims' allowances), and receipts for any valuables. You also need the documents necessary to obtain a residence permit plus certified copies, official translations and a number of passport-size photographs (students should take around a dozen).

After Arrival

The following checklist contains a summary of the tasks to be completed after arrival in Italy (if not done before arrival):

- On arrival at an Italian airport, port or border post, have your visa cancelled and your passport stamped, as applicable.

- If you aren't taking a car with you, you may wish to rent or buy one locally. Bear in mind that it's practically impossible to get around in rural areas without a vehicle.

- Apply for a permit to stay (see page 28) within eight days of your arrival.

- Register with your local social security office.

- Apply for a fiscal code (*codice fiscale*) from your local tax office (*intendenza di finanza*) – see page 181.

- Register with your local embassy or consulate (see page 169).

- Open a post office or bank account (see page 154) and give the details to your employer and any companies that you plan to pay by direct debit or standing order (such as utility companies).

- Register with a local doctor.

- Arrange schooling for your children.

- Arrange whatever insurance is necessary (see **Chapter 8**).

7.
TAXATION

An important consideration when buying a home in Italy is taxation, even for non-residents, which includes property tax, income tax (if you earn an income from a home) and possibly capital gains tax. You must also pay Italian income tax on all your earnings if you live permanently in Italy.

Italy is one of the highest taxed countries in the European Union when both direct and indirect taxes (including social security) are taken into consideration. If you own a holiday home there, you can employ a local accountant or tax adviser as your fiscal representative to look after your financial affairs in Italy and declare and pay your local taxes (see below).

Italy is also estimated to have the highest number of tax dodgers, including many of Italy's most famous names (tax evasion is **the** national sport). There seems to be a tax stamp (*bollo*) for everything in Italy (the Beatles must have had Italy in mind when they wrote their song *The Tax Man*). To make matters worse, Italian tax law is inordinately complicated (amazingly it has actually been simplified in recent years) and most Italians don't understand it. In fact, even the experts have difficulty agreeing with the tax authorities and tax advisers often give different advice. It's difficult to obtain accurate information from the tax authorities and, just when you think you have it cracked, (ho! ho!) the authorities change the rules or hit you with a new tax.

It's important to check tax information with an accountant or tax office (but get it in writing) in order to establish that it's correct, including the information contained in this book.

Before you decide to settle in Italy permanently, you should obtain expert advice regarding Italian taxes. This will (hopefully) ensure that you take maximum advantage of your current tax status and that you don't make any mistakes that you will regret later.

FISCAL CODE

All residents of Italy need a fiscal code (*codice fiscale*), which Italians receive at birth. This is required to apply for a job, open a bank account, register a car, buy or rent a home, and even pay utility bills. You can obtain a fiscal code card from your local tax office (*intendenza di finanza*), where you must present your passport and a copy of the pages containing your particulars.

Codes for individuals comprise letters and figures (figures only for companies). The code is made up of the first, third and fourth consonants of your surname (or fewer if there aren't enough), the year and month of your birth (the months being represented by the letters A to L), and your day of birth (1 to 31 for men, 41 to 71 for women). So, for example, if your name is Joe Bloggs and you were born on 1st January 1950, your fiscal code would be BGGS1950A1. Each *comune* has its own number for fiscal code purposes, although the country of birth is shown for foreigners. Husbands and wives have separate codes, as a wife in Italy retains and uses her maiden name after she is married.

You should inform your local tax office when you move home, although you retain the same fiscal code, which must be used on all official correspondence with the tax authorities and on tax declarations. It's useful to keep a note of your code with you at all times, as you never know when you may be required to provide it. If you lose your fiscal code card, the easiest way to obtain a new one is via the Finance Ministry's website (⌨ www.finanze.it).

INCOME TAX

Italy has a pay-as-you-earn (PAYE) system of income tax (*imposta sul reddito delle persone fisiche/IRPEF*), whereby employees' tax is withheld at source by employers. The tax year is the same as the calendar year and income is taxed in the year in which the payment or advantage is received. Each person is taxed individually and, although a married couple may file a joint tax return, they're taxed separately.

Italian income tax has traditionally been among the highest in the EU and, although the rates have been reduced in recent years, it's still above the EU average. On the other hand, tax allowances are more generous than in some other countries (see **Allowances** on page 225 and **Credits** on page 185). If you're able to choose the country where you're taxed, you should obtain advice from an international tax expert.

Moving to Italy (or another country) often offers opportunities for legal 'favourable tax planning'. To make the most of your situation, it's recommended that you obtain professional tax advice before moving,

as there are usually a number of things you can do in advance to reduce your tax liability, both in Italy and abroad. For example, you may be able to avoid paying tax on a business abroad if you establish both residence and domicile in Italy before you sell. On the other hand, if you sell a foreign home after establishing your principal residence in Italy, it becomes a second home and you may then be liable for capital gains tax abroad.

> ☑ SURVIVAL TIP
>
> Be sure to consult a tax adviser who's familiar with both the Italian tax system and that of your present country of (tax) residence.

You should inform the tax authorities in your former country of residence that you're going to live permanently in Italy.

Tax evasion (*l'evasione fiscale*) is rife in Italy, where avoiding taxes is more popular than soccer (Italians are world champions at soccer, but are masters of the universe when it comes to tax evasion). The worst offenders are businesses and the self-employed, and it's common knowledge that tax inspectors accept bribes to 'turn a blind eye' to tax evasion.

The tax authorities may estimate your taxable income based on your perceived wealth. All taxpayers must list (on a one-page *riccometro* form) their possessions and liabilities, such as homes, cars, boats and motorbikes, whether they employ household help, whether their spouse works, and whether they have dependent family members. This information is used to determine your financial situation and whether you're entitled to certain social services. Therefore, if you're a millionaire and declare the income of a shop assistant, it would be wise not to live in a *palazzo* and drive a Ferrari! Severe sanctions, including larger fines, were introduced for tax evasion in 2000.

Detailed information about Italian income tax is available from local tax offices in Italy.

Liability

Your liability for Italian income tax depends on where you're domiciled. Your domicile is normally the country you regard as your permanent home and where you live for most of the year. A foreigner working in Italy for an Italian company who has taken up residence in Italy and has no income tax liability abroad, is considered to have his tax domicile (*domicilio fiscale*) in Italy. A person can be resident in more than one country at any time, but can be domiciled in only one country. The domicile of a married woman isn't necessarily the same as her husband's but is determined using the same criteria as anyone capable of having an independent domicile.

Your country of domicile is particularly important regarding inheritance tax, as there's no longer inheritance tax in Italy (see **Inheritance Taxes** on page 189). Double taxation treaties (see below) contain rules that determine in which

country an individual is resident. Generally, you're considered to be an Italian resident and liable to Italian tax if **any** of the following applies:

● Your permanent home (i.e. family or principal residence) is in Italy;

● You spend over 183 days in Italy during any calendar year (not that most countries, e.g. the UK, limit visits by non-residents to 183 days in any one year, and in the case of the UK, an average of 91 days per tax year over a four-year period);

● You carry out paid professional activities or employment in Italy, except when secondary to business activities conducted in another country;

● Your centre of vital economic interest, e.g. investments or business, is in Italy.

If you're registered as a resident (*residenza anagrafica*) in your *comune*, you're automatically liable to pay income tax in Italy.

Those who intend to live permanently in Italy, should notify the tax authorities in their present country (you will be asked to complete a form, e.g. a form P85 in Britain). You may be entitled to a tax refund if you depart during the tax year, which usually necessitates completion of a tax return. The authorities may require proof that you're leaving the country, e.g. evidence of a job in Italy or of having purchased or rented a property there. If you're in doubt about your tax liability in your home country, contact your nearest embassy or consulate in Italy.

After moving to Italy to take up a job or start a business, you must register at your local tax office (*intendenza di finanza*) soon after your arrival.

Double Taxation Treaties

Italian residents are taxed on their world-wide income, subject to certain treaty

Where applicable, a double taxation treaty prevails over domestic law. Italy has double taxation treaties with over 60 countries, including all members of the EU, Australia, Canada, China, Iceland, India, Israel, Japan, Malaysia, Mexico, New Zealand, Norway, Pakistan, the Philippines, Russia, Singapore, South Africa, Sri Lanka, Switzerland, Turkey and the US.

Taxable Income

Taxable income in Italy is officially divided into the following six categories, each of which is defined by law:

● employment;

● self-employment;

● business;

● property (land and buildings – see below);

● capital (principally dividends and interest);

● and 'miscellaneous' income.

Income from employment includes bonuses (annual, performance, etc.), stock options, interest-free loans, overseas adjustments, cost of living allowances, housing allowance, education allowance, tax reimbursements and car allowance.

Taxable income also includes contributions to profit sharing plans, storage and relocation allowances, language lessons provided for a spouse, a personal company car, payments in kind (such as free accommodation or meals), home leave or holidays (paid by your employer), children's education, and property and investment income (dividends and interest).

Some income, such as certain social security benefits, isn't subject to income tax. However, income also includes unemployment benefits, redundancy pay, pensions, and benefits for cessation of employment (e.g. severance pay) over

exceptions. Non-residents are normally taxed only on income arising in Italy. The US is the only country that taxes its non-resident citizens on income earned abroad (American citizens can obtain a copy of a brochure, *Tax Guide for Americans Abroad*, from American consulates). Citizens of most other countries are exempt from paying taxes in their home country when they spend a minimum period abroad, e.g. one year.

Double taxation treaties are designed to ensure that income that has already been taxed in one treaty country isn't taxed again in another treaty country (not as you may imagine – that you taxed twice!). The treaty establishes a tax credit or exemption on certain kinds of income, either in the country of residence or the country where the income was earned.

and above the minimum required by law. Benefits in kind are valued for tax purposes at their fair market value.

Residents are taxed on their world-wide income and non-residents on income earned only in Italy. Bear in mind that although tax rates in Italy are relatively high, your net income tax can be considerably reduced by allowances and credits, as explained below.

Property Income

All property owners in Italy (whether residents or non-residents) must pay income tax based on a property's imputed income. Income from land and buildings is based on their cadastral value (*rendita catastale*), which is a nominal value attributed by the land registry (*catasto*). The value of land is calculated by multiplying the average ordinary income (fixed by the *catasto*) by the surface area, taking into consideration the location of the land. The value of buildings is calculated by multiplying the surface area by an amount (fixed by the *catasto*) that takes into consideration their location, age, condition and official category (see **Property Taxes** on page 187).

Income tax is also payable on rental income from an Italian property, even if you live abroad and the money is paid there. All rental income must be declared to the Italian tax authorities, whether you let a property for a few weeks to a friend or 52 weeks per year on a commercial basis.

Rental income is taxed as ordinary income (see **Tax Rates** on page 185). You're eligible for allowances such as repairs and maintenance, security, cleaning costs, mortgage interest (Italian loans only), management and letting expenses (e.g. advertising), local taxes, insurance and depreciation. You should seek professional advice to ensure that you're claiming everything to which you're entitled. Many people find that there's little tax to pay after deducting their expenses.

Property is also liable to a number of property taxes (see page 187).

Allowances

Certain allowances can be made against taxable employment income, including social security contributions, contributions to qualifying pension funds, travelling and other business expenses, maintenance payments, expenses related to property income. Personal 'allowances' are granted in the form of tax credits (see **Credits** below).

Tax Rates

Italian income tax is levied at the following rates on taxable income:

Taxable Income (€)	Tax Rate (%)
Up to 15,000	23
15,001 – 28,000	27
28,001 – 55,000	38
55,001 – 75,000	41
Over 75,000	43

In addition to the above state tax, regional tax is payable at between 0.9 and 1.4 per cent, depending on the region, and municipal tax at up to 0.5 per cent.

Credits

Personal allowances are granted in the form of tax credits, deducted from your tax due. The following allowances or credits can be made against taxable employment income:

● Mandatory social security contributions;

● Contributions up to €5,164.57 to Italian qualified pension funds;

- Reimbursement for travel and accommodation for business trips, up to a maximum of €46.48 within Italy and €77.47 abroad;

- Reimbursement for laundry, parking and telephone costs for work away from home;

- Reimbursement for food provision by an employer to his or her employees;

- Reimbursement for remuneration in kind, e.g. transport to and from the workplace provided by an employer;

- Share purchase plans granted under certain conditions;

- Maintenance payments to a spouse (from whom the taxpayer is legally separated or divorced);

- Expenses related to property income.

A tax credit of up to 19 per cent of the expenses mentioned below is also granted:

- Interest on a mortgage on a principal residence (*prima casa*) or land in Italy, provided that the loan is taken out in a European Union country, up to a maximum of €3,615.20;

- Medical expenses in excess of €129.11 for general medical expenses and €129.11 for specialist medical treatment, for both the taxpayer and his dependants;

- Funeral expenses up to a maximum of €1,549.37;

- Tuition expenses at universities up to the equivalent cost of attendance at a state establishment;

- Premiums which are for life insurance and health insurance, up to a total of €1,291.14;

- Veterinary expenses exceeding €129.11, up to €387.34;

- Contributions to non-profit entities, up to €2,065.83.

Tax Returns

The tax year in Italy is the same as the calendar year. If you're a resident, you must file an income tax return (*dichiarazione dei redditi*), unless **any** of the following applies:

- You have no income;

- Your income is exempt from tax, e.g. a war, old age or invalidity pension;

- You've already paid tax at source on income, e.g. dividends, bank interest, mortgage interest;

- You're an employee and are taxed on a PAYE basis and have no other income.

Non-residents with income arising in Italy must also file a tax return. The tax system is based on self-assessment and the tax office won't send you a tax return or chase you to complete one.

Tax returns are available free from your local council (*municipio*) or can be purchased from a tobacconist or stationer.

They can also be downloaded from the Ministry of Finance's website (💻 www.finanze.it). Declarations can also be made from abroad by registered post. Many people can obtain free income tax assistance at a Centro Assistenza Fiscale (CAF), including pensioners, part-time workers, certain categories of self-employed people, the disabled and those receiving unemployment benefit. See also **Using a Commercialista** below.

You must file a different tax return depending on whether you're employed or self-employed. Employees' returns (*modello 730*) for the previous year must be filed between the 1st May and the 30th June. If you've completed your own form, you may hand it in at a bank or post office and don't need to file it at the local *comune* or send it to a service centre (*intendenza di finanza*). However, forms completed by professionals using computer systems must be handed in or sent to a service centre.

Returns for the self-employed (*Unico*) should be 'filed' between 1st June and 31st July at a bank, post office or Centro Assistenza Fiscale (CAF) office (a kind of citizens' advice bureau for tax matters, listed in telephone books and on the CAF website, 💻 www.caaf-cia.it); it shouldn't be taken or sent to a service centre office. Late filing within 30 days of the due date is subject to a penalty of 15 per cent of the tax due; after 30 days penalties range from 120 to 245 per cent of the tax due! You should keep copies of tax returns and receipts for six years.

Payment

Advance tax payments must be made equal to 98 per cent of the tax paid for the previous year or the amount due for the current year (whichever is less). Forty per cent of the advance tax payments (called an *acconto*) must be made by 31st May and the remaining 60 per cent by 30th November. If you've earned less than your advance payment, you can claim a refund, although tax rebates can take years to be paid. Income tax can be paid in two six-monthly instalments, or in seven instalments (provided you don't pay VAT), in which case annual interest of 6 per cent is payable. Payment is due on the last day of each instalment period or, for those who pay VAT, on the 15th of the month. A portion of the total interest due (where applicable) must accompany each instalment. If you choose to pay in instalments, it must be noted on your income tax return.

☑ SURVIVAL TIP

Payments up to 20 days overdue attract a surcharge of 0.5 per cent; between 20 and 60 days, the surcharge is 3.75 per cent; if you're over 60 days late, you must pay a further surtax of 30 per cent plus 5 per cent annual interest.

Using a Commercialista

Because of the complexity of the Italian tax system, it's wise to use a *commercialista* (a combination of accountant and lawyer) to prepare your tax return, particularly if you're self-employed (obligatory unless you have a doctorate in Italian bureaucracy!). A *commercialista*'s fees are relatively low (although you should obtain a quotation) and he can also advise you on what you can and cannot claim regarding allowances and expenses.

PROPERTY TAX

Property tax (*imposta comunale sugli immobili/ICI* – pronounced 'itchy') is paid by everyone who owns property or land in Italy, whether resident or non-resident. It's levied at between 0.4 and 0.7 per

Category	Property Type
A/1	*Signorile* (refined)
A/2	*Civile* (civilian)
A/3	*Economico* (economical)
A/4	*Populare* (working class)
A/5	*Ultrapopolare* ('ultra-working class')
A/6	*Rurale* (rural)
A/7	*Villini* (small detached)
A/8	*Ville* (detached)
A/9	*Castelli, palazzi di eminenti pregiartistici o storici* (castle or building of eminent historic or artistic importance)
A/10	*Uffici e studi privati* (private offices and studios)
A/11	*Alloggi tipici dei luoghi* (typical housing of the region)

cent of a property's fiscal value (*valore catastale*), the rate being decided by the local municipality according to a property's size, location, age, condition and official category (*categoria*), as shown in the property deeds (*rogito*). Categories are decided by the land registry (*catasto*) according to the type of property (*abitazione di tipo*) as above.

A property's category has a relatively small influence on the amount of tax payable. If a property is unfit for habitation, property tax is reduced by 50 per cent.

Property tax is usually paid in two instalments: 90 per cent by 30th June and the remaining 10 per cent between 1st and 20th December (for uninhabitable properties, the figures are 45 per cent and 5 per cent respectively). If it isn't paid on time, you can be fined in the form of a surcharge or additional tax (*sopratassa*) of up to 200 per cent of the amount due. The form for paying tax is complicated and many people (particularly foreigners) employ a *commercialista* (see above) or agent to do it for them. You can also pay property tax from abroad using registered post, addressing payment to the tax office of your *comune*. Payments must be up to date when a property is sold and you should check this before buying.

Other property-related taxes include communal services (*servizio riscossione tributi ruoli*) for owners of condominiums and other community properties, refuse tax (*tassa comunale dei rifiuti*) and water rates. Property owners also pay income tax on their property, which is based on its cadastral value.

CAPITAL GAINS TAX

Capital gains tax (*imposta comunale sull'incremento di valore degli immobili/INVIM*) has been abolished for new property owners. Where applicable, CGT is payable to the local community and varies from 3 per cent to 30 per cent according to the capital gain made on a sale, as shown in the table below.

CGT is reduced by 50 per cent when a property is sold to a principal residence (*prima casa*) buyer.

The capital gain is the difference between the purchase and sale prices declared in the deeds of sale (*rogito*), less expenses for renovation, improvements, repairs, etc., and is based on the increase in the cadastral value (*rendita catastale*) of a

Capital Gain	CGT Payable
Up to 20%	3 – 5%
20–50%	5 – 10%
50–100%	10 – 15%
100–150%	15 – 20%
150–200%	20 – 25%
Over 200%	25 – 30%

property, not the increase in its market value. It isn't wise to under-declare the value (too much), or the authorities may arbitrarily assess a new sale price, although you can appeal against this. Where applicable, CGT is deducted from the amount payable to the vendor by the notary (*notaio*) handling the sale. Calculating GCT is complicated and it's recommended to employ a *commercialista* (see page 187) to assess the sum payable.

A new capital gains tax was introduced on 1st January 1999 and applies to gains made on stocks and shares. The tax is levied at two rates, 12.5 and 27 per cent, according to the type of gain and is based on the value of your assets at the beginning of the year. Capital gains from managed (as opposed to speculative) savings are subject to CGT at 12.5 per cent, levied on the actual gain (selling price less purchase price re-valued to account for inflation), and capital losses are deductible from capital gains and may be carried forward for five years.

Gains derived from qualified sales are subject to CGT at 27 per cent. (A qualified sale is a sale of more than 2 per cent of the issued shares of a company quoted on the primary or secondary markets, or of more than 5 per cent of the shares of a non-listed company.) Capital losses cannot be recovered for qualified sales. The increased value of a pension fund is taxed at 11 per cent (called a substitute tax), instead of the usual rate of 12.5 per cent.

INHERITANCE TAXES

Taxes have been abolished for inheritances and gifts made after October 25th 2001. However, some experts believe that the abolition was a political concession and may be reinstated, particularly if the government finds that it needs to raise more taxes (which it always does)! However, a mortgage and registration tax of 3 per cent applies to inherited property and gifts.

● **Inheritances** – Any property inherited is subject to mortgage and registration tax on the cadastral value of the property, and the tax is reduced to €129.11 if the property is the first home of the heir or beneficiary.

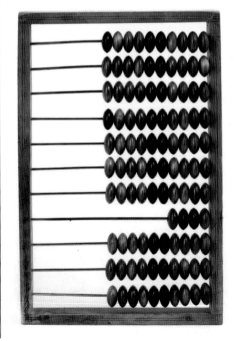

- **Gifts** – Gifts are also subject to a mortgage and registration tax, although in the case of gifts to distant relatives or unrelated people, registration tax is levied at 7 per cent (for property) or 15 per cent (for land) on amounts above €185,759.91.

Non-residents owning assets in Italy, including property, are subject to the inheritance law in their country of residence, where inheritance tax may be payable.

You should consult an expert in current inheritance law both in Italy and in your home country, for further information./

Wills

'Immovable' property in Italy, i.e. land and buildings, **must** be disposed of in accordance with Italian law. All other belongings in Italy or elsewhere (defined as 'movables') may be disposed of in accordance with the law of your home country or domicile. Therefore, it's important to establish where you're domiciled under Italian law. One solution for a non-resident wishing to avoid Italian inheritance laws is to buy a home through a company, in which case the shares of the company are 'movable' assets and are therefore governed by the succession laws of the owner's country of domicile.

Italian law gives the immediate family, i.e. spouse, children and parents (called the *legittima*) an absolute right to inherit a share of an estate and it isn't possible to disinherit them. However, a foreigner who wishes to dispose of his estate (other than immovable property) according to the laws of his home country, can state this in an Italian will.

If you have a large estate in Italy, it's wise to consult a lawyer (*avvocato*) when drawing up a will. Most lawyers agree that it's best to have an Italian will for your Italian property (and a separate will for any other country where you own immovable property), which

will speed up and reduce the cost of probate in Italy. If you have an Italian and a foreign will (or wills), make sure that they don't contradict one another. Bear in mind that a will written in a foreign language must be translated into Italian (a certified translation is required) and proven in Italy in order to be valid there.

You need someone to act as the executor of your estate, which can be particularly costly for modest estates. Under Italian law, the role of the executor is different from that in many other countries. Your bank, lawyer or other professional will usually act as the executor, although this should be avoided if at all possible, as the fees can be astronomical. It's recommended to make your beneficiaries the executors, as they can then instruct a lawyer after your death should they require legal assistance. Bear in mind that probate (the proving of a will) can take a long time in Italy.

Keep a copy of your will(s) in a safe place and another copy with your lawyer or the executor of your estate. Don't leave them in a safe deposit box, which in the event of your death is sealed for a period under Italian law. You should keep information regarding bank accounts and insurance policies with your will(s), but don't forget to tell someone where they are!

☑ **SURVIVAL TIP**

Italian inheritance law is a complicated subject and it's important to obtain professional legal advice when writing or altering your will(s).

Chalet, Dolomites

Leaning Tower of Pisa, Tuscany

8.
INSURANCE

An important aspect of owning a home in Italy is insurance, not only for your home and its contents, but also health insurance for your family when living in or visiting Italy. It's vital to ensure that you have sufficient insurance when visiting your home abroad, which includes travel insurance, building and contents insurance and health insurance (covered in this chapter), as well as continental car insurance (including breakdown insurance) and third party liability insurance.

If you live in Italy permanently you will require additional insurance. It's unnecessary to spend half your income insuring yourself against every eventuality, from the common cold to being sued for your last Euro, although it's important to insure against any event that could precipitate a major financial disaster, such as a serious accident or your house being demolished by a storm. The cost of being uninsured or under-insured can be astronomical.

Insurance Companies

As with anything connected with finance, it's important to shop around when buying insurance. Simply collecting a few brochures from insurance agents or companies (listed in the yellow pages under *Assicurazioni*) or making a few telephone calls could save you a lot of money. The entire insurance industry has been going through a crisis in recent years and (at long last) is becoming more consumer driven. One major change has been the advent of telephone and Internet insurers, which allow you to obtain and compare estimates in minutes. Some Internet brokers allow you to compare rates online (💻 www.

diagramma.it) or you can contact individual insurance companies such as Genertel (☎ 800-202 020, 💻 www.genertel.it), Linear (☎ 800-992 222, 💻 www.onlinear. it), Genialloyd (💻 www.genialloyd.it) and Zuritel (💻 www.zuritel.it).

Not all insurance companies are equally reliable or have the same financial stability and it may be better to insure with a large international company with a good reputation than with a small (e.g. Italian) company, even if this means paying higher premiums. Regrettably you cannot insure yourself against being uninsured or sue your insurance agent for giving you bad advice!

Read insurance contracts carefully and ensure that you understand the terms and the cover provided before signing. Some insurance companies will do almost anything to avoid paying claims and will use any available legal loophole, so it pays to deal with reputable companies only (not that this provides a guarantee). Note that insurance policies are automatically renewed unless you cancel them in writing; Italian insurance companies can compel you to renew your insurance for a further year if you don't give adequate written notice (e.g. up to three months) of your intention to terminate it, although most companies allow policyholders to cancel on renewal. Check in advance.

If you wish to make a claim on an insurance policy, you may be required to report an incident to the police within 24 hours (this may also be a legal requirement). If you're uncertain of your rights, you're advised to obtain legal advice for anything other than a minor claim. Under EU rules, an insurance company registered in an EU member country can sell its policies in any other EU country.

☑ SURVIVAL TIP

In all matters regarding insurance, you're responsible for ensuring that you and your family are legally insured in Italy. The law in Italy may differ considerably from that in your home country or your previous country of residence, and you should never assume that it's the same.

HEALTH INSURANCE

If you're visiting or living or working in Italy, it's extremely risky not to have health insurance for your family; if you're uninsured or under-insured, you could be faced with some very high medical bills. When deciding on the type and extent of health insurance, make sure that it covers **all** your family's present and future health requirements in Italy **before** you receive a large bill. A health insurance policy should cover you for **all** essential health care whatever the reason, including accidents (e.g. sports accidents) and injuries, whether they occur in your home, at your place of work or while travelling. Don't take anything for granted, but check in advance. When travelling in Italy, you should carry proof of your health insurance with you.

Visitors

Visitors spending short periods in Italy (e.g. up to a month) should have a travel health insurance policy (see page 200), particularly if you aren't covered by an international health policy, although you may be covered by a reciprocal agreement between your home country and Italy (see below). If you plan to spend up to six months in Italy, you should either take out a travel policy, a special long-stay policy or an international health policy.

Reciprocal Health Agreements

If you're entitled to social security health benefits in another EU country or in a country with a reciprocal health agreement with Italy, you will receive free or reduced cost emergency medical treatment in Italy. Participating countries include all EU member states and most other European countries, **excluding** Albania, Switzerland and Turkey. The USA doesn't have a reciprocal health agreement with Italy, so American students and other Americans who aren't covered by the Italian national health service **must** have private health insurance in Italy.

EU residents must apply for a European Health Insurance Card (EHIC, which has replaced the old form E111), usually around two weeks before they plan to travel to Italy. An EHIC covers emergency hospital treatment but doesn't include prescribed medicines, special examinations, X-rays, laboratory tests, physiotherapy and dental treatment. Bear in mind that you can still receive a large bill from an Italian hospital, as your local health authority assumes only a percentage of the cost.

British visitors, or Britons planning to live in Italy, can obtain information about reciprocal health treatment in Italy (and EHIC cards) from the EHIC Information

Service (☎ 0871-050 0509, ⌨ www. ehicard.org).

Residents

If you're planning to take up residence in Italy, your family will be entitled to subsidised or free medical treatment under the National Health Service or Servizio Sanitario Nazionale (SSN). The SSN provides hospital accommodation and treatment (including tests, surgery and medication during hospitalisation), visits to family doctors (GPs), specialist medical assistance provided by paediatricians, obstetricians and other specialists, discounted medicines, laboratory services, appliances, ambulance services, and free services at a local health unit (*consultorio*).

If you qualify for health care under the SSN, your dependants will receive the same benefits and will be listed on your membership card. Dependants include your spouse (if she isn't personally insured), your children under 16 (or 26 if they're students or unable to work through illness or invalidity); and ascendants, descendants and relatives by marriage, supported by you and living in the same household.

Many residents also have a private health insurance policy (assicurazione sulla salute), which pays the portion of medical bills that isn't paid by SSN. If you aren't entitled to public health benefits, you should have private health insurance, which may be mandatory for non-EU residents when applying for a visa or residence permit. Some foreign health insurance policies may not provide sufficient cover to satisfy the authorities, so you should check the minimum cover necessary with a Italian consulate in your country of residence.

If you're a retired EU national planning to live permanently in Italy, you need form E121. EU citizens who retire before qualifying for a state pension can receive free health cover for two years by obtaining form E106 from their country's social security department. If the temporary cover expires before you reach retirement age, you must make voluntary social security contributions or take out private health insurance. For more information see *Living and Working in Italy* (Survival Books).

Private Health Insurance

Italian Companies

Most Italian health insurance policies don't pay family doctors' fees or pay for medication that isn't provided in a hospital, or charge an excess (deductible), e.g. the equivalent of around €100 for each 'illness', which may exceed the cost of treatment. Most, however, pay for 100 per cent of specialists' fees and hospital treatment in the best Italian hospitals. Private policies

vary considerably in cost but are generally from €1,300 to €2,500 per year (but they can be as high as €4,000) for a family of four, although costs are higher for the elderly. Many companies, retirement groups and other organisations offer lower group rates.

You should avoid a company that reserves the right to cancel (*recesso* or *facoltà di rescissione*) a policy unilaterally when you have a serious illness or when you reach a certain age (shown as *età massima assicurabile* – 'maximum insurable age – in policies), as it may prove difficult or impossible to find alternative cover. You should also steer clear of a one-year contract, which a company can refuse to renew. Policies often have a period (e.g. five years) during which the insurance company cannot exclude you from cover (*rinuncia al diritto di recessione*), even if you have a serious illness costing the insurance company a lot of money.

The largest insurers in Italy include the National Insurance Institute (Instituto Nazionale delle Assicurazioni/INA), formerly state-owned but now privatised, Europa Assistance, Filo Diretto, Pronto Assistance and Sanicard. Shop around and compare policies, which vary considerably, from good to terrible! Most Italian polices are supplementary policies for residents who are covered by the national health service, and aren't intended for foreigners who aren't covered by the SSN and are seeking a comprehensive health policy.

As in many countries, Italian insurance companies are loathe to pay claims (one of the reasons they don't insist on a medical examination is so that they can refuse to pay a claim because you omitted to tell them you had a heavy cold three years previously). When completing the questionnaire (*questionario sanitario*), be sure to list **ALL** previous illnesses, hospitalisation, current ailments and treatment.

Foreign Companies

There are a number of foreign health insurance companies with agents or offices in Italy, including AXA PPP Healthcare, Baltica (Denmark), BUPA International, Columbus Healthcare, Exeter Friendly Society and International Health Insurance (Denmark). These companies offer special policies for expatriates and usually include repatriation to your home country and international cover.

☑ SURVIVAL TIP

If you aren't covered by Italian social security and need comprehensive private health insurance to obtain a residence permit, you must ensure that your health policy will be accepted by the authorities.

The main advantages of a foreign health insurance policy are that treatment is unrestricted and you can usually choose any doctor, specialist, clinic or hospital in Italy, and often abroad as well. A policy may also pay for repatriation of your body for burial in your home country.

Premiums vary considerably and it's important to shop around. Most international health policies include repatriation or evacuation (although it may be optional), which may also include shipment (by air) of the body of a person who dies abroad to his home country for burial. An international policy also allows you to choose to have non-urgent medical treatment in the country of your choice.

Most international insurance companies offer health policies for different areas, e.g. Europe, worldwide excluding North America, and worldwide including North America. Most companies also offer different levels of cover, e.g. basic, standard, comprehensive and 'prestige'. There's always a limit on the total annual medical costs, which should be at least €300,000 (although many companies provide cover of up to €2m) and some companies limit the charges for specific treatment or care such as specialists' fees, operations and hospital accommodation. A medical examination isn't usually required for international health policies, although 'pre-existing' health problems are excluded for a period, e.g. two years.

Claims are usually settled in major currencies and large claims are usually settled directly by insurance companies (although your choice of hospitals may be limited). Always check whether an insurance company will settle large medical bills directly; if you're required to pay bills and claim reimbursement from an insurance company, it can take several months before you receive your money (some companies are slow to pay). It isn't usually necessary to translate bills into English or another language, although you should check a company's policy. Most international health insurance companies provide emergency telephone assistance.

The cost of international health insurance varies considerably with your age and the extent of cover. With most international policies, you must enrol before you reach a certain age (usually between 60 and 80) to be guaranteed continuous cover in your old age. Premiums can sometimes be paid monthly, quarterly or annually, although some companies insist on payment annually in advance. When comparing policies, carefully check the extent of cover and exactly what's included and excluded from a policy (often indicated only in the **very** small print), in addition to premiums and excess charges. In some countries, premium increases are limited by law, although this may apply only to residents in the country where a company is registered.

Although there may be significant differences in premiums, generally you get what you pay for and can tailor premiums to your requirements. The most important questions to ask yourself are: does the policy provide the cover required and is it good value? If you're in good health and are able to pay for your own out-patient treatment, such as visits to a GP and prescriptions, the best value is usually a policy covering only specialist and hospital treatment.

If you have existing private health insurance in another country, you may be able to extend it to include Italy. If you already have a private health insurance policy, you may find you can save a substantial amount by switching to another company without losing any benefits – you may even gain some. To compare policies, it's best to visit an insurance broker offering policies from a number of companies.

Changing Employers or Insurance Companies

When changing employers or leaving Italy, you should ensure that you have continuous health insurance. If your family is covered by a company health scheme, your insurance will probably cease after your last official day of employment. If you're planning to change your health insurance company, you should ensure that important benefits aren't lost; for example, existing medical conditions won't usually be covered by a new insurer for a period. When changing health insurance companies, it's wise to inform your old company if you have any outstanding bills for which they are liable.

HOUSEHOLD INSURANCE

There's no requirement to have cover for your home or belongings and most Italians don't bother to insure their home or its contents, although if you have a mortgage (*ipoteca*), your lender will require you to have building (*edificio*) insurance. Nevertheless, it's highly recommended to take out insurance covering damage to the building due to fire, water, explosion,

storm, freezing, snow, theft, vandalism and natural catastrophes. Household insurance (*assicurazione sulla casa*) generally constitutes a multi-risk policy for building and contents, although some companies require separate policies for fire and theft (*assicurazione contro furto e fuoco*) and for liability (*assicurazione contro terzi*), and others offer fire and damage (*incendio ed altri danni ai beni*) with an extra premium for theft and liability. Special conditions apply to holiday homes (see below).

It's possible (and legal) to take out building and contents insurance in another country for a property in Italy, although the policy may still be written under Italian law (so always check). The advantage is that you have a policy you can understand and you're able to deal with claims in your own language (you may also be more likely to be paid or be paid earlier). This may seem like a good option for a holiday home in Italy, although it may be more expensive than insuring with an Italian company, and can lead to conflicts if the building is insured with an Italian company and the contents with a foreign company.

Building Insurance

It's particularly important to have insurance against storm damage in Italy, which can be severe in some areas. Read the small print and check that you're covered for natural disasters, such as floods. Bear in mind that if you live in an area that's hit by a succession of natural disasters, your insurance may be cancelled or the premiums increased dramatically. Also note the following:

● Water damage caused by burst pipes due to old age or freezing may be excluded; under Italian law you're required to turn off the water at the mains if a property is left empty for more than 24 hours (although almost nobody does).

- If you use bottled gas, you must inform your insurance company, as there's an extra premium to pay.

- You must also specifically insure electrical systems and major apparatus against risk such as lightning strikes, otherwise an insurance company won't pay for damage.

- Italian policies usually exclude trees in your garden damaging your house and garden walls falling down.

- You cannot insure against earthquakes with an Italian policy, although a foreign insurance provider may offer cover for an exorbitant premium (e.g. Lloyd's of London). If there's an earthquake, the Italian government assumes responsibility, which is limited to the value stated in the land registry (well below a property's actual value), although the insured value of your home is also taken into consideration.

> ☑ SURVIVAL TIP
>
> In the event of total loss, building insurance payments are based on the cost of rebuilding your home, so make sure that you insure your property for the current cost of rebuilding.

If you have a property restored or modernised, you must obtain a professional valuation on completion for insurance purposes.

Apartments: If you own an apartment or a property that shares common elements with other properties, building insurance is included in your service charges, although you should check exactly what's covered. You must, however, still be insured for third party risks in the event that you cause damage to neighbouring apartments, e.g. through flood or fire. Having insurance also helps you claim against a neighbour if they cause damage to your apartment.

Rented Property: Your landlord will usually insist that you have third party liability insurance, as detailed in the rental contract. A lease requires you to insure against 'tenant's risks', including damage you may make to a rental property and to other properties if you live in an apartment, e.g. due to flood, fire or explosion. You can choose your own insurance company.

Contents Insurance

Contents (*contenuto*) are usually insured for the same risks as a building (see above) and are insured for their replacement value. Contents polices are restrictive with regard to security, including locks, window shutters or grilles (all windows less than 3m/10ft from the ground must be barred), armoured doors, etc. All security requirements must be adhered to or claims are reduced or won't be paid, and there's usually an excess of between €125 and €250 for each claim. Bear in mind that Italian policies usually exclude loss of frozen food (after a power cut).

You cannot normally insure valuables (e.g. antiques, jewellery and other precious objects) unless they've been valued by an approved Italian expert and they generally need to be stored in a safe (in which case you may not need insurance?), which must be approved by your insurance company. You should insist on a safe being approved by your insurer and a certificate being issued to verify this (otherwise your insurance company is liable to use the argument that your safe was insecure to avoid paying a claim).

Valuables are usually covered only when you're present, rather than abroad or on holiday. Due to the many loopholes, you may be better off keeping your valuables in a bank safety deposit box. When claiming for contents, you should produce the original bills (keep bills for expensive items) and bear in mind that imported items may be much more expensive in Italy.

Holiday Homes

Premiums are generally higher for holiday homes, due to their high vulnerability (particularly to burglaries), and are usually based on the number of days each year that a property is inhabited and the interval between periods of occupancy. Cover for theft, storm, flood and malicious damage may be suspended when a property is left empty for more than three weeks at a time. It's possible to negotiate cover for periods of absence for a hefty surcharge, although valuable items are usually excluded.

If you're absent from your property for long periods, e.g. more than 60 days per year, you may also be required to pay an excess on a claim arising from an occurrence that takes place during your absence (and theft may be excluded). You should read the small print in policies. Where applicable, it's important to ensure that a policy specifies a holiday home and not a principal home.

In areas with a high risk of theft (e.g. most major cities and resort areas), you may be required to fit extra locks and employ other security measures. Some companies may not insure holiday homes in high risk areas. It's unwise to leave valuable or irreplaceable items in a holiday home or a home that's vacant for long periods. Some insurance companies do their utmost to find a loophole which makes you negligent and relieves them of their liability. Always carefully check that the details listed in a policy are correct, otherwise your policy could be void.

Premiums

Premiums are usually calculated on the size of the property (either the habitable area in square metres or the number of rooms), rather than its value. Usually the sum insured (house and contents) is unlimited, provided the property doesn't exceed a certain size and is under a certain age. Premiums depend on the area, although you should expect the premium for a policy that includes theft to be around double what you would expect to pay in another western European country. The cost of multi-risk property insurance in a low-risk area is around €100 per year for a property with one or two bedrooms, €180 for three or four bedrooms and around €375 per year for five or six bedrooms. Premiums can be much higher in high-risk areas. If you have an index-linked policy, cover is increased each year in line with inflation.

Claims

If you wish to make a claim, you must usually inform your insurance company in writing (by registered letter) within two to five days of an incident or 24 hours in the case of theft. Thefts should also be reported to the local police within 24 hours, as the police statement (*denuncia*), of which you receive a copy for your insurance company, usually constitutes irrefutable evidence of your claim.

> ☑ **SURVIVAL TIP**
>
> **Check whether you're covered for damage or thefts that occur while you're away from the property, and are therefore unable to inform your insurance company immediately.**

HOLIDAY & TRAVEL INSURANCE

Holiday and travel insurance (*assicurazione sul viaggio*) are recommended for anyone who doesn't wish to risk having their holiday or travel ruined by financial problems, or to arrive home broke. As you probably know, anything can and often does go wrong with a holiday, sometimes

before you even get started (particularly when you **don't** have insurance). The following information applies equally to residents and non-residents, whether you're travelling to or from Italy or within Italy. Nobody should visit Italy without travel (and health) insurance.

Travel insurance is available from many sources, including travel agents, insurance companies and brokers, banks, motoring organisations and transport companies (airline, rail and bus). Package holiday companies and tour operators also offer insurance policies, some of which are compulsory, overpriced **and don't provide adequate cover.** You can also buy 24-hour accident and flight insurance at major airports, although it's expensive and doesn't offer the best cover. Before taking out travel insurance, you should carefully consider the range and level of cover you require and compare policies.

Short-term holiday and travel insurance policies may include cover for holiday cancellation or interruption; missed flights and departure delay at both the start and end of a holiday (a common occurrence); delayed, lost or damaged baggage; lost belongings and money; medical expenses and accidents (including evacuation home); personal liability and legal expenses; and default or bankruptcy, e.g. a tour operator or airline going bust. You may also need cover for transport strikes in Italy!

Always check any exclusion clauses in contracts by obtaining a copy of the full policy document, as all relevant information won't be included in an insurance leaflet. High risk sports and pursuits should be specifically covered and **listed** in a policy (there's usually an additional premium). Special winter sports policies are available and more expensive than normal holiday insurance ('dangerous' sports are excluded from most standard policies). Third party liability cover should be €3m in North America and €1.5m in the rest of the world. However, this doesn't usually cover you when you're driving a car or other mechanically propelled vehicle.

Health Cover

Medical expenses are an important aspect of travel insurance and you shouldn't rely on insurance provided by reciprocal health arrangements, charge and credit card companies, household policies, or private medical insurance (unless it's an international policy), none of which usually provide adequate cover – although you should take advantage of what they offer. The minimum medical insurance recommended by experts is €400,000 for Italy and the rest of Europe and €1.5m for the rest of the world (many policies have limits of between €2.5m and €7.5m). If applicable, check whether pregnancy-related claims are covered and whether there are any restrictions for those over a certain age, e.g. 65 or 70 (travel insurance is becoming increasingly expensive for those aged over 65, although they don't usually need to worry about pregnancy – particularly the men!).

Visitors

Travel insurance for visitors to Italy should include personal liability and repatriation expenses. If your travel insurance expires while you're visiting Italy, you can buy further insurance from a local insurance agent, although this won't include repatriation expenses. Flight and comprehensive travel insurance are available from insurance desks at most airports, including travel accident, personal accident, worldwide medical expenses and in-transit baggage.

Cost

The cost of travel insurance varies considerably depending on where you buy it, how long you intend to stay in Italy and your age. Generally the longer the period covered, the cheaper the daily cost, although the maximum period covered is usually limited, e.g. three to six months. With some policies, an excess must be paid for each claim; with others, the excess applies only to certain items, such as luggage, money and medical expenses. As a rough guide, travel insurance for Italy (and most other European countries) costs from around €45 for one week, €60 for two weeks and €85 for a month for a family of four (two adults and two children under 16). Premiums may be higher for those aged over 65 or 70.

Annual Policies

For people who travel abroad frequently, whether on business or pleasure, an annual travel policy usually provides the best value, but check carefully exactly what it includes. Many insurance companies offer annual travel policies for around €150 to €300 per year for an individual (the equivalent of around two to three months' insurance with a standard travel insurance policy), which are excellent value for frequent travellers.

☑ SURVIVAL TIP

Some insurance companies also offer an 'emergency travel policy' for holiday homeowners who need to travel abroad at short notice to inspect a property, e.g. after a severe storm or burglary.

The cost of an annual policy may depend on the area covered, e.g. Europe, worldwide (excluding North America) and worldwide (including North America), although it doesn't usually cover travel within your country of residence. There's also a limit on the number of trips per year and the duration of each trip, e.g. 90 or 120 days. An annual policy is usually a good choice for owners of a holiday home in Italy who travel there frequently for relatively short periods.

Carefully check exactly what's covered (or omitted), as an annual holiday and travel insurance policy may not provide adequate cover.

Claims

If you need to make a claim, you should provide as much documentary evidence as possible to support it. Travel insurance companies gladly take your money, but they aren't always so keen to pay claims and you may need to persevere before they pay up. Always be persistent and make a claim **irrespective** of any small print, as this may be unreasonable and therefore invalid in law. Insurance companies usually require you to report a loss (or any incident for which you intend to make a claim) to the local police or carriers within 24 hours, and obtain a written report. Failure to do so may mean that a claim won't be considered.

Positano, Campania

Colosseum, Rome

9.
LETTING

Many people planning to buy a holiday home are interested in owning a property that will provide them with an income from letting to cover the running costs, and help pay the mortgage payments. Letting a home for a few weeks or months in the summer can more than recoup your running costs (see page 113) and pay for your holidays. However, if you're planning to let a property, it's important not to overestimate the income, particularly if you're relying on letting income to help pay the mortgage and running costs.

If you're planning on holiday lets, don't overestimate the length of the season, which varies with the region. The letting season is longest in southern Italy (e.g. on the Amalfi Coast and in Sicily) and in the major cities and resorts, where it may be as long as 16 weeks, while in others it's ten or less. However, you're unlikely to achieve this many weeks' occupancy and you should budget for around half these figures, even when letting full time. Apartments in major tourist cities (e.g. Florence, Rome and Venice) and ski resorts may have almost year-round letting potential, while villas (especially large ones) are in demand from Easter to late autumn plus Christmas.

Nevertheless, you may be unable to meet all your mortgage payments and running costs from rental income, even if a property is available to let year-round. Most experts recommend that you don't purchase a home in Italy if you need to rely on rental income to pay for it. The holiday rental market is extremely volatile and subject to highs and lows at short notice; a good rental season can easily be followed by a very poor one.

It's difficult to make a living providing holiday accommodation in most areas, as the season is too short and there's often too much competition.

This is particularly true of Tuscany and Venice, where there's a surfeit of property for rent and competition for clients is intense. If you buy a property in these areas and plan to let it successfully, you will need to restore and furnish the property to the highest standards and preferably include a unique selling point (e.g. an original da Vinci in the bedroom!). If you wish to let a property in Tuscany or Venice, you should be prepared to invest a considerable amount in it before you get any rental return.

Bear in mind that tax must be paid **in Italy** on rental income earned in Italy (see page 184), and long-term rental properties must be registered with the authorities.

Buyers who over-stretch their financial resources often find themselves on the rental treadmill, constantly struggling to earn enough money to cover their running costs and mortgage payments. In the early '90s, some overseas buyers lost their Italian homes after they defaulted on their mortgage payments, often because rental income failed to meet expectations. Buying property in Italy (and in most other countries) isn't usually a good investment compared with the return on income that can be achieved by investing elsewhere.

RULES & REGULATIONS

If you let a property in Italy, you're required by law to pay tax on your rental income in Italy and not in the country where the income is received (e.g. in the UK). The authorities find it difficult to oblige foreign, non-resident owners to comply with these regulations and many simply turn a blind eye, although there are heavy fines for offenders. See also **Taxation Of Property Income** on page 184.

If you provide bed and breakfast (*casa per vacanza* or *affittacamere*) or something similar in a rural property, you must have a certificate of habitability (*certificato di abitabilità*) and obtain a licence from the local authorities (*comune*), who will inspect the property before approving the licence.

All tenants renting for longer than a month must be registered with the authorities and in some communes **all** tenants, however short their stay, must register. The onus is on the owner to register the property's tenants and there are forms for this purpose. In some communes the police make periodic visits on rental properties and bed and breakfast businesses to check the registration. Confirm the latest regulations with the local authorities. You should also have third party insurance (costing at least €150 a year) covering accidents and injury for guests (or anyone) using your property.

If you're planning to buy a community property (see page 121), you must check whether there are any rules that prohibit or restrict short-term letting. You may also be required to notify your insurance company.

Contracts

Most people who do holiday letting have a simple booking form that includes a property description, the names of the clients, and the dates of arrival and departure. However, if you do regular letting you may wish to check with a lawyer that your agreement is legal and contains all the necessary safeguards. If you plan to let to non-English speaking clients, you must have a letting agreement in Italian or other languages. If you use an agent, he will provide a standard contract. If you receive rent and accept a lessee without protest, you're deemed under Italian law to have entered into a contractual relationship, even if there's no written contract.

If you do 'long-term' lets (usually three months or more), you must ensure that you or your agent uses the correct contract (*contratto di locazione*).

> ☑ SURVIVAL TIP
>
> The minimum period of validity of a long-term rental contract in Italy is usually four years, even if you're letting for only a few months. Because of the danger of a tenant refusing to leave after the period expires, some foreign landlords (and many Italians) are wary of letting to Italians.

LOCATION

If income from an Italian home has a high priority, the location should be one of your main considerations when buying (see also page 71). When considering the location for a property you plan to let, you should bear in mind the following criteria.

Climate

Properties in areas with a pleasant year-round climate, such as the Ligurian Riviera, Sardinia, parts of Sicily and the much of the south of the country, have a greater rental potential, particularly outside high season. This is also important should you wish to use the property yourself outside the high season; for example, you could let a property over the summer months, when rental income is at its highest, and use it yourself in May or October and still enjoy fine weather.

Proximity to an Airport

A property should be situated within easy reach of a major airport, as most holidaymakers won't consider travelling more than 45 minutes to their destination after arriving at an airport. Choose an airport with frequent flights from your home country and preferably one with a range of scheduled and low-cost flights. However, it isn't wise to rely on an airport served only by budget airlines, as they may alter or cancel routes at short notice. See **Airline Services** on page 85 and **Appendix F**.

Accessibility

It's an advantage if a property is served by public transport or is situated in a town where a car is unnecessary. If a property is located in a town or village within a maze of streets, you should provide a detailed map. If it's in the country where signposts are all but non-existent, you will not only need to provide a detailed map with plenty of landmarks, but you may also need to erect signs; holidaymakers who spend hours driving around trying to find a place are unlikely to return or recommend it! Maps are also helpful for taxi drivers, who may not know the area.

Attractions

The property should be close to tourist attractions and/or a good beach, depending on the sort of clientele you wish to attract. If you want to let to families, a property should be close to leisure facilities such as theme parks, water parks, sports

grounds and nightlife. If you're planning to let a property in a rural area, it should be somewhere with good climbing or hiking possibilities, preferably near one of Italy's many natural parks. Properties in Venice, Florence and Rome are in demand all year round.

SWIMMING POOL

If you're planning to let your property, a swimming pool is obligatory in most areas, as properties with pools are much easier to let than those without (some private letting agencies won't handle properties without a pool), unless a property is situated on a beach, lake or river. It's usually necessary to have a private pool with a single-family home (e.g. a detached villa), although a shared pool is adequate for an apartment. If you plan to let mainly to families, it's wise to choose an apartment with a 'child-friendly' communal pool, e.g. with a separate paddling pool or a pool with a shallow area. You can charge a higher rent for a property with a private pool and it may be possible to extend the letting season even further by installing a heated or indoor pool, although the cost of heating a pool may be higher than the rental return.

There are strict regulations regarding pool safety (including private pools) in Italy and you must ensure that you comply with them.

LETTING RATES

Rental rates vary considerably depending on the time of the year, region or town, size and quality of a property. A house sleeping two to four people in an average area can be let for around €500 to €1,200 per week in high season. At the other extreme, a luxury property in a popular area with a pool and accommodation for 8 to 12 can be let for between €4,000 and €7,000 per week in the high season, which generally includes the months of July and August and possibly the first two weeks of September. The mid-season usually comprises June, September and October (and possibly Easter), when rents are around 20 to 25 per cent lower than the high season; the rest of the year is the low season.

In some cities, e.g. Florence and Venice, high season tends to be from April to June and September to October plus Christmas and, in Venice, Carnival time (February). July and August aren't popular months for lets in Florence and Venice.

For long-term lets in the low season, a house sleeping four to six usually rents for around €650 per month in most rural areas (except Tuscany and Umbria, where rents are higher).

Rates usually include linen, gas and electricity, although electricity and heating (e.g. gas bottles) are usually extra for long winter lets.

FURNISHINGS

If you let a property, it's wise not to fill it with expensive furnishings or valuable belongings. While theft is rare, items will eventually get damaged or broken. When furnishing a property that you plan to let, you should choose hard-wearing, dark-coloured carpets or rugs which won't show stains (although most properties have tiled or marble floors rather than carpets), and buy durable furniture and furnishings. Simple, inexpensive furniture is best in a modest home, as it will need to stand up to hard wear.

Small, two-bedroom properties usually have a sofa bed in the living room. You may also need a cot and/or high chair. Properties should be well equipped with cooking utensils, crockery and cutlery (including a kitchen knife that cuts!), and it's usual to provide bed linen and towels (some agents provide a linen hire service). Ensure that the bed linen and towels are of good quality and replace them before they wear out. You can buy good quality, inexpensive household linen at most

hypermarkets in Italy, and during sales in January and July or August.

Appliances should include a washing machine and microwave, and possibly a dishwasher and tumble-dryer. Depending on the rent and the quality of the property, your guests may also expect central heating, air-conditioning, covered parking, a barbecue and garden furniture (including loungers). Heating is essential if you want winter lets, while air-conditioning is an advantage when letting property in summer, although it's considered mandatory only when letting a luxury villa. Some owners provide bicycles and equipment for sports such as badminton and table tennis. It isn't usual to have a telephone, although you could install a credit card phone or one that just receives incoming calls.

KEYS

You will need several sets of spare keys (plus spare remote controls for electric gates, etc.), which will probably get lost at some time. If you employ a management company, their address and not the address of the house should be on the key fob. If you lose keys or if they can easily be copied, you should change the lock barrels regularly (at least annually). You don't need to provide guests with keys to all the external doors, only the front door (the others can be left in your home). If you arrange your own lets, you can send keys to guests in your home country or they can be collected from a caretaker or agent in Italy. It's also possible to install a security key-pad entry system, the code of which can be changed after each let.

CLEANING

A property should always be spotlessly clean when holidaymakers arrive and you should provide basic cleaning equipment. You will need to arrange for cleaning between lets and also at regular intervals, e.g. weekly or twice-weekly, for lets of more than a week. If you use a local agent, he will usually arrange cleaning, which costs around €12 per hour. If applicable, you must arrange pool cleaning and a gardener (see **Maintenance** on page 213).

USING AN AGENT

If you're letting a second home, the most important decision is whether to let it yourself or use a letting agent (or agents). If you don't have much spare time, you're better off using an agent, who will take care of everything and save you the time and expense of advertising and finding clients. An agent will charge commission of between 20 and 40 per cent of gross rental income, although some of this can be recouped through higher rents. If you want your property to appear in an agent's catalogue, you must contact him the summer before you wish to let it (the deadline is usually September).

☑ **SURVIVAL TIP**

Although self-catering holiday companies may fall over themselves to take on luxury properties in the most popular areas, top letting agents turn down as many as nine out of every ten properties they're offered.

Most agents don't permit owners to use a property during the peak letting season (July and August or spring and autumn in some cities, such as Florence and Venice) and may also restrict their use at other times, e.g. over the Christmas period.

There are numerous self-catering holiday companies, most of whom have agents in many countries (try your local travel agent). Some Italian estate agents in resort areas and cities also act as agents for holiday lets, and some specialise in long-term winter lets. Italian regional tourist agencies can put you in touch with letting agents.

If possible, make sure that your income is kept in an escrow account and paid regularly, or even better, choose an agent with a bonding scheme who pays you the rent before the arrival of guests (some do). It's essential to employ an efficient, reliable and honest company, preferably long-established. Bear in mind that anyone can set up a holiday letting agency and there are a number of 'cowboy' operators. Always ask a management company to substantiate rental income claims and occupancy rates, by showing you examples of actual income received from other properties. Ask for the names of satisfied customers and contact them.

Take care when selecting an agent, as it isn't uncommon for them to go bust or simply disappear, owing their clients thousands of Euros. Things to ask a letting agent include:

● when the letting income is paid;

● whether he provides detailed accounts of income and expenses (ask to see samples);

● what extras are charged;

● who he lets to, e.g. what nationalities and whether they include families, children or singles, etc.;

● how he markets properties and whether you're expected to contribute towards marketing costs;

● whether you're free to let the property yourself and use it when you want.

The main agents market homes via newspapers, magazines, overseas agents and colour brochures, and have representatives in many countries. Management contracts usually run for a year. A management company's services should include routine and emergency repairs; reading meters (if electricity is charged separately); routine maintenance of house and garden, including lawn cutting and pool cleaning; arranging cleaning and linen changes between lets; advising guests on the use of equipment; and providing guest information and advice (24 hours per day in the case of emergencies).

Agents may also provide someone to meet and greet clients, hand over the keys and check that everything is in order. A letting agent's representative should also make periodic checks when a property is empty to ensure that it's secure and that everything is in order. The services provided usually depend on whether a property is a basic cottage or a luxury villa costing thousands of Euros a week.

> ☑ SURVIVAL TIP
>
> Before buying a community property, you should check that letting is permitted. You may need to notify the property's administrator and your insurance company if a property is to be let (see Rules & Regulations on page 253).

DOING YOUR OWN LETTING

Some owners prefer to let a property to family, friends, colleagues and acquaintances, which allows them more control – and hopefully the property will also be better looked after. In fact, the best way to get a high volume of lets is usually to do it yourself, although many owners use a letting agency in addition to doing their own marketing in their home country. You will need to decide whether you want to let to smokers and whether you will accept pets and young children – some people won't let to families with children under five due to the risk of bed-wetting. Some owners also prefer not to let to young,

single groups. Note, however, that this will reduce your letting prospects.

Letting Rates & Deposits

To get an idea of the rent you can charge (see **Letting Rates** on page 208), simply ring a few letting agencies and ask them what it would cost to rent a property such as yours at the time of year you plan to let it. They're likely to quote the highest rent you can charge. You should also check advertisements. Set a realistic rent, as there's lots of competition. Add a returnable deposit (e.g. €150 to €500 depending on the rent) as security against loss (e.g. of keys) and breakages. A booking deposit is usually refundable up to six weeks before the booking, after which it's forfeited. Many people have a minimum two-week rental period in July and August.

Advertising

If you wish to let a property yourself, there's a wide range of Italian and foreign newspapers and magazines in which you can advertise, e.g. *Daltons Weekly* (💻 www.daltons.co.uk) and newspapers such as the *Sunday Times* in the UK. Many of the English-language newspapers and magazines listed in **Appendix B** include advertisements from property owners.

It can be prohibitively expensive to advertise a single property in a national newspaper or magazine, and you will need to experiment to find the best publications and days of the week or months to advertise.

A cheaper method is to advertise in property directories such as *Private Villas* (☎ UK 020-7955 3811, 💻 www.privatevillas.co.uk) or on websites such as those of Holiday Rentals (☎ UK 020-8743 5577, 💻 www.holiday-rentals.co.uk) and Owners Direct (☎ UK 01372-229 330, 💻 www.ownersdirect.co.uk), where you pay for the advertisement and handle the bookings yourself. Another option is to let through a company such as Brittany Ferries Holidays (✉ holiday homes@brittany-ferries.com), who provide a bond and include a discount on ferries. These need to be arranged the previous year.

You can advertise among friends and colleagues, in company and club magazines (which may even be free), and on notice boards in offices, shops and public places. The more marketing you do, the more income you're likely to earn, although you should ensure that you provide a quick and efficient response to any enquiries. It pays to work with local people in the same business and send surplus guests to competitors (they will usually reciprocate). In addition to advertising locally and in your home country, you can extend your marketing abroad (or advertise via the internet). Bear in mind that it's necessary to have a answering machine and preferably also a fax machine.

Internet

Advertising on the internet is an increasingly popular option for property owners. There are many tourism websites where you can advertise. Typical arrangements include posting your property's details (in up to four languages), photos and prices, and links from major search engines. Some companies will even provide you with your own website.

You may wish to consider having your own website, which is an excellent marketing tool and can include photographs, booking forms and maps, as well as comprehensive information about your property. You can also provide information about flights, car rental, local attractions, sports facilities and links to other website. A good website should be easy to navigate (avoid complicated page links or indexes) and must include contact details, ideally by email. It's wise to subscribe to a company that will submit your website to the main search engines, such as Google or Yahoo. You can also exchange links with other websites.

Brochures & Leaflets

If you don't have a website containing photographs and information, you should produce a coloured brochure or leaflet. This should contain external and internal pictures, comprehensive details of the property, the exact location, and local attractions and details of how to get to them (with a map included). You should enclose a stamped addressed envelope when sending out details and follow up within a week if you don't hear anything. It's necessary to make a home look as attractive as possible in a brochure or leaflet without distorting the facts – advertise honestly and don't over-sell the property.

Handling Enquiries

If you plan to let a home yourself, you must decide how to handle enquiries about flights and car rentals. It's best to let clients make bookings themselves, but you should be able to offer advice and put them in touch with airlines, ferry companies, travel agents and car rental companies.

INFORMATION PACKS
Pre-Arrival

After accepting a booking, you should provide guests with a pre-arrival information pack containing:

- a map of the local area and instructions how to find the property

- information about local attractions and the local area (available free from tourist offices);

- emergency contact numbers in your home country (e.g. the UK) and Italy for when guests have any problems or plan to arrive late;

- the keys or instructions on where to collect them on arrival.

It's ideal if someone can welcome your guests when they arrive, explain how things work, and deal with any special requests or problems.

Post-arrival

You should also provide an information pack in your home for guests explaining:

- how things work such as kitchen appliances, TV/video, heating and air-conditioning;

- security measures (see page 214);

- what not to do and possible dangers (for example, if you allow young children and pets, you should make a point of emphasising dangers such as pool safety, etc.);

- local emergency numbers and health services such as a doctor, dentist and hospital/clinic;

- numbers of useful services such as a general repairman, plumber, electrician and pool maintenance company (you may prefer to leave the telephone number of a local caretaker, who can handle any problems);

- recommended local shops, restaurants and attractions.

Many people provide a visitors' book for guests to write their comments and suggestions, and some send out questionnaires. If you want to impress your guests, you can arrange for fresh flowers, fruit, a bottle of wine and a grocery pack to greet them on their arrival. It's personal touches that ensure repeat business and recommendations; you may even find after the first year or two that you rarely need to advertise. Many people return to the same property year after year, so it pays to do an annual mail-shot to previous clients, who may also tell their family and friends – provided they had a good time.

MAINTENANCE

☑ SURVIVAL TIP

If you do your own letting, you will need to arrange for cleaning and maintenance, including pool cleaning and a gardener if applicable. Ideally you should have someone on call seven days a week.

Caretaker

If you own a second home in Italy, you'll find it beneficial or even essential to employ a local caretaker, irrespective of whether you let it. You can have your caretaker prepare the house for your family and guests, as well as looking after it when it isn't in use. If it's a holiday home, have your caretaker check it periodically (e.g. weekly) and allow him to authorise minor repairs. If you let a property yourself, your caretaker can arrange for (or do) cleaning, linen changes, maintenance, repairs, gardening and pay bills. If you employ a caretaker, you should expect to pay around €12 to €15 per hour.

Closing a Property for the Winter

Before closing a property for the winter, you should turn off the water at the mains (required by insurance companies), remove fuses (except those for a dehumidifier or air-conditioner if you leave them on), empty food cupboards and the fridge/freezer, disconnect gas cylinders and turn off mains gas, and empty bins. You should leave interior doors and a few small windows (with grilles or secure shutters), as well as wardrobes, open to provide ventilation. Lock the main doors, windows and shutters, and secure anything of value or leave it with a neighbour or friend. Check whether any work needs to be done before you leave and, if necessary, arrange for it to be done in your absence. Most importantly, leave a set of keys with a neighbour or friend, and/or arrange for them or a caretaker to check your property periodically.

SECURITY

Most people aren't security conscious when on holiday and you should therefore provide detailed instructions for guests regarding security measures and emphasise the need to secure the property when they're out. It's also important for them to be security conscious when in the property, particularly when having a party or in the garden, as it isn't unusual for valuables to be stolen while guests are outside. When leaving a property unattended, it's important to employ all security measures available, including:

- storing valuables in a safe (if applicable) – hiding them isn't a good idea, as thieves know ALL the hiding places;

- closing and locking all doors and windows;

- locking grilles on patio and other doors;

- closing shutters and securing any bolts or locks;

- setting the alarm (if applicable) and notifying the alarm company when you're absent for a long period;

- giving the appearance that a property is occupied, through the use of timers for lights and/or a TV or radio.

> ☑ **SURVIVAL TIP**
>
> Bear in mind that prevention is always better than cure, as stolen possessions are rarely recovered.

If you have a robbery, you should report it to your local police station, where you must make a statement. You will receive a copy, which is required by your insurance company if you make a claim. See also **Home Security** on page 220.

INCREASING RENTAL INCOME

Rental income can be increased outside high season by offering special interest or package holidays – which can be organised in conjunction with local businesses or tour operators – to broaden the appeal and cater for larger parties. These include:

- sporting activities such as golf, tennis, cycling or hiking;

- cooking, gastronomy and wine tours/tasting;

- arts and crafts such as painting, sculpture, photography and writing courses.

You don't need to be an expert or conduct courses yourself, but can employ someone to do it for you.

Agriturismo

If your property is rural and has at least five hectares (12.5 acres) of land, you may consider setting up an *agriturismo* business, similar to a farm bed and breakfast. *Agriturismo* holidays are popular with both Italians and foreigners in search of a holiday with a difference in the Italian countryside. There are strict qualifying conditions for *agriturismo* businesses; they must be of a certain size and some sort of 'farming' activity must take place on the property, although this may be fruit growing or riding lessons. There are government subsidies and grants available for establishing businesses, although these are generally awarded only in under-developed areas (i.e. mostly in southern Italy) and the paperwork involved can be considerable. Tax relief on income is also possible. Contact the authorities in your commune for further information.

Palace of Caserta, Naples

10.
MISCELLANEOUS MATTERS

This chapter contains miscellaneous, but nevertheless important, information for homeowners in Italy, including crime, heating and air-conditioning, postal services, public holidays, security, shopping, telephone, television and radio, and utilities.

CRIME

The crime rate in Italy varies considerably from region to region and is around average for Europe. Violent crime is rare in most areas, although muggings do occur in resort areas and cities. Despite the fearsome reputation of the Mafia, there's actually **less** violent street crime such as muggings and robbery with violence in most parts of Italy than in many other European countries, and it's generally a very safe place for children. Sexual harassment and even assault can be a problem for women in some areas, although most men draw the line at cat-calls and whistles. Foreigners should take care when travelling in the south of Italy, where highway robbery and kidnappings of foreigners occasionally take place.

Burglary is rife, and vacant holiday or second homes are a popular target. Many residents keep dogs as a protection or warning against burglars, and have triple-locked and steel-reinforced doors. However, crime in rural areas remains relatively low and it's still common for people in villages and small towns not to lock their cars and homes (in some small villages you still see the keys left nonchalantly in the front door).

Car theft and theft from cars is widespread in cities, where foreign-registered cars are a popular target, particularly expensive models, which are often stolen to order and spirited abroad. Theft of small items such as radios, luggage, mobile phones, cameras, briefcases, sunglasses and even cigarettes from parked cars is a major problem. Thieves in the south take items from cars at gas stations, often by smashing car windows. It's also possible to have your belongings stolen from an occupied vehicle while waiting in traffic or stopped at traffic lights. It's therefore wise to keep the windows closed (weather permitting) in cities and major towns, the doors locked, and to keep all valuables (such as cameras) out of sight. When parking a bicycle, moped or scooter, you should also use as many high-security locks as you can carry.

Italy is infamous for its organised crime and gang warfare, which is rife in some areas, although it has no discernible impact on the lives of most foreigners there (particularly in the north of the country). The term 'Mafia' is used to describe five distinct organised crime groups: the original Sicilian Mafia, the *Camorra* in

Naples and Campania, the *Ndrangheta* in Calabria, and the *Sacra Corona Unità* and *La Rosa* in Apulia. These groups operate both individually and together, and their activities range from drugs and contraband, to protection rackets, gambling and prostitution. They also monopolise lucrative contracts in most fields throughout the country and it's estimated that their combined turnover is billions of Euros, possibly over 10 per cent of Italy's GNP.

The Mafia holds a death grip on the south of Italy, where business people are often forced to pay protection money (*pizzo*) to mobsters to ensure their businesses are safe – it's estimated that half the businesses in Naples pay protection money! Loan sharking (*usurai*), lending money at extortionate rates of interest, is common in the south, where an association has been established to help those who cannot borrow money from banks. Despite many high profile arrests in recent years, rumours of the Mafia's demise or loss of influence are premature, and they reportedly have their fingers in every facet of government, right up to the Prime Minister's office in Rome! In recent years, Albanians, Russians and other foreign gangsters have challenged the Mafia in the north, where they're heavily involved in illegal drugs.

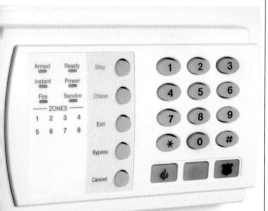

Don't let the foregoing catalogue of crime and mayhem put you off Italy. You can usually safely walk almost anywhere at any time of day or night and there's no need for anxiety or paranoia about crime. However, you should be 'street-wise' and take certain elementary precautions.

Precautions include avoiding high-risk areas at night (such as parks and car parks) and those frequented by drug addicts, prostitutes and pickpockets. You can safely travel on the underground (*metrò*) at any time, although some stations are best avoided late at night. When you're in an unfamiliar city, ask a policeman, taxi driver or other local person whether there are any unsafe neighbourhoods – and avoid them!

See also **Household Insurance** on page 198 and **Home Security** on page 220.

HEATING & AIR-CONDITIONING

Heating

Central heating systems in Italy may be powered by oil, gas, electricity, solid fuel (usually wood) or even solar power. Whatever form of heating you use, it's essential to have good insulation, without which up to 60 per cent of heating is lost through the walls and roof. Over half of Italian homes have central heating, which is essential in northern Italy if you plan to spend any time there outside the summer months. Many people keep their central heating on a low setting during short absences in winter to prevent freezing. Heating requirements in winter vary from six hours a day for around 14 weeks a year in the south to over 14 hours a day for six months or longer in the north.

Aluminium radiators are preferable to cast-iron, as they withstand extreme cold better and are less likely to leak or burst. Moreover, Italian insurance companies won't cover you for burst cast-iron radiators and the subsequent water damage.

An apartment block (*condominio*) usually has central heating (*riscaldamento*), which can be controlled separately in each apartment (*autonomo*) or centrally (*centrale*). With *riscaldamento autonomo* you're billed according to your use. With *riscaldamento centrale* you must pay the same as other residents, even if you occupy an apartment for only part of the year; the heating is turned on in autumn (October) and off in spring (March) and you have no control over this.

Electric

Electric central heating isn't common in Italy, as it's too expensive. However, many people with modern homes with good insulation and a permanent system of ventilation use electric storage heaters. Electric central heating isn't recommended for old properties with poor insulation. If you install an electric central heating system, you may need to increase your electricity rating to cope with the extra demand (see **Power Rating** on page 241). Stand-alone electric (e.g. halogen) heaters are relatively expensive to run and are best suited to holiday homes.

Gas

Mains gas central heating is popular, relatively cheap to run and widely used in the north of Italy. Gas is clean, economical and efficient, and the boiler is usually fairly small and can be wall-mounted. In rural areas where there's no mains gas, you can have a gas tank (*bombolone*) installed on your property (see page 245). The cost of heating with methane gas (*metano*) is between €5.50 and €7 per m3.

Oil

Oil-fired central heating isn't common in Italy due to the high cost of heating oil and the problems associated with storage and deliveries. Heating oil costs around €1.10 per litre and is among the most expensive in Europe (the price fluctuates with the price of crude oil). A family of four in a property in central Italy can expect to use around 1,700 litres a year. You also need space to install the storage tank. If you have a tank with a 2,000-litre capacity or larger, it must be buried in your garden or stored away from the house where it's sheltered from frost.

Solar Power

A solar power system can be used to supply all your energy needs, although it's usually combined with an electric or gas heating system, as solar power cannot be relied upon year-round for lighting, heating and hot water. A solar power system can be used to provide electricity in a remote rural home, where the cost of extending electricity is prohibitive. Solar power can also be used to heat a swimming pool. A solar power system must be installed by an expert.

The main drawback is the high cost of installation, which varies considerably according to the region and how much energy you require. The cost is between €2,000 and €5,000 for an installation sufficient to operate around eight lights and a small refrigerator.

☑ SURVIVAL TIP

The advantages of solar power are no running costs, silent operation, low maintenance and no electricity bills. A system should last 30 years (it's usually guaranteed for ten years) and can be uprated to provide more power in the future.

Continuous advances in solar cell and battery technology are expected to dramatically increase the efficiency and reduce the cost of solar power, which is forecast to become the main source of energy world-wide in this century.

Solid Fuel

Many people rely solely on wood-burning stoves or fireplaces for their heating and hot water, particularly in rural areas. Stoves come in a huge variety of sizes and styles, and may also heat radiators throughout a house and provide hot water. Most people burn wood (which should have been seasoned for at least two years), which is relatively inexpensive, rather than coal or coke. You can have it delivered cut and dried, or can collect it for free if you live in the country.

The main disadvantages are the chores of collecting and chopping wood, cleaning the grate and lighting fires. Smoke can also be a problem. Open fireplaces can be wasteful of heat and fuel; an enclosed hearth with a glass door is more efficient and often has the advantages of a hot-air chamber that warms other parts of a home, reduced fire risk, and less ash and dust.

Air-Conditioning

Few homes in Italy have air-conditioning (*aria condizionata*), despite the fact that summer temperatures often reach over 40°C (104°F) in some areas. Although properties are built to withstand the heat, you may find it beneficial to install air-conditioning, although there can be negative effects if you suffer from asthma or respiratory problems. You can choose from a huge variety of air-conditioners: fixed or moveable, indoor or outdoor installation, and high or low power. Air-conditioning units cost from around €800 (plus installation) for a unit that's sufficient to cool an average-size room. An air-conditioning system with a heat pump provides cooling in summer and heating in winter. For extra cooling in summer, many people fit ceiling fans (costing from around €80), which are standard fixtures in some new homes.

Humidifiers & De-humidifiers

Central heating dries the air and may cause your family to develop coughs. Those who find the dry air unpleasant can purchase a humidifier to add moisture to the air. Humidifiers that don't generate steam should be disinfected occasionally with a special liquid available from chemists (to prevent nasty diseases). Humidifiers range from simple water containers hanging from radiators to expensive electric or battery-operated devices.

If you're going to be using a holiday home only occasionally, it's worthwhile installing de-humidifiers, especially in the bedrooms, to prevent clothes and linen going mouldy.

HOME SECURITY

Security is of paramount importance when buying a home in Italy, particularly if it will be left empty for long periods. Obtain

advice from local security companies and neighbours. Bear in mind, however, that no matter how good your security, a property is rarely impregnable, so you should never leave valuables in an unattended home unless they're kept in a safe.

When moving into a new home, it's often wise to replace the locks (or lock barrels) as soon as possible, as you have no idea how many keys are in circulation for the existing locks. This is true even for new homes, as builders often give keys to sub-contractors. In any case, it's wise to change the external locks or lock barrels regularly, e.g. annually, particularly if you let a home. If not already fitted, it's best to fit high security (double cylinder or dead bolt) locks. Modern properties may be fitted with high security locks which are individually numbered. Extra keys for these locks cannot be cut at a local hardware store and you will need to obtain details from the previous owner or your landlord.

☑ SURVIVAL TIP

In areas with a high risk of theft (e.g. most major cities and coastal resorts, and isolated country homes), your insurance company will insist on extra security measures such as two locks on external doors, internal locking shutters, security bars on windows less than 3m (10ft) from the ground and grilles on patio doors.

An external door must usually be armoured (*porta blindata*), with a steel rod locking mechanism. An insurance policy may specify that all forms of protection must be employed when a property is unoccupied. If security precautions aren't employed, a claim may be reduced by half. It's usually necessary to have a safe for any insured valuables, which must be approved by your insurance company.

You may wish to have a security alarm fitted, which is usually the best way to deter thieves and may also reduce your household insurance (see page 198). It should include all external doors and windows, internal infra-red security beams, and may also include a coded entry keypad (which can be frequently changed and is useful for clients if you let a home) and 24-hour monitoring (with some systems it's even possible to monitor properties remotely from another country). With a monitored system, when a sensor (e.g. smoke or forced entry) detects an emergency or a panic button is pushed, a signal is sent automatically to a 24-hour monitoring station. The duty monitor will telephone to check whether it's a genuine alarm and, if he cannot contact you, will send someone to investigate.

You can deter thieves by ensuring that your house is well lit and not conspicuously unoccupied. External security 'motion detector' lights (that switch on automatically when someone approaches); random timed switches for internal lights, radios and televisions; dummy security cameras; and tapes that play barking dogs (etc.) triggered by a light or heat detector, may all help deter burglars.

You can fit UPVC (toughened clear plastic) security windows and doors, which can survive an attack with a sledge-hammer without damage, and external steel security blinds (which can be electrically operated), although these are expensive. A dog can be useful to deter intruders, although he should be kept inside where he cannot be given poisoned food. Irrespective of whether you actually have a dog, a warning sign with a picture of a fierce dog may act as a deterrent. If not already present, you should have the front door of an apartment fitted with a spy-hole and chain, so that you can check the identity of a visitor before opening the door.

Bear in mind that prevention is better than cure, as stolen property is rarely recovered.

Holiday homes are particularly vulnerable to thieves and in some areas they are regularly ransacked. No matter how secure your door and window locks, a thief can usually obtain entry if he's sufficiently determined, often by simply smashing a window or even breaking in through the roof or by knocking a hole in a wall! In isolated areas thieves can strip a house bare at their leisure and an unmonitored alarm won't be a deterrent if there's no-one around to hear it. If you have a holiday home in Italy, it isn't wise to leave anything of great value (monetary or sentimental) there.

If you vacate your home for a long period, it may be obligatory to notify your caretaker, landlord or insurance company, and to leave a key with the caretaker or landlord in case of emergencies. If you have a robbery, you should report it immediately to your local police station, where you must make a statement (*dichiarazione*). You will receive a copy, which is required by your insurance company if you make a claim.

When closing up a property for a long period, e.g. over the winter, you should ensure that everything is switched off and that it's secure (see **Closing A Property For The Winter** on page 214).

Another important aspect of home security is ensuring that you have early warning of a fire, which is easily accomplished by installing smoke detectors. Battery-operated smoke detectors can be purchased for around €30 (they should be tested regularly to ensure that the batteries aren't exhausted, although some emit a beep when the batteries are low). You can also fit an electric-powered gas detector that activates an alarm when a gas leak is detected.

There are many specialist home security companies who will inspect your home and offer free advice on security, although you should shop around and obtain at least two quotations before having any work done.

POSTAL SERVICES

The Italian post office (Poste Italiane S.p.A.) has the reputation of offering one of the slowest and least efficient postal services in western Europe, but it's currently undergoing radical restructuring, including vast investment in automated sorting, post office improvements and further computerisation. While not all of the promised improvements have been fully implemented, the introduction of a two-tier letter post service has done much to improve standards. Other innovations include an increasing range of online services.

> ☑ SURVIVAL TIP
>
> While the ordinary postal service is acceptable for everyday items, many people in Italy prefer to send important letters and parcels by registered post (*posta raccomandata*) or use a private courier service, as stories of post disappearing are legion.

The (independent) Vatican City post office in Rome is the most efficient and reliable in Italy, as it sends all its international post via Switzerland (with colourful Vatican stamps!). Many companies and courier services in Italy also use the Swiss and other foreign post offices to deliver their international post, e.g. Deutsche Poste World Net (🖳 www.dpwn.de). The American company, Mailboxes, Inc., has franchises in Rome and other major cities.

There's a post office (*ufficio postale*) in most towns and villages in Italy, a total of over 14,000, providing a wide range of services. In addition to the standard postal services, post offices offer facilities for telegram, fax and telex transmissions; exchange of foreign currency; domestic and international cash transfers; and the payment of utility bills, road tax and TV licences. A range of financial and banking services is available, including cheque and savings accounts, investment plans, tax-paying facilities, and the sale of post office shares and bonds. Telephone cards, lottery tickets, train and bus tickets, and pre-paid toll cards for Italian motorways are also sold at post offices. The post office also acts as an agency for the payment of social security benefits such as state pensions. There are public telephones in main post offices.

Main post offices have separate counters (*sportelli*) for different services, which are divided between those dealing with post and those handling financial services, with sometimes a third counter for telegrams, faxes and telexes. New layouts in main post offices include a single-queue system with an electronic board showing the number of the next available window. When this system isn't in operation, you must ensure that you join the correct queue (shown by a sign above the window), or you will need to start queuing all over again. If you require different services, you may need to queue at different counters at a main post office, although in rural towns and villages one or two counters usually provide all services.

The identifying colour of the Italian post office is currently red, although new documentation and office layouts use sky blue. Post vans may be red, white or brown, and the post office logo is a rhomboid-shaped envelope made up of horizontal lines with a diagonal flap. The sign above post offices is *Poste e Telecomunicazioni* or sometimes just the initials *PT*, while in phone books they're listed under *Poste Italiane*. In main towns and cities, there's a central post office for each district, as well as some smaller post offices (*agenzie*). The yellow pages list all post offices in a province. Post offices in Italy are always operated by post office employees and there are (as yet) no post offices run by private businesses or located in shops.

Information (in Italian only) about all postal services is available from the post office's website (💻 www.poste.it). For information about faxes see page 233.

SHOPPING

Italy is one of the world's great shopping countries, and Italian shops are designed to seduce you with their artful displays of beautiful and exotic merchandise.

Shopping is both an art form and a pleasure in Italy, particularly food shopping, most Italians preferring to shop in traditional small family stores (*botteghe*) rather than faceless supermarkets.

The major cities, where even the smallest shop windows are a delight, are a shopper's paradise. It's difficult to say which is Italy's finest shopping city; some say Milan or Rome, with their streets packed with designer boutiques, while others plump for Florence or Venice, with their more traditional shops – all have their unique attractions.

Sales (*saldi*) are an important event in the Italian shopping calendar and, although there aren't massive queues of shoppers outside department stores from the early hours of the morning, sales are nonetheless popular with bargain hunters. There are three kinds of sale in Italy, all of which are strictly regulated by local and national laws. The main sales are held twice a year: between 7th January and 7th March and between 10th July and 10th September. Shops don't need to hold sales for the whole of these periods, but sales must start and end within these periods. Only seasonal products (including fashion) can be sold at a discount, and sale prices must be displayed in shop windows.

You should try to avoid offering a shopkeeper a €50 or €100 note when you're buying something costing a few Euros and should also avoid using a credit card to pay for items costing less than around €15 (you may not be permitted to do so anyway). In Rome and other major cities and resorts, where there are lots of tourists, you must be wary of pickpockets and bag-snatchers. Never tempt fate with an exposed wallet or purse or by flashing your money around.

For further information about shopping in Italy, see *Living and Working in Italy* (Survival Books). There are a number of books for dedicated shoppers in Italy, including Frommer's *Born to Shop Italy* by Suzy Gersham and George McDonald (Macmillan), *Made in Italy* by Annie Brody and Patricia Schultz (Workman), *Bargain Hunting in Italy*, *Designer Bargains in Italy* and *Lo Scoprioccasioni* (the bargain hunter's bible in Italian, but easy enough to understand) – the last three written by Theodora van Meurs.

Opening Hours

Italians don't generally 'convenience shop' at all times of the day and night, and retail hours reflect this, although the only law limiting opening hours is one passed in 1998 that forbids retailers from opening for more than 13 hours daily between 7am and 10pm and on more than eight Sundays annually (even this restriction is relaxed in resort and tourist areas). Shopping hours vary depending on the region, city or town and the type of shop. However, in general, shops open Mondays to Saturdays from around 8.30 or 9am to 12.30 or 1pm and from 3.30 or 4pm to 7.30 or 8pm, although in some cities (particularly in the south) and during summer months, shops may not open until 5pm and may remain open until 9p, and afternoon shopping is virtually non-existent in small towns.

This long lunchtime break (*pausa*) may come as a surprise to many foreigners. The *pausa* makes good sense in the summer, when it's often too hot to do anything at midday and it allows time for lunch, traditionally the most important meal of the day for Italians. However, in winter you find yourself shopping in the dark, a practice that may seem odd to some foreigners. In the major cities there's a growing tendency for shops to stay open all day, and larger shops and department stores open from 9am to 7pm continuously (*orario continuato/non-stop*).

Most shops close on Wednesday or Thursday afternoons depending on the region, and department stores and supermarkets usually also close on Monday mornings, although this is becoming less common in the larger cities. Most shops close on Sundays throughout the country, although this tendency is changing and many supermarkets in tourist and coastal areas now open on Sunday mornings. However, even in popular tourist areas, many small shops close for holidays for a few weeks in summer; August is the most popular month, especially around 15th (*Ferragosto*).

Furniture & Furnishings

Furniture (*mobili*) is generally more expensive in Italy than in many other European countries, although a wide range of modern and traditional furniture is available. Modern furniture is popular and is sold in furniture shops in industrial zones and in hypermarkets throughout Italy, although there are few nation-wide chains of discount shops. Department stores also sell a wide range of (mostly up-market) furniture. UnoPiu and DuePiu have huge factory outlets north of Rome selling wooden furniture, garden and conservatory furniture (such as rattan and bamboo items), DIY furniture and household goods.

Tucano and Oltrefrontiera have a wide selection of furniture and home furnishings, many imported from around the world. Inexpensive chain stores include Coin, Habitat, Home Shop, Rinascente, Standa and Upim. At the other end of the scale, a number of international designer companies have elegant boutiques in Italy, including Biggie Best, English Home and Designers Guild.

Most stores make deliveries or loan or rent self-drive vans at reasonable rates. Pine furniture is inexpensive and popular. Beware of buying complicated home-assembled furniture with indecipherable instructions and too few screws. If you want reasonably priced, good quality, modern furniture, you need look no further than Ikea, a Swedish company manufacturing furniture for home assembly with a number of stores in Italy. There are also many good carpet stores in Italy, although, like most home furnishings, they can be expensive.

Exclusive modern and traditional furniture is available everywhere, although not everyone can afford the exclusive prices. Many regions of Italy have a reputation for quality hand-made furniture. Italian furniture and furnishing shops often offer design services (which may be free to customers), and stock a wide range of beautiful fabrics and materials, with patterns and colours usually ideally suited to Italian homes, the climate and conditions.

> ☑ **SURVIVAL TIP**
>
> If you're spending a lot of money, don't be reluctant to ask for a reduction, as most stores will give you a discount.

The best time to buy furniture and furnishings is during sales (particularly in winter), when the prices of many items are slashed. Most furniture shops offer special deals on furniture packages for a complete room or home. It's possible for residents to pay for furniture (and large household appliances) interest-free over a year or with interest over a longer period, e.g. five years. It may be worthwhile comparing the cost of furniture in a neighbouring country with that in Italy, although it usually doesn't pay to buy new furniture abroad to furnish an Italian home (particularly as you must usually add transport costs).

If you're looking for old furniture at affordable prices, you may find a few bargains at antique fairs (*fiera d'antiquariato*) and flea markets (*mercato delle pulci*), although genuine antiques are expensive and difficult to find. If you do come across anything worthwhile, you must usually drive a hard bargain, as the asking prices are often ridiculous, particularly in popular tourist areas during the summer. Markets are, however, good for fabric (e.g. for curtains), bed linen and wallpaper.

There's a reasonable market for second-hand furniture in Italy and many sellers and dealers advertise in the expatriate and local press (e.g. *Wanted in Rome*). Charity shops are an Aladdin's cave of household goods and furniture (and they hold periodic sales). You can also try the classified ads in newspapers such as *Porta Portese* (Rome – named after the city's famous flea market), *La Pulce* (Florence) and *Secondamano* (Milan) – there are equivalents in most cities.

The kind of furniture you buy depends on a number of factors, including how long you're planning to stay, whether you plan to take it with you when you leave, the style and size of your home, your budget, the local climate, and not least, your taste. If you intend to furnish a second home with antiques or expensive modern furniture, bear in mind that you will need adequate security and insurance. If you own a home abroad, it may be worthwhile shipping surplus items of furniture you have abroad (unless you live in Australia!).

DIY

There are do-it-yourself (DIY) hypermarkets in some areas, selling everything for the home, including DIY supplies, furniture, bathrooms, kitchens, decorating and lighting, plus services such as tool rental and wood-cutting. Look for the enormous Brico Io and Brico Centre stores, usually located in shopping centres on the outskirts of large cities. There are salvage and second-hand companies selling old doors, window frames, fireplaces, tiles, and other materials that are invaluable when restoring an old home or to add a special touch to a modern home. Note, however, that many modern DIY supplies and materials aren't as easy to find in Italy as in some other European countries and are more expensive, so you may be better off importing them.

Household Goods

Household goods in Italy are generally of good quality and there's a large choice.

Prices compare favourably with other European countries, and bargains can be found at supermarkets and hypermarkets. Not surprisingly in a nation where people spend much of their time in the kitchen (the rest is spent eating!), Italian kitchenware, crockery, cutlery and glasses can all be purchased cheaply, and the quality and design are usually excellent. It's recommended to buy white goods (such as refrigerators and washing machines) in Italy, as imported appliances may not function properly due to differences in the electrical supply (it may also be difficult to have them repaired).

☑ SURVIVAL TIP

Italian appliances, such as those made by Candy or Zanussi, usually have a good reputation for reliability, although German brands are generally better (and more expensive).

Note that most Italian kitchens don't come with cupboards or major appliances when you buy or rent a home long-term (unless you agree to purchase the existing kitchen from the previous tenant/owner), so you don't usually need to worry about whether you can fit an imported dishwasher or washing machine into the kitchen. However, you should check the size **and** the latest Italian safety regulations before shipping these items to Italy or buying them abroad, as they may need expensive modifications (see **Electricity** on page 241).

If you already own small household appliances, it's worth bringing them to Italy, as usually all that's required is a change of plug. If you bring appliances with you, don't forget to bring a supply of spares and refills such as bulbs for a refrigerator or sewing machine and spare bags for a vacuum cleaner (unless you have a bag-less

model!). If you're coming from a country with a 110/115V electricity supply, such as the US, you will need a lot of expensive transformers and it's usually better to buy new appliances in Italy. Small appliances such as vacuum cleaners, grills, toasters and electric irons are inexpensive in Italy and good quality. Don't bring a television without checking its compatibility first, as TVs from many countries won't work in Italy (see page 236).

If you need kitchen-measuring equipment and cannot cope with metric measures, you must bring your own measuring scales, jugs, cups and thermometers (or refer constantly to **Appendix D**). Note also that foreign pillow sizes (e.g. American and British) aren't the same as in Italy, and duvets are much more expensive in Italy than in some other countries and therefore worth bringing with you.

Shopping Abroad

Shopping abroad (e.g. in neighbouring Austria, France, Slovenia or Switzerland) makes a welcome change from all those Italian shops full of tempting and expensive luxuries. It can also save you money and makes an interesting day out for the family. Don't forget your passports or identity cards, car papers, children, dog's vaccination papers and foreign currency (if applicable). If you're travelling to Switzerland via motorway by car, you need to buy an annual motorway tax sticker at the border costing Sfr40 (around €25). Shopping in Switzerland is popular with Milan and Turin residents, particularly for dairy products and chocolate. Most shops in Swiss and Slovenian border towns accept Euros, but usually give you a lower exchange rate than a bank. Whatever you're looking for, compare prices and quality before buying. Bear in mind that if you buy goods that are faulty or need repair, you may need to return them to the place of purchase.

Since 1993, there have been no cross-border shopping restrictions within the European Union (EU) for goods purchased duty and tax paid, provided all goods are for personal consumption or use and not for resale. Although there are no restrictions, there are 'indicative levels' for certain items, above which quantities may be classified as commercial. For example, those entering Italy aged 17 or over may import the following amounts of alcohol and tobacco without question:

- 10 litres of spirits (over 22° proof);

- 20 litres of sherry or fortified wine (under 22° proof);

- 90 litres of wine (or 120 x 0.75 litre bottles/ten cases), of which a maximum of 60 litres may be sparkling wine;

- 110 litres of beer;

- 800 cigarettes, 400 cigarillos, 200 cigars and 1kg of smoking tobacco.

There's no limit on perfume or toilet water.

⚠ Caution

If you exceed the above amounts, you will need to convince the customs authorities that you aren't planning to sell them. There are fines for anyone who sells duty-paid alcohol and tobacco, which is classed as smuggling.

Duty-Free Allowances

Duty-free (*esente da dazio*) shopping was abolished within the EU on 1st July 1999 and duty-free allowances now apply only if you're travelling to Italy from a country outside the EU (which includes neighbouring Switzerland). For each such journey, travellers aged 17 or over are entitled to import the following goods purchased duty-free:

- One litre of spirits (over 22° proof) **or** two litres of fortified wine (under 22° proof) **or** two litres of sparkling wine;

- Two litres of still table wine;

- 200 cigarettes **or** 100 cigarillos **or** 50 cigars* **or** 250g of tobacco;

- 60ml of perfume;

- 250ml of toilet water;

- Other goods, including gifts and souvenirs to the value of €220.

*Non-EU residents are entitled to import 150 cigars.

Duty-free allowances apply to both outward and return journeys, even if both are made on the same day, and the combined total (i.e. double the above limits) can be imported into your 'home' country.

VAT Refunds

If you live outside the EU, you can obtain a VAT refund (20 per cent on most goods) on purchases provided the value of goods purchased in any one shop (excluding books, food, services and some other items) amounts to at least €154.94, including VAT (shops providing this service usually display a 'Tax-Free' sticker in their windows). Large department stores may have a special counter where non-EU shoppers can arrange for the shipment of duty-free goods. An export sales invoice (or 'tax-free shopping cheque') is provided by retailers, listing all purchases.

When you leave Italy, your purchases must be validated by customs (*dogana*) staff at the airport, port or railway station, so don't pack them in your checked baggage. Refunds may be made on the spot at 'tax-free' counters or by post, in which case they're usually made within 90 days of the date of purchase. On-the-spot refunds can take some time, which you should allow for before your plane, train

Nowadays tone dialling is the rule rather than the exception.

Telecom Italia (formerly SIP) was privatised in 1997, and used to be the only provider of telephone lines and fixed-line (non-mobile) telephones in Italy. Towards the end of the '90s, Tiscali, Wind and a number of other companies provided much-needed competition for long-distance domestic calls and international calls, and (surprise, surprise) calls charges started to fall dramatically. Telecom Italia used to have a monopoly on local calls from fixed-line phones, but since 2002 the company Infostrada (part of Wind) has provided some competition. Three separate companies provide mobile phone services.

or ship leaves. You can choose to have a refund paid to a credit card or bank account or to receive a cheque.

TELEPHONE SERVICES

Until recently, the use of telephones in Italy was hampered by two serious drawbacks: the first was that holding a phone interfered with the Italians' predilection for gesticulating with both hands when talking and the second was the unavailability of phone numbers.

The latter was due to an old-fashioned system that couldn't accommodate the number of lines that were needed. As a result, people in some areas had to literally wait for years for a phone line to be installed!

However, Italians gradually learned to gesticulate with one hand and a major modernisation of the telephone system in the early '90s saw the introduction of fibre optics and electronic switching that greatly increased the availability of phone lines. By around 1995, Telecom Italia had completed the conversion, although some remote areas still have mechanical switchboards.

Installation & Registration

To have a fixed-line phone installed – at least for the first time – you must visit your local Telecom Italia office (there's one in most large towns and cities and all provincial capitals). They can provide information about equipment and services, and help you complete the application form. However, staff usually speak only Italian, therefore if you don't you will need to take along an interpreter, plus your passport (and a photocopy) for identification purposes.

The fee for installing a line in a property where one wasn't previously installed is €250. Transfer of a telephone number to another location within the same code area is free of charge, as the fee is to change the name of the user of an existing telephone line. Additional charges apply depending on the distance involved if a phone is to be installed in a remote area which isn't considered 'inhabited' (*oltre perimetro abitato*). Nowadays, it usually takes just a few working days to have a line installed.

You're expected to lease or buy a telephone from Telecom Italia, but you can also replace it with another phone purchased elsewhere. Telecom Italia's 'INSIP' shops sell phones that have been approved by themselves (marked *omologato*), although it isn't illegal to sell non-approved phones and most electronics shops stock a wide variety. The contractual requirement that the subscriber must use equipment provided by Telecom Italia or approved by them is seldom enforced. In principle, Telecom Italia could confiscate a phone connected to its network that isn't *omologato*, but this is highly unlikely unless it's a cordless phone that uses frequencies allocated to the emergency services.

For ordinary analogue lines, Telecom Italia usually installs a standard three-prong socket with a standard telephone. It's up to the user to change the socket or use adapters for the equipment that will be used. Digital ISDN lines are growing in popularity and are usually marketed as a package with two lines. The cost (excluding VAT) of a new ISDN installation is around €110, and switching from an analogue line costs the same. The monthly fixed cost for two lines is around €18 for private users and €30 for business users. There are three categories of subscriber (*abbonati*) in Italy.

- **Category A** – All subscribers that aren't included in categories B and C. In practice, this means all business enterprises and professional offices.

- **Category B** – The first installation made in a private home where there's no business or professional activity, and the phone is in the name of a private person.

- **Category C** – Subsequent installations made after the first installation in category B, with the same user characteristics and the same subscriber.

Categories B and C can be installed as single user lines or as duplex lines when they will carry low traffic. Having a duplex line means you share a line (but not the phone number – so you cannot hear what is being said on the other line) with another party. This has the drawback that you won't be able to use your phone if the person with whom you're sharing is using the line. Otherwise it works like a normal phone line, with exactly the same costs for installation and calls. The difference is in the line rental for each two-month period Infostrada (🖳 www.infostrada.it) does not charge a fee for telephone installation, and offers a wide, ever-changing range of different customer packages, for private and business use, and internet access.

Using the Telephone

Using the telephone in Italy is much the same as in any other country, with a few Italian eccentricities thrown in for good measure. One unusual feature of the Italian phone system is that you must include the area code (*prefissi*) when making local calls, not just when making calls outside your local code area. If you leave out the

area code when making a call, you hear a recorded message telling you to dial it before the number. However, this message is (naturally) given in Italian, so visiting friends or relatives who try to call you from within the country (who leave out the code) may not understand why they cannot get through. If you don't know the area code, you can get it from the operator (dial 12 for domestic codes). A booklet listing area codes (and postcodes) is published by Telecom Italia and available from bookshops and stationers.

Since 1998 you've also had to include the '0' of the area code when calling from abroad, unlike when making calls to almost every other country (Italy doesn't care much for international standards). If you omit the zero when calling from abroad you hear an engaged tone, with no further explanation, which has caused a lot of confusion and upset many people who have often tried for days on end to call someone in Italy! When dialling a number in Italy from abroad, you dial the international access code of the country from which you're calling (e.g. 00), followed by Italy's international code (39), the area code **with** the first 0 (e.g. 02) and the subscriber's number (e.g. 12345678). Therefore using the previous example you would dial 00-39-02-12345678.

Telephone numbers in Italy are often written with a dash or forward slash (as in this book) after the area code and a space after each two or three digits, e.g. Milan 12345678, should be shown as 02-123 456 78 or 02-123 456 78. However, there may only be a space after the area code, or the code and number may be written with no spaces at all, e.g. 0212345678. Italian phone numbers vary in length; for example, Rome numbers may be between five and eight digits. Bear in mind that mobile phone (see page 289) numbers start with 03 and are more expensive to call than ordinary fixed lines.

Alternative Providers

In addition to Telecom Italia, there are a number of other providers of national and international long-distance phone calls, the largest of which include Tiscali and Wind, who also operate a mobile phone network. To access these you must dial a company's code (prefix) before dialling a number, e.g. 10030 for Tiscali and 1088 for Wind. Both require pre-registration and a minimum advance payment of around €50. This isn't a deposit but an advance payment of calls, which must be renewed when it's exhausted by having it charged automatically to a credit card or by obtaining a re-chargeable card from the carrier (the companies aren't taking any chances on you absconding without paying your bill).

Calls can only be made from the phone numbers specified in the contract with the carrier and you can only use the service from your home phone plus one additional number (e.g. your office), but not from anywhere else. The same access prefix can be used to call mobile phones at a lower cost than charged by Telecom Italia. Additional information about the tariffs and conditions of Tiscali and Wind is available on the Internet (⌨ www.tiscali.it and www. wind.it).

> ☑ SURVIVAL TIP
>
> There are also numerous other companies offering long-distance services in Italy, including AT&T (⌨ www.att.com), BT Italia (⌨ www.italia.bt.com), Infostrada (⌨ www. infostrada.it), MCI Worldcom (⌨ www.mci. com) and Tele2 (⌨ www.tele2.it).

Charges

Line rental and call charges in Italy are among the highest in Europe, although

the peak period (8am to 6.30pm), the charge for local calls is around €0.20 per minute for up to 15 minutes, after which it falls to €0.18 per minute. A cheaper rate of €0.10 for the first 15 minutes and €0.09 thereafter applies on weekdays outside the peak period, after 1pm on Saturdays, and all day on Sundays and public holidays.

For long-distance domestic calls, the cost depends on the distance, with tariffs increasing in steps for calls (a) within the local district, (b) up to 15km, (c) between 15 and 30km, and (d) beyond 30km. The cost also depends on the time of day, as noted above.

International calls can be particularly expensive via Telecom Italia and there is no longer an off-peak period. The charges for international calls also depend on the country – the world is divided into 12 zones. Generally, the 'connection' fee is around €3.20, plus the fee per minute, e.g. a call to the UK costs €1.90 per minute.

Telecom Italia's charges for calls from a fixed-line phone to a mobile phone depend on the type of mobile phone contract, which is indicated by the number's prefix. Cheaper rates usually apply on Saturdays and Sundays, but still vary depending on the phone number prefix – there are up to six different periods in a single day! For some prefixes there's also a higher charge between 8am and 1pm on Saturdays. This complex system is expected to be simplified in future, in line with the billing method used by independent long-distance carriers.

Emergency & Service Numbers

The general emergency number in Italy is 113. However, people are discouraged from using this except in cases where there's a real, serious danger for the caller or other persons, or in the event of a serious accident. Otherwise, the preferred emergency procedure is to call the relevant organisation directly. People witnessing

they've fallen considerably in recent years due to increased competition. Telephone charges from Telecom Italia include line rental, telephone and other equipment rentals, special services such as call transfer and three-way conversation, credit card calls, and general call charges. If you have a standard category B private line, the bimonthly line rental is around €30. If you have a line installed or reconnected, the charge appears on your first bill. The charges and tariffs below apply only to calls made via Telecom Italia, and when making long-distance or international calls you should compare Telecom's rates with those of alternative carriers, which are sometimes cheaper.

Call charges are based on the duration of the phone call in seconds, plus an initial 'connection' fee of around €0.06 for local calls and €0.07 for national long-distance calls. The charges for calls via analogue and ISDN (digital) lines are the same. The tariff per minute depends on the time of the day and the distance of the call.

For local calls there are two charging periods from Mondays to Fridays. During someone being assaulted at night and calling 113 on their mobile phones have been told to call 112 (the number for the *Carabinieri* – see below) instead. Even calling 112 may not produce the expected result. Some youngsters once called this number when they saw a car being stolen in the early morning hours. The reply was, 'We only have two cars and they're not for that sort of thing', from which you may conclude that car theft isn't a particularly high priority for the Italian police. The most important emergency numbers are shown below:

Local telephone operators usually only speak Italian, although a translation service (in Arabic, English, French or German) is available if you dial 170.

Fax

Fax is widely available in Italy, where messages can be sent and received from post offices and many private offices offering business services. Faxes sent nationally and internationally from a post office cost around €1.30 per page. Tobacconists, stationery shops, and other establishments also send and receive faxes (and may also provide photocopying services), and many petrol stations on motorways also provide access to fax machines. Unlike the post office (which charges by the page), private businesses charge according to the number of telephone units used and therefore the price may be lower.

There are no special rules for fax machines, except that they should conform to the international G3 standard. The cost of a fax machine varies according to the make, the kind of paper used (e.g. fax rolls or plain paper), the features (such as an answer phone) and multiple-use features. For example, some fax machines can be used as a scanner and colour printer when connected to a computer. An average price for a standard, middle-of-the-range machine is around €150. If you bring a fax machine to Italy it should work without any problems, provided it operates on a 220v power supply, although some machines need modifying.

Public Telephones

Public telephones (*telefono pubblico* or *cabina telefonica*) are located in bus

---

Emergency & Useful Numbers

112 Paramilitary police (*carabinieri*) for crimes and traffic accidents;
113 General emergency number for serious emergencies only (*soccorso pubblico di emergenza*);
115 Fire brigade (*vigili del fuoco*);
118 Ambulance or first aid (*emergenza sanitaria*).

Calling the above numbers from public phones is usually free of charge. Other useful numbers include:

12 Directory enquiries (*informazioni elenco abbonati*);
110 Information (*informazioni*);
116 Vehicle breakdown assistance (*soccorso stradale*) – Automobile Club d'Italia (ACI);
176 International operator (*informazioni internazionali*), who can provide general information in English;
197 For urgent phone calls (*chiamate urgenti*) – if a number is busy you can ask the operator to interrupt an ongoing call.

depots, railway stations and airports, bars, cafés and restaurants, motorway rest areas, business premises, main post offices, and in streets in cities and towns. All payphones allow International Direct Dialling (IDD) and international calls can also be made via the operator. Some public phones are coin operated, but these are now being phased out and replaced by phones that only accept phone cards (*scheda telefonica prepagata*) or Telecom debit cards. Telecom Italia also provides pre-paid, international phone cards and credit cards. Phone cards are available from bars, news kiosks, tobacconists, post offices, shops and dispensing machines in various small denominations, most commonly €5, €10 and €20.

You can usually make both national and international calls from public phones, provided you have sufficient credit on your phone card. Bear in mind that calling a mobile phone from a public phone includes a connection fee of around €0.50. Normally the minimum amount accepted by payphones is €0.10, although if you phone a mobile you must insert over €0.50 to cover the additional cost.

There are *posto telefonico* offices in small towns throughout the country, where you can obtain assistance when making calls, and automatic telecommunication centres (*centri di telecomunicazione automatici*) offering self-service, automatic calls (no assistance) in major cities and resorts. In cities and many towns in Italy there are also private telephone offices operated by a range of companies, including AT&T, Infostrada, Italia Blu, MCI, Teledue and Wind Telecom, from where you can make international calls.

Mobile Phones

There are four mobile phone networks in Italy: H3G (🖥 www.tre.it), Omnitelvodafone (🖥 www.190.it), TIM (🖥 www.privati. tim.it) and Wind (🖥 www.wind.it). The best national cover is provided by TIM, although this is countered by a reluctance to provide access to international calls on a rechargeable phone (phones with a contract can be used to make international calls in Italy and world-wide). Omnitelvodafone and Wind don't cover the whole of Italy, although they're more generous with international access, which they provide through the TIM network.

☑ **SURVIVAL TIP**

When you're considering which mobile phone company to sign up with, you must ensure that its network covers your home area and any other areas where you travel frequently or do business.

All the mobile phone companies provide the option of either having a contract for access or using a rechargeable card. A rechargeable card usually costs €55, half of which is for the card itself and half credit for calls. Cards can usually be recharged with up to €250 of credit, but most people recharge for €25 or €50, which is valid for 12 months. Many shops offer recharging, which can also be done via some cash-dispensing machines (ATMs) or through your mobile phone (if your contract provides it). There's usually a separate fee for the actual recharging, the cost of which depends on the network provider.

The cost of mobile phones themselves, affectionately called 'little phones' (*telefonini*), is quite high in Italy. Unlike countries such as Germany and the UK, where mobile phones are often provided 'free' (although they remain the property of the provider) on signing a contract with a provider, Italians must buy their phones at the market price. However, the cost of a 'free' phone and a one-year contract in the UK, is equal to around the same as the price of a mobile phone in Italy. The cost of a phone varies depending on the manufacturer and its level of sophistication (and whether it's a new model), and ranges from as little as around €50 to €800, with most costing around €175.

Mobile phone retailers advertise in newspapers and magazines, where a wide range of special offers is promoted. There's also an active market in second-hand mobile phones. Good places to look are the classified advertisements in newspapers such as *Porta Portese* (Rome – named after the city's famous flea market), *La Pulce* (Florence) and *Secondamano* (Milan) – there are equivalents in most cities. There are also a number of 'bazaars' on the internet offering used mobile phones at competitive prices – search on *cellulari usati* or *di seconda mano*. Bear in mind, however, that as well as buying a phone, you must negotiate a contract with a service provider (or buy rechargeable cards).

Internet

Perhaps due to the relatively high cost of telecommunications, Italy has been slower than many other European countries to adapt to the internet. However, this is changing and most large and medium-sized companies now quote an email address and often a website in their advertising. Private consumers are also joining up, lured by the recent arrival of a number of free internet service providers (ISPs), although only just over half of Italians were connected by 2006.

The most popular ISP is Tin (🖥 http://tin.alice.it), a subsidiary of Telecom Italia, which offers two services, one of which, ClubNet, is free. This provides you with one email address, 20 MB of home page space and access to the internet via a local phone number. The other Tin service, Premium, is similar to CompuServe and AOL, in that it provides special content for subscribers only and you're charged a monthly subscription fee. Like CompuServe and AOL (although unlike ClubNet), Premium gives you international access to the internet from places outside Italy, with some 400 nodes worldwide.

CompuServe and AOL also have local access in Milan and Rome, although unless you live in one of these two cities your access will be through long-distance calls (which can be very expensive). The long-distance phone company, Wind, also provides free internet access (🖥 www.inwind.it).

Telecom Italia offers four different internet tariffs: €2 per hour; €9.95 per month; €19.95 per month; and €36.95 per month, each with different conditions. Tiscalinet (🖥 www.tiscali.it) is a free access provider, with local access numbers in most areas. They give you one free email address and 30 MB of homepage space and, unlike some free services, your email can be accessed directly using third party software such as Microsoft Outlook. One drawback with free services is that there can be a lot of traffic on the networks, particularly during the evenings and weekends, which can slow things down considerably and sometimes means you cannot connect at all. Furthermore, the telephone support available is of variable quality and availability, and may be charged at extortionate rates (even by Italian standards). You may therefore be better off choosing a subscription service.

Most computer shops have agreements with local ISPs and act as agents for them. They will sell you a software kit, access numbers and so on, and the service is usually activated within a few hours. The cost is quite reasonable at around €100 per year, which usually includes one email address and unlimited internet access. The actual provider depends on where you live, with some areas well covered by local ISPs and others not at all.

If you already have internet access (e.g. at work) and don't want to pay for an email account of your own, you can sign up with one of the free web-based email services such as Yahoo Mail (🖳 www.yahoo.com) or Microsoft Network's Hotmail (🖳 www.hotmail.com). One advantage of these services is that you can access your email from any computer with internet access, e.g. at a library or cybercafe. Note, however, that mail sent to and from such services isn't secure.

TELEVISION & RADIO

☑ **SURVIVAL TIP**

Before taking a television (TV), video cassette recorders (VCRs) or DVD player to Italy, you should consider both costs and compatibility. Further details of television and radio services in Italy are contained in *Living and Working in Italy* (Survival Books).

TV Standards

The standards for television reception in Italy aren't the same as in some other countries. Due to the differences in transmission standards, TVs and video recorders operating on the British (PAL-I) French (SECAM) or North American (NTSC) systems won't function in Italy, which, along with most other continental European countries, uses the PAL-BG standard. It's possible to buy a multi-standard European TV (and VCR) containing automatic circuitry that switches between different systems.

Some multi-standard TVs also offer the NTSC standard and have a jack plug connection, allowing you to play back American videos. A standard British, French or US TV won't work in Italy, although British TVs can be modified. The same applies to foreign video recorders, which won't operate with an Italian TV unless the VCR is dual-standard. Some expatriates opt for two TVs, one to receive Italian programmes and another (e.g. SECAM or NTSC) to play their favourite videos.

A portable 36cm (14in) colour TV can be purchased in Italy for around €150, a 55cm (21in) TV costs from around €250 and a 71cm (28in) model from around €500. Many TVs feature Nicam stereo sound, and high-quality, digital sound is available in most of Italy. Digital (HD) wide-screen TVs are also widely available and, although still relatively high, prices are falling, and a good quality, widescreen HD TV can now be purchased from around €1,000. Most new TVs offer a teletext system, which apart from allowing you to display programme schedules, also provides a wealth of useful and interesting information. Teletext information is called *Televideo* on RAI stations and *Mediavideo* on Italia Uno, Rete 4 and Canale 5 stations.

TV Licence

A TV tax (*canone*) is payable in Italy of €104 per year for a colour TV; it can be paid quarterly, half-yearly or annually (at a post office). A single licence covers any number of TVs in a household. When you buy a TV in Italy, your name is automatically registered with the authorities, although many people avoid tax by buying a second-hand TV or making an 'arrangement' with the vendor. The tax must be paid to customs if you personally import a TV. The authorities have powerful detector vans to identify homes where people are watching TV and whether they've paid the tax. There are fines for non-payment, but the **maximum** fine is just 50 per cent of the licence fee, so it isn't surprising that many people avoid paying.

Satellite Television

Domestic

There's currently little competition in the Italian pay television market, since the closure of Telepiu. Sky Italia (which is owned by News Corporation, 🖳 www.skylife.it) controls around 93 per cent of the market, with 2.5m subscribers. Subscribers to Sky Italia are bound to a 12-month contract that auto-renews every year and in order to cancel the subscription, you must cancel at least 60 days before the termination of the contract. Subscription costs vary according to the channel package and begin at €24 per month. The decoder is free and it costs €99 to have the satellite dish installed (which is periodically discounted).

Sky offers four types of 'mixing packages': Mondo, Cinema, Sport and Calcio. The first is a mixed basic entertainment package (music, children's, teenage, culture and some sport). The second has nine movie channels, the third has a range of sports and Calcio has 17

channels aimed at football (although quite how this is possible – or desirable – is anyone's guess!).

As of 2006, individual Italian football clubs have had the right to sell their own broadcast rights, unlike most European clubs. Three broadcasters are currently 'in play': Sky Italia and two terrestrial broadcasters, Mediaset and La7 (owned by Telecom Italia), which have pay television services. They currently sublease rights back to Sky.

International

There are a number of satellites positioned over Europe carrying over 200 stations broadcasting in a variety of languages. Satellite TV has been growing apace in Europe in the last decade, particularly in Italy, which has no cable TV. TV addicts (easily recognised by their antennae and square eyes) are offered a huge choice of English and foreign-language stations, which can be received via the Astra satellites throughout Italy with an 85cm dish. A bonus is the availability of radio stations, including the major BBC stations.

Among the many English-language stations available on Astra are Sky One,

Movimax, Sky Premier, Sky Cinema, Film Four, Sky News, Sky Sports (several channels), UK Gold, Channel 5, Granada Plus, TNT, Eurosport, CNN, CNBC Europe, UK Style, UK Horizons, the Disney Channel and the Discovery Channel. Other stations broadcast in Dutch, German, Japanese, Swedish and various Indian languages. The signal from many stations is scrambled (the decoder is usually built into the receiver) and viewers must pay a monthly subscription fee to receive programmes. You can buy pirate decoders for some channels. The best served by clear (unscrambled) stations are German-speakers (most German stations on Astra are clear).

Sky: You must buy a receiver with a Videocrypt decoder and pay a monthly subscription to receive Sky stations except Sky News (which isn't scrambled). Various packages are available costing from around GB£15 to around GB£45 per month for the premium package offering all movie channels plus Sky Sports. To receive scrambled channels such as Movimax and Sky Sports, you need an address in Britain. Subscribers are sent a coded 'smart' card (similar to a credit card), which must be inserted in the decoder to activate it (cards are periodically updated to thwart counterfeiters).

Sky won't send smart cards to overseas viewers, as they have the copyright for a British-based audience only (Italian homeowners need to obtain a card via a UK address or through a friend or relative there).

However, a number of satellite companies in Italy (some of which advertise in the expatriate press) supply genuine Sky cards – at a premium.

BBC: The BBC has stopped encrypting (scrambling) its channels coming from the Astra satellite that it shares with Sky, which means that you don't need a Sky Digibox to receive the BBC channels, including BBC interactive services. The BBC's commercial subsidiary, BBC World Television (formerly BBC Worldwide Television) broadcasts two 24-hour channels: BBC World (24-hour news and information) and BBC Prime (general entertainment). BBC World is free-to-view, while BBC Prime is encrypted.

BBC World is normally included as part of the 'international' offering with basic cable or digital satellite services in Italy. A subscription to BBC Prime costs GB£85 a year, plus a one-time charge of GB£30 for a smart card and VAT, making a total of £135.13 (💻 see www.bbcprime.com/ManagedMedia/Files/BBC_Prime_Subscription_Form_EU.pdf). Both BBC World and BBC Prime have their own websites (💻 www.bbcworld.com and www.bbcprime.com), where you can view programme schedules; you must choose the country (e.g. Italy) so that schedules are displayed in local time.

Equipment: A satellite receiver should have a built-in Videocrypt decoder (and others such as Eurocrypt, Syster or SECAM if required) and be capable of receiving satellite stereo radio. A system with an 85cm dish (to receive Astra stations) costs from around €350 plus the cost of installation, which may be included in the price. Shop around, as prices can vary considerably. With a 1.2 or 1.5 metre motorised dish, you can receive up to 500 stations in a multitude of languages from around the world. If you wish to receive satellite TV on two or more TVs, you can buy a satellite system with two or more receivers. To receive stations from two or more satellites simultaneously, you need a motorised dish or a dish with a double feed antenna (dual LNBs). There are many satellite sales and installation companies in Italy, some of which advertise in the expatriate press. Alternatively, you can import your own satellite dish and receiver and install it yourself. Before buying a system, ensure that it can receive programmes from all existing and planned satellites.

Location: To receive programmes from any satellite, there must be no obstacles between the satellite and your dish, i.e. no trees, buildings or mountains must obstruct the signal, so check before renting or buying a home. Before buying or erecting a satellite dish, check whether you need permission from your landlord or the local municipality. Some towns and buildings (such as apartment blocks) have laws or regulations regarding the positioning of antennae, although generally owners can mount a dish almost anywhere without attracting any complaints. Dishes can usually be mounted in a variety of unobtrusive positions and can also be painted or patterned to blend in with the background. Individual dishes will eventually be banned in apartment buildings

(*palazzine*) and substituted with a single communal antenna with a cable connection to apartments.

Programme Guides: A number of satellite TV magazines are published in the UK, including the weekly *TV & Satellite Week* (💻 www.ipcmedia.com/brands/tvsatweek) and the monthly *What Satellite and Digital TV* magazine, both available on subscription.

Videos & DVDs

Videos are widely available to rent (*noleggiare*) or buy from video shops in all main towns and cities, which are listed in yellow pages under *Audiovisivi*. To rent videos you usually need to join a club and pay an annual fee and you can then rent videos from €2 per night (for an old 'classic') up to €5 to €7.50 per night for the latest Hollywood blockbuster. Many shops also sell videos from €10 to €50. The American video rental company Blockbuster has stores in major cities with a wide selection of films (both VCR and DVD) in the original language. In some places you may also be offered pirate videos of new films that haven't yet been released on video, which should be avoided as the quality is usually terrible – they're also illegal!

You may be able to buy or swap English-language videos with other foreigners through expatriate clubs, and you can buy English-language videos via the Internet and through mail-order video catalogues. Choices UK, Southgate House, Southgate Way, Orton Southgate, Peterborough, PE2 6YG, UK (☎ 0870-400 3838, 💻 www.choicesuk.com), who are licensed by the BBC to sell their videos, will search for anything you want if you don't have it in their catalogue; if you order from their website, you don't pay postage.

DVDs are becoming increasingly popular in Italy. Although they're still more expensive than videos, they often offer additional features such as extra scenes, multiple language soundtracks and subtitling. Be particularly careful, however, to buy DVDs for the correct 'zone', as films intended for an American audience (Zone 1) won't play back in a European (Zone 2) DVD player unless it has been modified, and Zone 1 versions often don't contain the alternate soundtracks and subtitling. There are multi-zone DVD players available and it's also possible to modify many single-zone players to read multiple-zone DVDs.

Radio

Radio is popular in Italy with an estimated audience of some 35m people, over a third of whom listen exclusively to popular music stations.

Radio was deregulated in Italy in 1976, at the same time as television. Since then there has been an explosion in the number of stations available; there are now some 2,500, from large national stations to small local stations with just a 'handful' of listeners. The three main channels are Radio 1, 2 and 3 operated by the state controlled company RAI. Radios 1 and 2 are split into light (dance) music and general entertainment on one wavelength and popular music on another, while Radio 3 broadcasts serious discussion programmes and classical music.

The favourite station among young listeners is Radio DJ, which also features famous club disc jockeys (mostly on Friday and Saturday nights), while Radio Italia offers a selection of Italian singers and bands, and Radio Globo plays mostly dance music.

English-Language Stations

During the summer, RAI broadcasts daily news in English, and Vatican Radio also broadcasts news in English at various times. There are also expatriate English-language radio stations in the major cities.

The BBC World Service is broadcast on short wave on several frequencies (e.g. short wave 12095, 9760, 9410, 7325, 6195, 5975 and 3955 KhZ) simultaneously and you can usually receive a good signal on one of them. The signal strength varies according to where you live in Italy, the time of day and year, the power and positioning of your receiver, and atmospheric conditions. The BBC World Service plus BBC Radio 1, 2, 3, 4 and 5 are also available on the Astra (Sky) satellite. For a free BBC World Service programme guide and frequency information write to BBC World Service, Bush House, Strand, London WC2B 4PH, UK (☎ 020-7240 3456, 🖳 www.bbc.co.uk/worldservice).

Many other foreign stations can be received in Italy, including Radio Australia, Radio Canada, Denmark Radio, Radio Nederland, Radio Sweden International and the Voice of America. Schedules can be found via the Internet, and you can often download broadcast material.

Satellite Radio

If you have satellite TV, you can receive many radio stations via your satellite link. For example, BBC Radio 1, 2, 3, 4 and 5, BBC World Service, Sky Radio, Virgin 1215 and many foreign-language stations are broadcast via the Astra satellites.

UTILITIES

Immediately after buying or renting a property (unless utilities are included in the rent), you should arrange for your meters (if applicable) to be read, contracts (e.g. electricity, gas and water) to be registered in your name and services switched on (e.g. mains gas). Always check before buying or renting a property that all outstanding bills have been paid by the previous owner, or you will be liable for any debts (see **Conveyancing** on page 161). Registration usually entails a visit to the company's office, although some companies allow you to register online or by telephone.

If you go to the utility company's office, you must take with you some identification (passport or residence permit), and the contract and bills paid by the previous owner. The registration procedure for water connection is sometimes via the local town hall (see **Water** on page 247). If you've purchased a home in Italy, the estate agent may arrange for the utilities to be transferred to your name or go with you to the offices (no charge should be made for this service).

If you're a non-resident owner, you should also give your foreign address in case there are any problems requiring your attention, such as a bank failing to pay the bills. You may need to pay a deposit.

See also **Heating & Air-Conditioning** on page 218.

Electricity

Most electricity in Italy is supplied by Ente Nazionale per l'Energia Elettrica (ENEL, 🖥 www.enel.it), which had a monopoly on providing electricity before being privatised in 1998, with competition currently provided by Edison Edipower, Endesa and ENI, along with some smaller companies. Most electricity is generated by burning oil, none of the country's four nuclear power plants having been in operation since a public vote against the use of nuclear power in a referendum in 1987. Italy imports around 15 per cent of its electricity from France and Switzerland. In major cities, electricity may be controlled by a local municipal energy board, e.g. the Azienda Energetica Municipale (AEM) in Milan. Electricity and other utility offices are listed in telephone directories under Numeri di Pubblica Utilità.

After buying or renting a property in Italy (unless utilities are included in the rent),

you must sign a contract (*volturazione delle utenze*) at the local office of your electricity company. You need to take with you some identification (passport or residence permit), a copy of the deeds or rental contract, the registration number of the meter (*contatore*), the previous tenant's electricity contract or a bill paid by the previous owner, and a good book as queues can be long. If you've purchased a home in Italy, the real estate agent may arrange for the utilities to be transferred to your name or go with you to the office.

Make sure all previous bills have been paid and that the contract is transferred to your name from the day you take over. If you're a non-resident owner, you should also give your foreign address or the address of a representative in Italy, in case there are any problems requiring your attention such as your bank refusing to pay the bills. You need to cancel (*disdire*) the contract when you move home.

Power Supply

The electricity supply in Italy is generally 220 volts AC with a frequency of 50 hertz (cycles) and either two or three phase, although in some areas older buildings may still use 125 volts. Not all appliances, e.g. TVs made for 240 volts, will function with a power supply of 220 volts. Power cuts are frequent in many areas of Italy (many lasting just a few micro-seconds or just long enough to crash a computer), particularly in rural areas, and the electricity supply is also unstable, with power surges commonplace.

If you use a computer you should have an uninterrupted power supply (UPS) with a battery backup, which allows you time to shut down your computer and save your work after a power failure. If you live in an area where cuts are frequent and rely on electricity for your livelihood, e.g. for operating a computer, fax machine and other equipment, you may need to install a backup generator.

☑ SURVIVAL TIP

Even more important than a battery backup is a power surge protector for appliances such as TVs, computers and fax machines, without which you risk equipment being damaged or destroyed.

In remote areas you must install a generator or solar power system if you want electricity, as there's no mains electricity, although some people make do with gas and oil lamps (and without TV and other modern conveniences).

Wiring Standards & Connection

Most modern properties in Italy (e.g. less than 20 years old) have decent electrical installations. However, old rural homes may have no electricity or may need totally rewiring. You should ensure that the electricity installations are in good condition well in advance of moving house, as it can take some time to have a new meter installed or get the electricity reconnected. The wiring in a new or renovated house (that has been rewired) must be inspected and approved by an ENEL inspector before a contract is issued and connection (*allacciato*) is made.

If you have any electrical work done in your home you should ensure that you employ an electrician (*elettricista*) who's registered at the local chamber of commerce or a member of an official body such as Uane, who works to ENEL's standards. There are safety regulations for all domestic electrical and gas systems and appliances, which must be inspected annually. Householders must have a certificate of inspection and there are fines of up to €5,000 for offenders who break the law.

If you buy a rural property without electricity that's over 500 metres from the nearest electricity pylon, you must pay to have the service extended to the property. The cost of connecting a rural property to mains electricity can be prohibitively expensive or even be impossible, in which case you will need to install a generator or solar power system (see page 241). The good news is that the wiring doesn't need to be installed to the high standard required by ENEL. A generator should be powered by diesel and secured against theft.

Meters

In an old apartment block there may be a common meter, with the bill shared among the apartment owners according to the size of their apartments. However, all new properties have their own meters, which for an apartment block or townhouse development may be installed in a basement in a special room or be housed in a meter 'cupboard' in a stairwell or outside a group of properties. A meter should be located outside a home so that it can be read by electricity company staff when you aren't at home.

Plugs

Depending on the country you've come from, you will need new plugs (*spine*) or a lot of adapters. Plug adapters for most foreign electrical apparatus can be purchased in Italy, although it's wise to bring some adapters with you, plus extension cords and multi-plug extensions that can be fitted with Italian plugs. There's often a lack of electricity points in Italian homes, with perhaps just one per room (including the kitchen), so multi-plug adapters may be essential. Electricity points don't usually have their own switches.

Most Italian plugs have two or three round pins (when present, the middle pin of three is for the earth or ground) and come in various sizes depending on the power consumption of the appliance. Small low-wattage electrical appliances such as table lamps and small TVs, don't require an earth. However, plugs with an earth must be used for high-wattage appliances such as fires, kettles, washing machines and refrigerators, and must be used with earthed sockets.

▲ **Caution**

Electrical appliances that are earthed have a three-core wire and must never be used with a two-pin plug without an earth socket. Always make sure that a plug is correctly and securely wired, as bad wiring can be fatal.

Fuses

In modern properties, fuses (*fusibili*) are of the earth trip type. When there's a short circuit or the system has been overloaded, a circuit breaker is tripped and the power supply is cut. If your electricity fails, you should suspect a fuse of tripping off, particularly if you've just switched on an electrical appliance (usually you will hear the power switch off). Before reconnecting the power, switch off any high-power appliances such as a stove, washing machine or heater. Make sure you know where the trip switches are located, and keep a torch handy so you can find them in the dark (see also **Power Rating** below).

Bulbs

Electric light bulbs in Italy are of the Edison type with a screw fitting. If you have lamps requiring bayonet bulbs you should bring some with you, as they cannot be readily purchased in Italy. You can, however, buy adapters to convert from bayonet to screw fitting (or vice versa). Bulbs for non-standard electrical appliances (i.e. appliances that aren't made for the Italian market), such as refrigerators and sewing machines, may not be available in Italy, therefore you should bring some spares with you.

Power Rating

If the power keeps tripping off when you attempt to use a number of high-power appliances simultaneously, e.g. an electric kettle, heater and cooker, it means that the power rating of your property is too low. This is a common problem in Italy. If this is the case, you may need to contact your electricity company and get them to upgrade the power supply to your property (it can also be downgraded if the power supply is higher than you require). Bear in mind that it can take some time to get your power rating changed. The power rating to a private dwelling in Italy can be 3kw, 4kw or 6kw (the maximum).

The minimum rating is 3kw, which is sufficient for a few lights only and even with a 4kw rating you're unable to run more than two or three high-powered appliances simultaneously. Consequently many people are now switching to 6kw. The maximum is generally unrestricted, although in some remote areas (e.g. mountainous areas) you may be limited to just 4kw and to increase it you need to take out another contract for another 2kw (making a maximum of 6kw). If you have a low supply, you can install a generator to increase it and use timers to ensure that no more than one high-powered apparatus is in operation at one time.

Your standing charge depends on the power rating of your supply, which is why owners tend to keep it as low as possible. Of the over 22m electrical service contracts in Italy, over 18m are for 4kw, including most apartments. The basic service cost depends on your power rating and whether your usage is low, medium or high, with current costs (subject to change) as shown in the table below:

Converters & Transformers

If you have electrical equipment rated at 110 volts AC (for example, from the US) you will require a converter or a step-down transformer to convert it to 220 volts. However, some electrical appliances are fitted with a 110/220 volt switch. Check for the switch, which may be inside the casing, and make sure it's switched to 220 volts **before** connecting it to the power supply. Converters can be used for heating appliances, but transformers are required for motorised appliances. Total the wattage of the devices you intend to connect to a transformer and make sure that its power rating **exceeds** this sum.

Generally all small, high-wattage, electrical appliances such as kettles, toasters, heaters and irons, need large transformers. Motors in large appliances such as cookers, refrigerators, washing machines, dryers and dishwashers, need replacing or fitting with a large transformer. In most cases it's simpler to buy new appliances in Italy, which are of good quality and reasonably priced (and sell them when you leave if you cannot take them with you).

The dimensions of cookers, micro-wave ovens, refrigerators, washing machines, dryers and dishwashers purchased abroad may differ from those in Italy, and therefore may not fit into an Italian kitchen.

Tariffs

The cost of electricity in Italy is relatively high compared with many other EU countries. The tariff depends on your usage and power rating (see above), which is used to calculate your monthly standing charge, which is payable irrespective of whether you use any electricity during the billing period. Your actual consumption is charged per KwH and the cost depends on the amount of usage: around ¢21 per kWh for low usage, ¢14 for medium usage and ¢12 for high usage. In other words, the basic cost (standing charge) increases with the power rating, but the actual cost of

Power Rating	Basic Service Cost (€)		
	Low Use	Medium Use	High Use
3kw	4	10	15
4kw	8	20	30
6kw	15	40	60

electricity consumption is reduced the more you use.

ENEL charges non-residents a higher rate and a residence permit (*certificato di residenza*) is necessary to obtain a resident's contract. You can buy energy-friendly appliances that consume less energy than average and energy saving devices can also be installed in appliances such as washing machines, dishwashers and dryers.

Bills

You're billed for your electricity usage every two months. Bills (*conti* or *bolletta*) are based on estimated consumption and adjusted twice per year when meters have been read. Consumption is usually estimated for four months (two bills) and then adjusted (*conguaglio*) when a meter reading is taken. This may result in a larger than expected bill, and therefore if you're a non-resident, you should ensure that you have sufficient funds in your bank account. If you've overpaid, you receive a refund in the form of a postal order, which can be cashed at a post office.

Half the bill contains account information and how to pay the bill, and the other half a payment slip and a receipt for your records. Bills show the account number (*numero utente*), amount payable (*importo*), due date (*scadenza*) and the utility company's account number (*conto corrente*). Bills may be paid at banks, post offices and electricity company offices, although ENEL prefers to be paid by direct debit (*domiciliazione*) from a bank account (for which there's a small surcharge).

Italian utility companies are notorious for over-charging, although customers rarely, if ever, receive a refund. It's recommended that you check that your meters remain static when services are turned off and learn to read your electricity bill and meter, and check your consumption to ensure that you aren't being overcharged.

Gas

Mains gas (*gas di città* or *metano città*) in Italy is supplied by Eniltalgas (⌨ www.italgas.it), which is now deregulated, with competition from Edison and ENEL, among others. The country has the third-largest gas market in Europe (behind Germany and the UK), and gas provides some 30 per cent of Italy's total energy requirements. It's widely available in cities and large towns in the north of the country, but isn't available in the south or in rural areas (e.g. in Tuscany and Umbria).

When moving into a property with mains gas, you must contact *SIG* to have the gas switched on and the meter read, and have the account changed to your name. You need to give the gas company the registration number of the meter and (if known) the name of the previous tenant. As with electricity, there are different contracts for residents and non-residents. The cost of mains gas is around €38 per megacalorie (MCAL) plus a standing charge of around €2.35 per month. You're billed every two

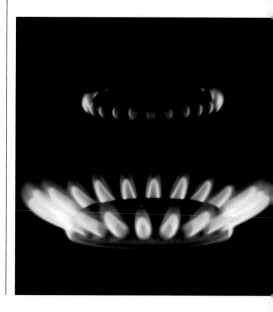

months and bills can be paid at banks, post offices and *SIG* offices, or by direct debit (*domiciliazione*) from a bank account.

Mains gas is mostly used just for central heating and cooking. All gas appliances must be approved by *SIG* and installed by your local gas company.

Gas water heaters cannot be installed in bathrooms for safety reasons, although many people do so, often with fatal consequences.

Old gas water heaters can leak carbon monoxide and have been the cause of a number of deaths in Italy and other countries, although this is unlikely with a modern installation. Gas water heaters must be regularly serviced and descaled annually. You can have a combined gas hot water and heating system installed (providing background heat), which is relatively inexpensive to install and cheap to run.

Bottled Gas

Bottled gas is mostly used for cooking, but can also be used to provide hot water and heating. The use of gas bottles (*bombole*) is common in rural areas and they're also frequently used for portable gas fires in cities. Cooking by bottled gas is cheaper than electricity and there's no standing charge (as with mains gas). Cookers often have a combination of electric and (bottled) gas rings (you can choose the mix). If your gas rings are sparked by electricity, keep some matches handy for use during power cuts.

You must pay a deposit on the first bottle and thereafter can exchange an empty bottle for a full one; the most common bottle size is 15kg, which cost around €22.50. Check when moving into a property that the gas bottle isn't empty and keep a spare bottle or two handy. Make sure you know how to change bottles – if necessary, ask the previous owner or your estate agent to show you. Bottles are delivered in many areas and you can also buy them from agents and supermarkets. A bottle used just for cooking lasts an average family around six weeks.

Some people keep their gas bottles outside, often under a lean-to. If you do, you must buy propane gas rather than butane, as it can withstand a greater range of temperatures than butane, which is for internal use only. Although bottled gas is very safe, if you use it you must inform your household insurance company, as there's an extra premium to pay.

If you live in a rural area, you can have a gas tank (*bombolone*) installed. Tanks come in various sizes and can be installed by gas companies. It isn't necessary to buy the tank as it remains the property of the gas company who make their money through the sale of gas (although you can also buy your own tank and buy gas from whichever supplier is cheapest). When a tank is installed free, you must sign a contract to purchase a minimum amount of gas per year, e.g. to the value of €500 to €1,000. Gas can officially be used only for heating and hot water, although many people also use it for cooking and gas fires.

A gas tank usually holds between 750 and 1,500 litres of liquid gas (1,000 litres is the most common size) and bulk gas costs around €5.50 per m3. The installation of gas tanks is strictly controlled and they must be at least 25m (82ft) from a house or road. If you have a gas tank installed on your property, you must inform your insurance company, as it increases your home insurance premium.

Water

Water is supplied by local companies, e.g. a *Società d'Acquedotto* (*SADA*) or *Azienda Comunale Energia e Ambiente* (*ACEA*), and each commune has its own rules concerning the use of water, which vary from area to area. Water, or rather the lack of it, is a major concern in many areas of Italy and the price paid for those long, hot summers. There's generally sufficient water in the north, but central and southern areas (and the islands) often experience acute shortages in the summer. Water shortages are exacerbated by poor infrastructure (up to 50 per cent is lost due to leaking pipes in some areas) and wastage due to poor irrigation methods.

Water is usually metered and the meter installed at the householder's expense. If water is metered, as in most of northern Italy, it's usual to have a contract for a limited number of cubic metres per household, per year (e.g. 300m3), irrespective of the number of occupants. You're charged a higher rate for consumption above this limit.

> ☑ **SURVIVAL TIP**
>
> You cannot use 'household' water for a garden or swimming pool, for which you need a special contract (called *uso vario*) and a separate meter.

In rural areas, you may have access to 'agricultural' water for garden use and you should check this, as a *uso vario* contract can cost €500 to €1,000 per year. In some regions, the cost is prohibitive and therefore few residents have swimming pools, although there are alternatives:

● You can recycle water for the garden

● You can have a pool filled by tanker (*autobotte*).

● In some areas, you can build an artificial water basin (*vasca*) that fills with rainwater during the winter and can also be fed by a spring or well. With a lining and filtering system, a *vasca* can even double as a swimming pool in summer.

Cost

The price of water varies considerably from region to region according to its availability, and is among the most expensive in Europe. In central Italy, water costs around €0.40 per m3. When moving into a new home, ask the local water company to read your meter. Where no water meter is installed, water is calculated on the size of a home (in square metres). Apulia has the highest average water bill – €330 per year – while Molise has the lowest, €138.78. You receive a bill (*acquedotto comunale*) every six months after your meter has been read. Like other utility bills, water bills may be paid by direct debit (*domiciliazione*) from a bank account; unlike in some other countries, in Italy your water is unlikely to be cut off if you're late paying a bill.

Most apartment blocks (*condomini*) have a single meter for the whole block, where the cost is shared equally between owners and included in the fees or expenses (*spese*), which isn't recommended if you have a holiday home in Italy.

Shortages

Water shortages are rare in towns, although they do occur occasionally, but are common in rural areas during the summer, when the water is periodically switched off. In areas with prolonged droughts, water may be switched off from 6pm to 6am daily to conserve supplies. Water shortages are exacerbated in resort areas in summer, when the local population may swell tenfold, and coincides with the hottest and driest period of the year. The use of sprinklers and hose-pipes is banned in many areas in summer. If you plan to maintain a garden in a region with low rainfall, you need a reserve supply for dry periods (you can also use waste water). In some areas, water shortages create low water pressure, resulting in insufficient water to take a bath or shower.

If you live in an area where cuts are common, you can have a storage tank (*cassone*) installed, which is topped up automatically when the water is switched on.

A 500 litre tank is usually large enough for a family living in an apartment in a city or in a rural area that doesn't suffer water shortages. In a rural area without mains water, it may be necessary to install an underground tank of 500,000 or one million litres (1,000m3) which is large enough to supply a family for up to six months. This is filled by tanker and is expensive.

Quality

When water isn't drinkable it's usually marked 'non-drinking' (*acqua non potabile*). Water from wells and springs isn't always safe to drink. You can have well or spring water analysed by the public health department or the local water authority. It's possible to install filtering, cleansing and softening equipment to improve water quality, but you should obtain independent advice before installing a system, as not all equipment is equally effective. While boiling water kills any bacteria, it won't remove any toxic substances contained in it.

⚠ **Caution**

Although mains water in Italy is usually drinkable, it may be contaminated by industrial chemicals and nitrates, although supposedly not enough to harm your health. However, many Italians consider it undrinkable and drink bottled water (when not drinking wine!).

In general, water is hard in Italy with a high calcium content. In some areas the iron, calcium and other minerals stain sinks and porcelain, which can be removed only by rubbing regularly with a soft pumice stone. You can use a water softener to soften hard water and a filter to prevent the furring of pipes, radiators and appliances. Water in Italy may be fluoridated, depending on the area.

Wells

Beware of the quaint well (*pozzo*) or spring (*sorgente*) as they can dry up, particularly in parts of central and southern Italy. Always confirm that a property has a reliable water source. If the water supply is from a spring or well (possibly on a neighbour's land), make sure that there's no dispute over its ownership and your rights to use it, e.g. that it cannot be stopped or drained away by your neighbours. However, well water is usually excellent (and free), although you may need a pump (manual or electric) to bring it to the surface. You can also create your own well if land has water.

Dowsing (finding water by holding a piece of forked wood) is as accurate as anything devised by modern science and has an 80 per cent success rate. A good dowser or water diviner (*rabdomante*) can estimate the water's yield and purity to within 80 or 90 per cent accuracy. Before buying rural land without a water supply, engage an experienced dowser with a successful track record to check it. Rural homes with their own well or spring are at a premium in Italy.

Mains Connection

If you own a property in or near a town or village, you can usually be connected to a mains water system. However, connection can be expensive as you must pay for digging the channels required for pipes.

Obtain a quotation (*preventivo*) from the local water company for the connection of the supply and the installation of a water meter. Expect the connection to cost at least €800 and possibly much more, depending on the terrain and soil (or rock!) which must be excavated to lay pipes. If you're thinking about buying a property and installing a mains water supply, obtain a quotation before signing the contract.

Water Heaters

If you need to install a hot water boiler or immersion heater, ensure that it's large enough for the size of property, e.g. one room studio (100 litres), two rooms (150 litres), three to four rooms (200 litres) and five to seven rooms or two bathrooms (300 litres). Many holiday homes have quite small water boilers that are often inadequate for more than two people. If you need to install a water heater or a larger water heater, you should consider the merits of both electric and bottled gas heaters. An electric water boiler with a capacity of 75 litres (sufficient for two people) usually takes between 75 to 125 minutes (in winter) to heat water to 40°C (104°F).

A (bottle) gas flow-through water heater is more expensive to purchase and install than an electric water boiler, but you get unlimited hot water immediately whenever you want it and there are no standing charges. A gas heater should have a capacity of 10 to 16 litres per minute if it's to be used for a shower. There's usually little difference in quality between heaters, although a gas water heater with a permanent flame may use up to 50 per cent more gas than one without. A resident family with a constant consumption is usually better off with an electric heater, while non-residents using a property for short periods will find a self-igniting gas heater more economical. A solar power system can also be used to provide hot water.

Security Measures

Before moving into a new home you should check where the main stop-valve or stopcock is located, so that you can turn off the water supply in an emergency. If the water stops flowing for any reason, you should ensure that all the taps are turned off to prevent flooding when the supply starts again. In community properties the tap to turn the water on or off is usually located outside the building.

☑ SURVIVAL TIP

Water damage caused by burst pipes due to old age or freezing may be excluded from insurance policies and, under Italian law, you're required to turn off the water at the mains if a property is left empty for more than 24 hours.

When leaving a property empty for an extended period, particularly during the winter when there's the possibility of freezing, you should turn off the main stopcock, switch off the system's controls and drain the pipes, toilets (you can leave salt in the toilet bowls to prevent freezing) and radiators. It's also recommended to have your cold water tank and the tank's ball valves checked periodically for corrosion, and to check the hosing on appliances such as washing machines and dishwashers. It can be very expensive if a pipe bursts and the leak goes undiscovered for a long time!

Sunset over St. Paul's, Rome

Campania

APPENDICES

APPENDIX A: USEFUL ADDRESSES

Embassies & Consulates

Foreign embassies in Italy are located in Rome, although many countries also have consulates in other major cities. Bear in mind that office business hours vary considerably and all embassies close on their national holidays as well as on Italy's public holidays (see page 116). It's advisable to telephone and check the business hours before visiting. A selection of embassies is listed below:

Australia: Via Antonio Bosio 5, 00161 Rome (☎ 06-8527 21, 💻 www.australian-embassy.it).

Austria: Via G.B. Pergolesi 3, 00198 Rome (☎ 06-844 0141, 💻 www.bmeia.gv.at).

Belgium: Via dei Monti Parioli 49, 00197 Rome (☎ 06-3609 511, 💻 www.diplomatie.be/rome).

Canada: Via G.B. de Rossi 27, 00161 Rome (☎ 06-4459 81, 💻 www.international.gc.ca/canada-europa/italy/).

Czech Republic: Via dei Gracchi 332, 00192 Rome (☎ 06-3244 459, 💻 www.mfa.cz/rome).

Denmark: Via dei Monti Parioli 50, 00197 Rome (☎ 06-3200 441, 💻 www.danishembassy.it).

Finland: Via Lisbona 3, 00198 Rome (☎ 06-8522 31, 💻 www.finland.it).

France: Piazza Farnese 67, 00186 Rome (☎ 06-6860 11, 💻 www.missioneco.org/italie).

Germany: Via di Villa Sacchetti 4–6, Rome (☎ 06-809 511, 💻 www.deutschebotschaft-rom.it).

Greece: Via Mercadante 36, 00198 Rome (☎ 06-8549 630, 💻 www.ambasciatagreca.it).

Hungary: Via Villini 12/16, 00161 Rome (☎ 06-4402 032).

Ireland: Piazza di Campitelli 3, 00186 Rome (☎ 06-6792 354).

The Netherlands: Via Michele Mercati 8, 00197 Rome (☎ 06-3228 6011, 💻 www.olanda.it).

Poland: Via Rubens 20, 00197 Rome (☎ 06-3224 455).

Portugal: Via Liege N21, 00198 Rome (☎ 06-8073 801).

South Africa: Via Tanaro 14, 00198 Rome (☎ 06-8525 41).

Spain: Largo Fontanella Borghese 19, 00186 Rome (☎ 06-6840 401).

United Kingdom: Via XX Settembre 80, 00187 Rome (☎ 06-4220 0001, 💻 www.britishembassy.gov.uk).

United States of America: Via Vittorio Veneto 119/A-121, 00187 Rome (☎ 06-4674 1, 💻 www.usembassy.it).

British Provincial Consulates

Bari: Anglo Italian Shipping, Via Dalmazio 127, 70121 Bari (☎ 080-5543 668).

Cagliari: Viale Colombo 160, 09045 Quartu SE (☎ 070-828628).

Florence: Lungarno Corsini 2, 50123 Florence (☎ 055-284133).

Genoa: Piazza G Verdi 6/A, Genova (☎ 010-5740 071).

Milan: Via San Paolo 7, 20121 Milan (☎ 02-7230 01).

Naples: Via dei Mille 40, 80121 Naples (☎ 081-4238 911).

Palermo: Via Cavour 121, 90133 Palermo (☎ 091-3264 12).

Rome: Via XX Settembre 80ª, 00187 Rome (☎ 06-4220 0001, ✉ ConsulEnquiries@rome.mail.fco.gov.uk).

Trieste: Via Roma 15, Trieste (☎ 040-3478 303, ✉ jododds@tin.it).

Venice: Piazzale Donatori di Sangue 2/5, Venice (☎ 041-5055 990, ✉ britconvenice@tin.it).

Property Exhibitions

Property exhibitions are common in Britain and Ireland, which include Italian property. Below is a list of the main exhibition organisers in Britain and Ireland.

Homebuyer Show (☎ UK 020-7069 5000, 🖥 www.homebuyer.co.uk). Homebuyer stage annual Homebuyer and Investor property exhibitions in March in London (Excel) and Birmingham (NEC), respectively.

Homes Overseas (☎ UK 020-7324 1599, 🖥 www.homesoverseas.co.uk/ events). Homes Overseas is one of the largest organisers of international property exhibitions, and stages a number of exhibitions each year at various venues in Britain and Ireland.

International Homes Show (☎ UK 01245-358877, 🖥 www.international-homes.com). The International Homes Show is held several times a year at venues around Britain.

A Place in the Sun (☎ UK 01737-786800, 🖥 www.aplaceinthesun.com). A Place in the Sun is both a TV programme (Channel 4) and magazine publisher, which organises property shows in London, Manchester and Birmingham.

World of Property (☎ UK 01323-726040, 🖥 www.worldofproperty.co.uk). World of Property organise a number of large UK property exhibitions a year, in addition to emigration exhibitions.

APPENDIX B: FURTHER READING

Newspapers & Magazines

Casa per Casa, Via Valtellina 21, 20092 Cinisello Balsamo/MI (☎ 02-660 6161, 🖳 www.casapercasa.it). Free weekly property magazine published in Milan and Rome regional editions.

Dimore-Homes and Villas of Italy, Via Cristoforo Colombo 440, 00145 Rome (☎ 06-5422 5128, 🖳 www.dimore.com). Magazine dedicated to luxury homes and properties for sale, with English/Italian text.

English Yellow Pages, Via Belisario 4/B, 00187 Rome (☎ 06-4740 861, 🖳 www.englishyellowpages.it).

Grapevine, CP 62, 55060 Guamo/LU (☎ 0583-909 012, 🖳 www. luccagrapevine.com). Monthly English-language magazine for Lucca and the surrounding area.

Hello Milano (☎ 02-2952 0570, 🖳 www.hellomilano.it). Free monthly entertainment magazine.

Homes Overseas, Globespan Media Ltd, 1st Floor, 1 East Poultry Avenue, London EC1A 9PT, UK (☎ 0207-002 8300, 🖳 www.homesoverseas.co.uk). Monthly property magazine.

The Informer, Via dei Tigli 2, 20020 Arese/MI (☎ 02-9358 1477, 🖳 www. informer.it). A monthly online magazine for expatriates, and the best source of online information available for those buying property and living and working in Italy.

International Homes, 3 St Johns Court, Moulsham Street, Chelmsford, Essex CM2 0JD, UK (☎ 01245-358877, 🖳 www.international-homes. com). Bi-monthly magazine.

Italian Magazine (☎ 01225-786850, 🖳 www.merricksmagazines.co.uk). Monthly lifestyle and property magazine.

Italy (☎ 01305-266360, 🖳 www.italymag.co.uk). Monthly magazine that covers all aspects of visiting and living in Italy, including property.

Panorama Casa, Edizioni Panorama, Viale Spartaco Lavagnini 42, 50129 Florence (☎ 055-50701, 🖳 www.panoramacasa.it). Free weekly property guide to Tuscany.

Più Case, Viale Tunisia 41, 20124 Milan (☎ 06-620 291, 🖳 www.piucase. it). Weekly property guide covering Rome and Lazio, Milan and Lombardy, Turin and Piedmont, and Genoa and Liguria.

Ville e Casali, Edizioni Living International, Via Anton Giulio Bragaglia 33, 00123 Rome (☎ 06-3028 2202, 🖳 www.villeecasali.com). Glossy monthly home magazine containing a catalogue of luxury properties, with summaries of articles and house descriptions in English.

Wanted in Rome, Via dei Falegnami 79, 00186 Rome (☎ 06-6867 967, 🖳 www.wantedinrome.com). Fortnightly magazine published in Rome with classified ads, jobs, accommodation (rentals, properties for sale, holiday properties), what's on and lifestyle articles.

Where Rome, Via Ostiense 172, 00154 Rome (☎ 06-5781 615, 🖳 www. whererome.it). Free monthly entertainments magazine.

Books

Listed below are a selection of the many books of interest to those planning to buy a home or live in Italy. Some titles may be out of print but may still be available from bookshops and libraries. Note that some books may have different publishers in the UK and the USA.

Food

Bringing Italy Home, Ursula Ferrigno (Mitchell Beasley)

Celebrating Italy, Carol Field (Harper Perennial)

Cheap Eats in Italy, Sandra Gustafson (Chronicle)

The Classic Italian Cookbook, Marcella Hazan (Macmillan)

The Dictionary of Italian Food and Drink, John F. Mariani (Broadway Books)

The Edible Italian Garden, Rosalind Creasy (Periplus)

Essentials of Classic Italian Cooking, Marcella Hazan (Knopf)

Floyd on Italy, Keith Floyd (Penguin)

A Food Lover's Companion to Tuscany, Carla Capalbo (Chronicle)

Francesco's Kitchen, Francesco da Mosto (Ebury Press)

Gastronomy of Italy, Anna del Conte (Pavilion)

Italy for the Gourmet Traveler, Fred Plotkin (Kyle Cathie)

Jamie's Italy, Jamie Oliver (Michael Joseph)

Little Italy Cookbook, David Reggurio & Melanie Acevedo (Artisan)

Michelin Red Guide Italy (Michelin)

Return to Tuscany, Giancarlo & Katie Caldesi (BBC Books)

Slow Food Nation, Carlo Petrini (Rizzoli)

Tasting Tuscany: Exploring and Eating Off the Beaten Track, Beth Elon (Bantam)

Walking and Eating in Tuscany & Umbria, James Ladsun & Others (Penguin)

World Food Italy, Matthew Evans & Gabriella Cossi (Lonely Planet)

Houses, Gardens and Villages

Edith Wharton's Italian Gardens, Vivian Russell (Ecco Press)

Gardens of the Italian Lakes, Judith Chatfield (Rizzoli)

Gardens of Tuscany, Ethne Clark (Weidenfeld & Nicolson)

Great Houses of Tuscany: The Tuscan Villas (Viking)

The Hill Towns of Tuscany, Richard Kauffman & Carol Field (Chronicle)

Italian Country Style, Robert Fitzgerald & Peter Porter (Fairfax)

Italian Villas and Gardens, Paul van der Ree

Italian Villas and Their Gardens, Edith Wharton (Da Capo)

Italy: A Complete Guide to 1,000 towns and Cities and Their Landmarks (Touring Club Italiano)

Italy: The Hill Towns, James Bentley (Aurum)

The Most Beautiful Villages of Tuscany, James Bentley & Hugh Palmer (Thames & Hudson)

Restoring a Home in Italy, Elizabeth Helman Minchilli (Artisan)

Traditional Houses of Rural Italy, Paul Duncan (Collins & Brown)

Urban Land and Property Markets in Italy, Gastone Ave (UCL Press)

Living

After Hannibal, Barry Unsworth (Penguin)

Bella Tuscany, Frances Mayes (Bantam)

Desiring Italy, Susan Neunzig Cahill (Fawcett Books)

Extra Virgin: Among the Olive Groves of Liguria, Annie Hawes (Penguin)

Francesco's Italy, Francesco da Mosto (BBC Books)

Francesco's Venice, Francesco da Mosto (BBC Books)

The Hills of Tuscany: A New Life In An Old Land, Ferenc Matè (Harper & Collins)

A House in Sicily, Daphne Phelps (Carroll & Graf)

An Italian Education: The Further Adventures of an Expatriate in Verona, Tim Parks (Avon Books)

Italian Neighbours, Tim Parks (Fawcett Books)

Journey to the South, Annie Hawes (Penguin)

Living and Working in Italy, edited by Graeme Chesters (Survival Books)

No Going Back: Tuscan Living, Sarah Frazer (Cassell)

North of Naples, South of Rome, Paolo Tullio (Lilliput Press)

A Place in Italy, Simon Mawer (Sinclair Stevenson)

Private Tuscany, Elizabeth Helman-Minchilli & Others (Rizzoli)

Ripe for the Picking, Annie Hawes (Penguin)

A Small Place in Italy, Eric Newby (Picador)

Survival Guide to Milan, Jessica Halpern (Informer)

A Thousand Days in Tuscany, Marlena de Blasi (Virago)

A Thousand Days in Venice: An Unexpected Romance, Marlena de Blasi (Virago)

A Tuscan Childhood, Kinta Beevor (Penguin)

Under the Tuscan Sun, Frances Mayes (Broadway Books)

A Valley in Italy: The Many Seasons of a Villa in Umbria, Lisa St. Aubin de Terán (Harperperennial)

Venice: the Most Triumphant City, George Bull

Views from a Tuscan Vineyard, Carey More (Pavillion)

Within Tuscany, Matthew Spender (Penguin)

Wine

Guide to Italian Wine, Burton Anderson (Mitchell Beazley)

The Italian Wine Guide (TCI/Abbeville Press)

Italian Wines, Victor Hazan (Kyle Cathie)

Italian Wines, Gamberro Rosso (Gambero Rosso)

Slow Food Guide to Italian Wine (GRUB)

Touring in Wine Country: Northwest Italy, Maureen Ashley (Mitchell Beazley)

A Traveller's Wine Guide to Italy, Stephen Hobley (Traveller's Wine Guides)

Vino, Burton Anderson (Little, Brown)

Vino Italiano, Joseph Bastianich & David Lynch (Random House)

Wines of Italy, Michele Shah (Mitchell Beazley)

APPENDIX C: USEFUL WEBSITES

There are dozens of websites dedicated to Italy, many of them targeted specifically at expatriates living in Italy, a selection of which is listed below. A useful feature found on most expatriate websites is the 'message board' or 'forum', where expatriates answer questions based on their experience and knowledge, offering an insight into what living and working in Italy (or in a particular region or town) is really like.

Alitalia (🖥 www.alitalia.it). The site of the country's state airline.

Citizens Portal (🖥 www.italia.gov.it). Useful information about Italian administration (in Italian only).

Datasport (🖥 www.datasport.it). A comprehensive site dedicated to Italian sport (in Italian only).

Dolce Vita (🖥 www.dolcevita.com). Dubs itself 'the insider's guide to Italy' and covers fashion, design, cuisine, travel and events (in English).

Enit Online (🖥 www.enit.it). The official Italian tourist board site available in several languages, including English.

Hello Milano (🖥 www.hellomilano.it). Information on just about everything to do with Milan.

Informer Magazine (🖥 www.informer.it). Comprehensive information for expatriates living and working in Italy, including a useful 'Ask John' question and answer service and an excellent guide to Italian red tape.

In Italy Online (🖥 www.initaly.com). Over 4,000 pages of information about Italy, its regions, places to visit and things to do, as well as practical advice about day-to-day living.

Italian Automobile Club (🖥 www.aci.it). The site of Italy's leading motoring organisation has plenty of useful information about driving in the country (in Italian only).

Italian Government (🖥 www.governo.it). The Italian government's website, with information about all aspects of life in the country (in Italian only).

Italian Institute for Foreign Trade (🖥 www.italtrade.com). An organisation that promotes trade, business opportunities and industrial cooperation between Italian and foreign companies.

Italian Telephone Directory (🖥 www.pb.alice.it).

Italian Tourism USA (🖥 www.italiantourism.com). The Italian government's site for North American visitors, packed with information about Italy.

Italian Yellow Pages (🖥 www.paginegialle.it). The site has an English-language search facility.

Know Italy (🖥 www.knowital.com). Holiday rental information for most areas and travel and tourist information.

Made In Italy (🖥 www.made-in-italy.com). Useful guide to travel and shopping in Italy.

Museums Online (🖥 www.museionline.com). A guide to Italy's museums and their exhibits, including an English version.

Romebuddy.com (🖥 www.romebuddy.com). A general guide to all aspects of living in Rome and Italy.

Ticket Italy (🖥 www.tickitaly.com). A portal through which you can book tickets for museums and art galleries.

Travel Italy (🖥 www.travel.it). Contains information about everything from archaeology to thermal spas and religious tourism.

APPENDIX D: WEIGHTS & MEASURES

Italy uses the metric system of measurement. Those who are more familiar with the imperial system of measurement will find the tables on the following pages useful. Some comparisons shown are only approximate, but are close enough for most everyday uses.

In addition to the variety of measurement systems used, clothes sizes often vary considerably with the manufacturer. Try all clothes on before buying and don't be afraid to return them if, when you try them on at home, you decide they don't fit (most shops will exchange goods or give a refund).

Women's Clothes

Continental	34	36	38	40	42	44	46	48	50	52
UK	8	10	12	14	16	18	20	22	24	26
US	6	8	10	12	14	16	18	20	22	24

Pullovers

	Women's						Men's					
Continental	40	42	44	46	48	50	44	46	48	50	52	54
UK	34	36	38	40	42	44	34	36	38	40	42	44
US	34	36	38	40	42	44	sm	med	lar	xl		

Men's Shirts

Continental	36	37	38	39	40	41	42	43	44	46
UK/US	14	14	15	15	16	16	17	17	18	-

Men's Underwear

Continental	5	6	7	8	9	10
UK	34	36	38	40	42	44
US		sm	med		lar	xl

Note: sm = small, med = medium, lar = large, xl = extra large

Children's Clothes

Continental	92	104	116	128	140	152
UK	16/18	20/22	24/26	28/30	32/34	36/38
US	2	4	6	8	10	12

Children's Shoes

Continental	18 19 20 21 22 23 24 25 26 27 28 29 30 31 32
UK/US	2 3 4 4 5 6 7 7 8 9 10 11 11 12 13
Continental	33 34 35 36 37 38
UK/US	1 2 2 3 4 5

Shoes (Women's and Men's)

Continental	35 36 37 37 38 39 40 41 42 42 43 44
UK	2 3 3 4 4 5 6 7 7 8 9 9
US	4 5 5 6 6 7 8 9 9 10 10 11

Weight

Imperial	Metric	Metric	Imperial
1oz	28.35g	1g	0.035oz
1lb*	454g	100g	3.5oz
1cwt	50.8kg	250g	9oz
1 ton	1,016kg	500g	18oz
2,205lb	1 tonne	1kg	2.2lb

Length

British/US	Metric	Metric	British/US
1in	2.54cm	1cm	0.39in
1ft	30.48cm	1m	3ft 3.25in
1yd	91.44cm	1km	0.62mi
1mi	1.6km	8km	5mi

Capacity

Imperial	Metric	Metric	Imperial
1 UK pint	0.57 litre	1 litre	1.75 UK pints
1 US pint	0.47 litre	1 litre	2.13 US pints
1 UK gallon	4.54 litres	1 litre	0.22 UK gallon
1 US gallon	3.78 litres	1 litre	0.26 US gallon

Note: An American 'cup' = around 250ml or 0.25 litre.

Area

British/US	Metric	Metric	British/US
1 sq. in	0.45 sq. cm	1 sq. cm	0.15 sq. in
1 sq. ft	0.09 sq. m	1 sq. m	10.76 sq. ft
1 sq. yd	0.84 sq. m	1 sq. m	1.2 sq. yds
1 acre	0.4 hectares	1 hectare	2.47 acres
1 sq. mile	2.56 sq. km	1 sq. km	0.39 sq. mile

Temperature

°Celsius	°Fahrenheit	
0	32	(freezing point of water)
5	41	
10	50	
15	59	
20	68	
25	77	
30	86	
35	95	
40	104	
50	122	

Notes: The boiling point of water is 100°C / 212°F.

Normal body temperature (if you're alive and well) is 37°C / 98.6°F.

Temperature Conversion

Celsius to Fahrenheit: multiply by 9, divide by 5 and add 32. (For a quick and approximate conversion, double the Celsius temperature and add 30.)

Fahrenheit to Celsius: subtract 32, multiply by 5 and divide by 9. (For a quick and approximate conversion, subtract 30 from the Fahrenheit temperature and divide by 2.)

Oven Temperatures

Gas	Electric °F	°C
-	225–250	110–120
1	275	140
2	300	150
3	325	160
4	350	180
5	375	190
6	400	200
7	425	220
8	450	230
9	475	240

Air Pressure

PSI	Bar
10	0.5
20	1.4
30	2
40	2.8

Power

Kilowatts	Horsepower	Horsepower	Kilowatts
1	1.34	1	0.75

Trevi Fountain, Rome

APPENDIX E: MAPS

The map opposite shows the 20 administrative regions of Italy, which are listed below with the 110 provinces (and their official abbreviations). The maps on the following pages show transport links.

Region	Provinces
Abruzzo (*Abruzzi*)	Chieti (CH), L'Aquila (AQ), Pescara (PE), Teramo (TE)
Basilicata (*Lucania*)	Matera (MT), Potenza (PZ)
Calabria	Cantazaro (CZ), Cosenza CS), Reggio di Calabria (RC)
Campania	Avellino (AV), Benevento (BN), Caserta (CE), Naples/Napoli (NA), Salerno (SA)
Emilia Romagna	Bologna (BO), Ferrara (FE), Forli-Cesena (FC), Modena (MO), Piacenza (PC), Parma (PR), Ravenna (RA), Reggio Emilia (RE)
Friuli-Venezia Giuila	Gorizia (GO), Pordenone (PN), Trieste (TS), Udine (UD)
Lazio (*Latium*)	Frosinone (FR), Latina (LT), Rieti (RI), Rome/Roma (ROMA),Viterbo (VT)
Liguria	Genova (GE), Imperia (IM), La Spezia (SP), Savona (SV)
Lombardy (Lombardia)	Bergamo (BG), Brescia (BS), Como (CO), Cremona (CR), Mantua/Mantova (MN), Milan/Milano (MI), Pavia (PV), Sondrio (SO), Varese (VA)
Marche	Ancona (AN), Ascoli Piceno (AP), Macerata (MC), Pesaro (PS)
Molise (*Molize*)	Campobasso (CB), Isernia (IS)
Piedmont (*Piemonte*)	Alessandria (AL), Asti (AT), Cuneo (CN), Novara (NO), Turin/Torino (TO), Verbania-Cusio-Ossola (VB), Vercelli (VC)
Puglia (*Apulia/ Le Puglie*)	Bari (BA), Brindisi (BR), Foggia (FG), Lecce (LE), Taranto (TA)
Sardinia (*Sardegna*)	Cagliari (CA), Nuoro (NU), Oristano (OR), Sassari (SS)
Sicily (*Sicilia*)	Agrigento (AG), Caltanissetta (CL), Catania (CT), Enna (EN), Messina (ME), Palermo (PA), Ragusa (RG), Syracuse/Siracusa (SR), Trapini (TP)
Tuscany (*Toscana*)	Arezzo (AR), Florence/Firenze (FI), Grosseto (GR), Leghorn/Livorno (LI), Lucca (LU), Massa Carrara (MS), Pisa (PI), Pistoia (PT), Sienna (SI)
Trentino-Alto Adige	Bolzano (BZ), Trento (TN)
Umbria	Perugia (PG), Terni (TR)
Val d'Aosta	Aosta (AO)
Veneto	Belluno (BL), Padua/Padova (PD), Rovigo (RO), Treviso (TV), Venice/Venezia (VE), Verona (VR), Vicenza (VI)

AIRPORTS & PORTS

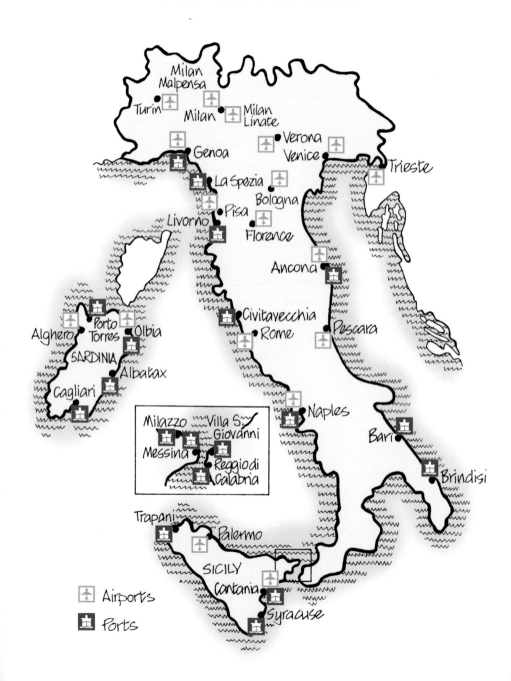

RAIL NETWORK

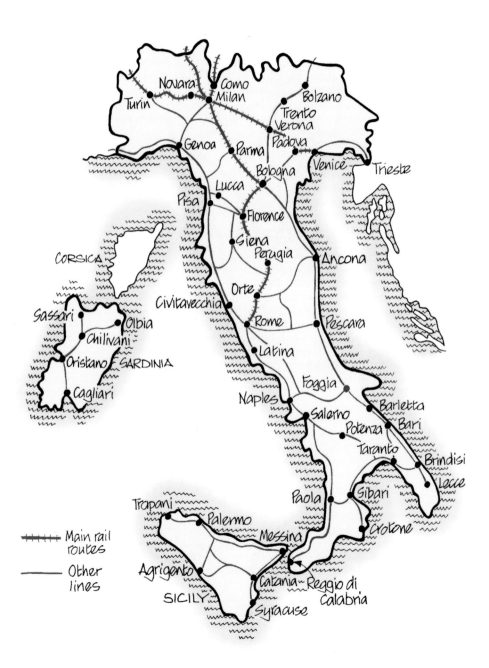

MOTORWAYS & MAJOR ROADS

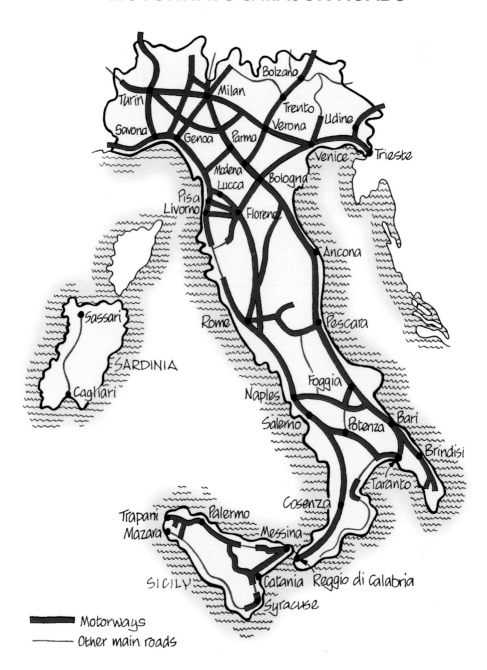

APPENDIX F: AIRLINE SERVICES

The tables on the following pages indicate scheduled flights from UK and Irish airports to Italy. Details were current in mid-2007. Airlines are coded as shown below (note that these aren't all official airline codes).

Code	Airline	Telephone	Website
AL	Aer Lingus	+353 (0)818-365000	www.aerlingus.com
AI	Air Italy	+356-2364 5300	www.airitaly.eu
AT	Alitalia	0870-544 8259	www.alitalia.com
BA	British Airways	0870-850 9850	www.britishairways.com
		(199-7122 66 in Italy)	
BM	BMI	0870-6070 555	www.flybmi.com
BI	bmibaby	0870-264 229	www.bmibaby.com
EJ	Easy Jet	0871-244 2366	www.easyjet.com
		(899-234 589 in Italy)	
XL	Excel	0870-320 7777	www.xl.com
FC	First Choice Airways	0871-200 7799	www.firstchoice.co.uk
FL	FLYBE	0871-522 6100	www.flybe.com
J2	Jet2	0871-226 737	www.jet2.com
ME	Meridiana	+39 0789-52600	www.meridiana.it
MO	Monarch	0870-040 5040	www.flymonarch.com
MT	My Travel Airways	45-3247 7200	www.mytravelairways.com
RA	Ryanair	0871-246 0000	www.ryanair.com
SA	SATA	351-296 209 720	www.sata.pt
TC	Thomas Cook	0870-243 0416	www.thomascookairlines.co.uk
TF	Thomsonfly	0870-1900 737	www.thomsonfly.com

Airport	Belfast	Birmingham	Bristol	Dublin	East Midlands	Edinburgh
Alghero				RA	RA	BM
Ancona						
Bari						
Bologna			AL	RA		
Brindisi						
Cagliari						
Catania						
Florence						
Forli			RA			
Genoa						
Lamezia Terme						
Milan Linate				AL		
Milan Malpensa		FL	EJ	AL		EJ
Naples	FC, MT	MO, TF	FC, MT	AL	FC, TC	
Olbia						
Palermo						
Palma						
Perugia						
Pescara						
Pisa	J2		EJ		RA	J2
Rimini					RA	
Rome Ciampino	EJ		EJ	RA	EJ, RA	
Rome Fiumicino		BI		AL, AT		
Trapani				RA		
Trieste						
Turin						
Venice Marco Polo	EJ		EJ	AL	EJ	
Venice Treviso				RA		
Verona		TF	TF			

Airport	Glasgow	Leeds/Bradford	Liverpool	London Gatwick	London Heathrow	London Luton
Alghero			RA	TC, TF		
Ancona			RA			
Bari				BA		
Bologna				BA		
Brindisi						
Cagliari				BA, ME		EJ
Catania				BA, MO		EJ
Florence				ME		
Forli						
Genoa						
Lamezia Terme				FC		
Milan Linate				EJ	AT, BA	
Milan Malpensa					AT, BA	
Naples	TF			BA, MO	BM	
Olbia				EJ, FC, ME, MT		
Palermo				EJ		
Palma						
Perugia						
Pescara						
Pisa	RA	J2	RA	BA, EJ, SA, TF		
Rimini						EJ
Rome Ciampino	RA		RA	EJ		RA
Rome Fiumicino		J2		BA	AT, BA	
Trapani						
Trieste						
Turin				BA		EJ
Venice Marco Polo		J2		BA, EJ	BM	
Venice Treviso	BM		RA	MO		
Verona	TF			BA, FC, TF		

Airport	London Stansted	Manchester	Newcastle
Alghero	RA		
Ancona	RA		
Bari	RA		
Bologna			
Brindisi	RA		
Cagliari			
Catania		MO, TC, TF	
Florence			
Forli	RA		
Genoa	RA		
Lamezia Terme	RA		
Milan Linate			
Milan Malpensa		AT, FL	
Naples	EJ	FC	TF
Olbia	J2		
Palermo	RA		
Palma	RA		
Perugia	RA		
Pescara	RA		
Pisa	RA	J2, TF	J2
Rimini		MT	
Rome Ciampino	RA		EJ
Rome Fiumicino		J2	
Trapani			
Trieste	RA		
Turin	RA		
Venice Marco Polo		J2, TF	
Venice Treviso	RA	MO	
Verona	AI, RA	EX, FC, TF	

APPENDIX G: GLOSSARY

Abbonamento: Standing charge, e.g. for electricity, gas, telephone or water services; subscription, e.g. to a magazine; season ticket for public transport

Abitabile: Habitable

Abitazione (tipo di): The housing category that determines the level of property and other taxes

Abusivo: Abusive (the word is used to denote illegal building or alterations to a building)

Acqua: Water

Acqua di sorgente: Spring water

Acquedotto comunale: Municipal water supply

Acquistare su carta: Buying off plan, i.e. before a property has been built

Affittacamere: Rooms for rent (usually cheaper than a *pensione* and not part of the official classification system)

Affittasi: To let; for rent

Affresco: Fresco

Agenzia immobiliare: (real) Estate agency/brokers

Agriturismo: Working farm with rooms for guests; a structure for rural tourism

Albo degli artigiani: Official list of artisans; tradesmen

Albergo: Hotel with up to five stars

Alimentari: General food shop; grocer's

Alloggio: Lodging (usually cheaper than a *pensione* and not part of the official classification system)

Amministratore di condominio: Administrator of a community property, e.g. an apartment block

Ammobiliato: Furnished

Ammortizzare: Amortisation; the process of systematically reducing debt in equal payments (as in a mortgage), comprising both principal and interest, until the debt is paid in full

Anagrafe/Ufficio di Stato Civile: Bureau of vital statistics or census office

Angolo cottura: Cooking corner or small corner kitchen

Annessi: Annex; attached (usually small) outbuildings

Annesso: Annex; extension

Antico: Antique

Anticipo di pagamento: Deposit sometimes paid before signing a preliminary contract

Apparecchio: Appliance; machine

Appartamento: Apartment; flat

Appartamento ammobiliato: Furnished apartment

Appartamento in affitto: Rented apartment

Appartamento (di lusso) nell'attico: Penthouse; luxury apartment

Appartamento su due piani: Duplex (apartment on two floors)

Appartamento vacanze: Holiday apartment

Arcate: Row of free-standing arches carried on columns or piers forming a covered walk

Architetto: Architect

Arco: Arch

Aria condizionata/Condizionamento d'aria: Air-conditioning

Arredamento: Furnishings

Arredato: Furnished

Ascensore: Lift (elevator)

Assicurazione: Insurance

Assicurazione contro i terzi: Third party liability insurance

Astenersi agenzie: Without an agent, i.e. for rent/sale by owner

Attico: Top floor apartment or penthouse in a city or town; attic in the country

Atto di compravendita: Property conveyance document (also called *atto notarile*)

Attrezzata: Equipped

Autorimessa: Garage

Autostrada: Motorway (freeway), usually a toll road

Avvocato: Lawyer; solicitor

Azienda agricola: Farm

Bagno: Bathroom; toilet (restroom)

Balcone: Balcony; terrace

Barocco: Baroque

Bellissima: Beautiful

Ben conservata: Well preserved

Ben tenuto: Well maintained

Bifamiliare: Semi-detached (two-family building)

Bilocale: Consisting of two rooms

Bolletta: Bill

Bollo: State tax stamp

Bombola: Gas bottle

Bombolone: Gas tank used to store liquid gas

Borgo/Borghi: Ancient town or village, often walled

Borgo: A suburb (or city neighbourhood) or a street leading into a suburb from the centre of town; also a village

Bosco: Wood

Bovindo: Bay (or bow) window

Breve periodo: Short period or term

Buona posizione: Good position

Buono stato: Good condition

Cabina: Cabin

Calce: Lime

Caldaia: Boiler; water heater

Camera: Room

Camera di commercio: Chamber of commerce

Camera doppia: Twin room

Camera matrimoniale: Double room

Camera singola: Single room

Camera sul davanti (sul dietro): Front room (back room)

Cameretta: Small bedroom

Camino: Chimney; fireplace

Cantina: (wine) Cellar

Capannone: Barn

Caparra: Deposit

Caratteristico: Typical; characteristic

Carpentiere: Carpenter

Carta bollata: An official paper with a tax stamp

Carta d'Identitià: Identity card

Carta da parati: Wallpaper

Casa: House

Casa colonica: Farmhouse

Casa canonica: Old church house

Casa d'epoca: Period house

Casa gemella: Semi-detached house

Casa padronale: Country house

Casa popolare: Public, low-rent accommodation for low-income families

Casa di ringhiera: A traditional Milanese apartment block with apartment entrances off a long balcony above an internal courtyard

Casa rurale: Rural property

Casa signorile: Luxury home

Casa urbana: Urban property (note, however, that many rural country properties are classified as urban!)

Casale: Farmhouse

Cascina: Farmstead

Casetta: Small house

Casette a schiera: Terrace of a small worker's house

Cassone: Water storage tank

Castello: Castle

Catasto: Land registry

Cemento (bianco): Cement (white)

Centralissimo: Central

Centro: Centre

Centro storico: Historic centre; old town

Ceramica: Ceramic tiles

Certificato di matrimonio: Marriage certificate

Certificato di morte: Death certificate

Certificato di nascita: Birth certificate

Certificato di residenza: Residence permit

Chiave: Key

Cipollino: Onion marble with veins of green or white

Circoscrizione: A subdivision of a *comune*, e.g. Rome is one *comune* but has 20 *circoscrizioni*

Clausola (condizionale): (conditional) Clause in a contract

Codice fiscale: Fiscal or tax number

Colombaia: Pigeon house; dovecote

Colonna: Column

Colonnato: Row of columns placed at regular intervals, possibly carrying arches

Coltivatore diretto: Farmer

Commercialista: Accountant who completes tax returns

Comodissimo per i mezzi e negozi: Convenient for public transport and shops

Complesso residenziale: Residential complex

Compromesso (di vendita): Preliminary contract of sale

Comune: An administrative area, e.g. a self-governing town or city; a municipality or county, town or city council

Concessione edilizia: Planning permission

Concio d'angolo: Dressed stones at the corners of buildings

Condotta d'acqua: Water pipes

Con gusto: With taste; tastefully, e.g. furnished or decorated

Condizione: Condition

Condominio: Condominium or apartment; apartment block

Convivere: Sharing, e.g. an apartment or house

Congelatore: Freezer

Conguaglio: Adjustment – the term utility companies use to refer to a bill (issued twice a year) based on actual rather than estimated consumption

Consegna: Exchange of contracts

Conservatorio: Conservatory

Costruttore: Builder; developer

Costruzione: Building

Contatore: Meter, e.g. electricity

Contenuto dell' abitazione: House contents; inventory

Conto: Bill; account

Conto estero: Foreign currency bank account

Contrada: District

Contraente: Contracting party

Contratto: Contract

Contratto di affitto: Rental lease

Contratto preliminaire di vendita: Preliminary contract of sale

Coppi (vecchi): Roof tiles (old)

Corridoio: Hall; corridor

Corso: Main street; avenue; boulevard

(in) Corso di costruzione: Being built; in the process of being constructed

Cortile: Galleried courtyard; cloisters

Cotto: Terracotta

Cucina: Kitchen; cooker

Cucina abitabile: Eat-in kitchen

Cucina a gas: Gas cooker

Cucinotto: Small kitchen

Cupola: Dome

Decoratore: Decorator

Denuncia: Legal or police statement

Deposito: Deposit

Deruralizzato: The process whereby a rural agricultural building (such as a barn) is legally converted into a dwelling

Diritto di passaggic: Right of passage/way

Disdire: Cancel (a contract)

Disponibile: Available

Doccia: Shower

Dogana: Customs

Domiciliazione: Direct debit payment (from a bank)

Domicilio: Address

Doppi servizi: Two bathrooms

Doppi vetri: Double-glazing

Doppio garage: Double garage

Due piani: On two floors, e.g. a duplex or maisonnette

Edificio: Building; structure

Edilizia: Builder's yard

Elettricista: Electrician

Emergenza: Emergency

Ente Nazionale per l'Energia Electtrica (ENEL): The national electricity company

Elettrodomestici: Appliances, e.g. cooker, washing machine

Ente Nazionale Italiano del Turismo (ENIT): The Italian state tourist office

Entrata: Entrance

Entroterra: Hinterland

Equo canone: Fair rent or rent control

Ettaro (ha): Hectare (2.47 acres)

Fabbricato: Building

Fabbricato rurale: A rural or agricultural building that cannot be used as a dwelling until it has been 'de-ruralised'

Facciata: Façade

Fai da te: Do-it-yourself (DIY)

Falegname: Carpenter

Farmacia: Chemists (pharmacy)

Fattoria: Farm; farmhouse

Ferramenta: Hardware store

Ferrovia: Railway

Ferrovie dello Stato (FS): The Italian state railway company

Finiture di lusso: Luxury finish

Finestra: Window

Fisco: Italian tax authorities

Fiume: River

Fondamenta: Foundation of a house; a street beside a canal in Venice

Fontana: Fountain

Fornello: Cooker

Forno: Oven

Forno a legna: Wood-burning oven

Fossa settica: Septic tank

Francobollo: Postage stamp

Frigorifero: Refrigerator

Fronte mare: On the seafront

Frontone: Gable

Frutteto: Orchard

Fusibli: Fuses

Gabinetto: Toilet; WC

Geometra: Surveyor

Gesso: Plaster

Gettone: Telephone token

Ghiaia: Gravel

Giardiniere: Gardener

Giardino: Garden

Gotico: Gothic

Granaio: Barn

Grande: Large

Grattacielo: Skyscraper; tower block

Grezzo: Uncut stone

Grisaille: A style of painting on walls or ceilings in greyish tints, in imitation of bas-relief

Idraulico: Plumber

Idromassaggio: Jacuzzi; hot tub

Imbianchino: House painter

Impianto: Fixtures

Imposta: Tax; shutter (on windows)

Imposta Comunale sugli Immobili (ICI): Property tax set by a town

Imposta Comunale sull'Incremento di Valore degli Immobili (INVIM): Capital gains tax

Imposta Regionale sulle Attività Produttive (IRAP): Regional tax

Imposta sul Reddito delle Persone Fisiche (IRPEF): Personal income tax

Imposta sul Reddito delle Persone Guiridiche (IRPEG): Corporation tax which applies to companies and partnerships

Imposta di registro: Stamp duty

Imposta Servizio Comunale (ISCOM): Tax on communal services

Imposta sulle Successioni e Donazioni (ISD): Inheritance and gift tax

Imposta sul Valore Aggiunto (IVA): Value added tax

Indipendente: Detached

Indirizzo: Address

Ingegnere: Engineer

Ingresso: Entrance hall

Inquilino: Tenant

Installatore: Installer; electrician

Intarsio: Inlaid wood, marble or metal

Interrato: Basement

Intonacatore: Plasterer

Intonaco: Plaster

Inventario: Inventory

Ipoteca: Mortgage

IVA (Imposta sul Valore Aggiunto): Value added tax

Lago: Lake

Lampadina: Light bulb

Largo: Square; wide

Lavabo: Wash basin

Lavanderia: Laundry

Lavastoviglie: Dishwasher

Lavatoio: Public washhouse

Lavatrice: Washing machine

Lavoro di idraulico: Plumbing

Legname: Timber

Legno: Wood

Libero: Unoccupied; free

Libretto di lavoro: Work booklet or permit

Locanda: Inn; small hotel (usually cheaper than a *pensione*)

Loggia: Covered area on the side of a building; gallery or balcony open on one or more sides, sometimes arcaded; small garden house

Luce: Electricity; lights

Lungomare: Sea-front road; promenade

Lusso: Luxury

Maniero: Manor

Mansarda: Attic

Manutenzione: Maintenance

Marca da bollo: Tax stamp

Mare: Sea

Marmi: Marble

Mattone: Brick

Mensile: Monthly

Merceria: Haberdashery shop

Mercato: Market

Metrature: Size

Metri quadri (mq): Square metres

Mezza pensione: Half board

Mezzogiorno: Noon; colloquial name for the southern part of Italy

Millesimi: Term used to express the portion (in thousandths) of a community property owned by each owner

Misura: Size; measure

Mobilio: Furniture

Modernizzare: Modernisation

Monolocale (con servizi): Studio apartment

Monte: Mountain

Moquette: Carpet

Multiproprietà: Timeshare

Municipio: Town hall

Muratore: Mason; bricklayer

Muratura: Stonework

Muro: Wall

Mutuo compreso: Mortgage included

Notaio: Notary

Nuova: New

Occasione: Bargain; special offer

Officina: Workshop

Oliveto: Olive grove

(in) Ordine: (In) order, i.e. good condition

Originali: Original

Ostello: Hostel

Ottima posizione: Excellent position

Ottime condizioni/ottimo stato: Excellent condition

Padrone/Padrona: Landlord/landlady

Paese: Town; village; area

Paesino: Small village

Pagamento: Payment

(di) Paglia: Thatched

Palazzo: Palace; mansion; large building of any kind, including an apartment block

Parco: Park

Parquet: Parquet flooring

(in) Parte ristrutturato: Partly restored

Partita IVA: VAT registration number

Parzialmente arredato: Partially furnished

Pavimenti in cotto: Terracotta floors

Pavimento: Floor

Pazienza: Patience (something you will need in abundance when dealing with Italian bureaucracy!)

Pensione: Small hotel, often with board

Perfette condizioni: Perfect condition

Periferie: Suburbs

Perito agronomo: Land surveyor

Permessi comunali: Planning permission (granted by commune or town)

Permesso di soggiorno: Permit to stay

Piano: Floor (of a multi-storey building), e.g. *primo* (first), *secondo* (second), *terzo* (third)

Piano nobile: Main floor of a palace, usually the first floor (USA = second floor)

Piano regolatore: Zoning plan

Piano terra: Ground floor (USA = first floor)

Piastrelle: Tiles

Piastrellista: Tiler

Piazza: Square (in town or city)

Piazzale: Large open square

Piccolo: Small

Pietra/legno originale: Original stone/wood

Pietra serena: Soft, grey sandstone that's easily carved (common in Sienna)

Piscina: Swimming pool

Pitture: Paint

Più spese: Plus expenses

Poggiolo: Balcony

Polizia: Police

Ponte: Bridge

Pontile: Wharf for boats

Portico: Porch; covered walkway, usually attached to the outside of a building; roofed space, open or partly enclosed, forming the entrance and centre-piece to a façade

Portiere: Porter; doorman; janitor in an apartment block

Portinaio: Caretaker; concierge of an apartment block

Portineria: Porter's house

Porta: Door

Porta blindata: Armoured door

Porto: Port

Portone: Main entrance; door

(a) Posto: Everything in order; in good condition

Posto auto/macchina: Parking space

Pozzo: Well (for water)

Pozzo nero: Cesspit

Pratica: File; conveyancing

Prato: Lawn

Premio: Premium, e.g. insurance

Prestito: Loan

Preventivo: Estimate or quotation, e.g. for building work

Prezzo: Price

Prima casa: Principal home (as opposed to a second or holiday home) where you're resident

Primo piano: First floor (USA = second floor), called the *Piano nobile* in a *palazzo*

Procura: Power of attorney

Progetto approvato: Approved plans

Pronta consegna: Ready to move in

Proprietà: Property

Questura: Police station

Quotazione: Quotation

Rabdomante: Water diviner

Radiatori: Radiators

Ragioniere(a): Accountant

Referenziati: References required

Regolamento di condominio: Regulations for a community property

Rendita catastale: Cadastral value

(da) Restaurare/Ristrutturare: In need of restoration

Restaurato: Restored

(da) Ricostruire: In need of reconstruction

Rilevamento: Land survey

Rinascimento: Renaissance

Rinnovamento: Renovation

Riparazione: Repair

Ripostiglio: Store; junk room

Riscaldamento: Heating

Riscaldamento autonomo: Independent heating, which can be regulated or switched off by the tenant or the owners of the apartment

Riscaldamento centrale: Central heating. (In an apartment block, this is provided centrally for all apartments, with the cost divided equally between them.)

Rivo: Stream

Rocca: Fortress

Rococò: Rococo

Rogito: Act or contract, signed in front of notary

Romanico: Romanesque

Rovina/Rudere: Ruin (usually in a historical sense)

Rustico: Rustic building; old home requiring restoration or finishing

Sala: Room; hall

Sala da pranzo: Dining room

Salone: Sitting room; lounge; hall

Salotto: Sitting room; lounge

Salvavita: Electricity circuit breaker or trip switch

Sassi: Stones; houses in grottos in the town of Matera

Scala/Scalinata: Stairway; staircase

Scaldabagno: Hot water heater or system (gas or electric)

Scrittura privata: Privately produced conveyance document

Scuderia: Stable

Semi arredato: Semi-furnished

Semicentro: The area just outside the centre of a city

Seminterrato: Basement apartment

Senza: Without

Serrande: Metal curtains or shutters (on windows)

(i) Servizi: Kitchen and bathroom (which are excluded from the number of rooms quoted in an advertisement)

Servizi allacciati: Services connected

Servizi zonali: Neighbourhood services

Servizio riscossione ruoli: Community fees for a property (e.g. an apartment) that shares building elements or services with other properties

Sfratto: Eviction

Sindaco: Mayor

(da) Sistemare: To be put in order, i.e. requiring work

Società: Building society

Soffitta: Attic

Soffitto (a volta): Ceiling (vaulted)

Soggiorno: Sitting room; lounge

Soggiorno pranzo: Combined living and dining room

Sorgente: Spring

Spese: Expenses

Spese agenzia: Agent's fees

Spese del condominio: Community fees for a property (e.g. an apartment) that shares building elements or services with other properties

Spese condominiali comprese: Community fees included

Spiaggia: Beach

Spiaggia libera/pubblica: Public beach

Spiaggia privata: Private beach

Stanza: Room

Stanza da letto: Bedroom

Stato: Condition

Stato di famiglia: Family status documents

Stazione: Station, e.g. railway

Stima: Estimate; valuation

Strada: Street; road

Struttura: Structure

Strutturalmente: Structurally

Stucco: Plaster made from water, lime, sand and powdered marble, used for decorative work

Studio: Study (den)

Suolo: Ground

Supermercato: Supermarket

Tapparelle: Metal or wooden shutters

Tappeto: Carpet

Tassa comunale dei rifiuti: Refuse (garbage) tax

Telefono: Telephone

Termoautonomo: Independent, automatic heating system

Terra: Ground floor

Terrazza: Terrace

Terreno: Land

Terreno alberato: Land with trees

Terreno boschivo: Wooded land

Terreno coltivato: Cultivated land; farmland

Testamento: Will

Tetto: Roof

Tinello: Small dining room; family room

Titolo di proprietà: Title deed

Toiletta: Toilet; WC

Torre: Tower

Torrente: Stream

Traghetto: Ferry

Trattabile: Negotiable

Travertino: Travertine (light-coloured limestone widely used as a building material in both ancient and modern Rome)

Travi a vista: Exposed beams

Travi di legno: Wooden beams

Ufficio Anagrafe: General registry office (e.g. in a *comune*), where records of residence, birth, death, etc. are kept

Ufficio delle Imposte Dirette: Provincial tax office (also known as *Fisco*)

Ufficio postale: Post office

Ultimo piano: Top floor

Umidità dal basso: Rising damp

Valore: Value

Valore catastale: Cadastral or fiscal value (the assessment of a property's value for tax purposes)

Vano: Room

Vasca: Artificial water basin or bath

Vecchio: Old

Vendesi: For sale

Veranda: Porch

Vetro: Glass

Via: Street; road (followed by the name in addresses)

Viale privato: Private road

Vigili urbani: Local town police

Vigneto: Vineyard

Villa: Villa. Detached town or country house, usually with a large estate

Villa fattoria: Villa-farmhouse of a landowner

Villaggio: Village

Villino: Cottage; small detached house with a garden

Vista: View

Vista sul mare: Sea view

Vista sul monte: Mountain view

Vuoti: Empty; unfurnished

Zona censuaria: Zone into which large towns and cities are divided for registration tax purposes (small towns usually have only one zone)

Zona tranquilla: Quiet area

INDEX

A

Abruzzo (Abruzzi) 43
Agriturismo 214
Air-conditioning 220
Airline Services 78
Airports 80
Avoiding Problems 94
    Buying Land 99
    Buying Off Plan 98
    Finance 98
    Galoppino 97
    Illigal Building 97
    Legal Advice 96
    Professionals 97
    Subrogation 98

B

Banks 153
    Offshore Banking 155
    Opening An Account 154
Basilicata (Lucania) 45
Before Arrival 178
Building Insurance 198
Building a Home 142
Bus Services 87
Buying 118
    For Investment 20
    Land 99, 142
    A New Home 118
    Off Plan 98, 119
    An Old Home 120
    A Resale Home 119
    Through a Company 166

C

Calabria 46
Campania 47
Capital Gains Tax 188
Caretaker 213
Castles, Monasteries,
    Estates & Villages 116
Checklists 178
    After Arrival 179
    Before Arrival 178
Cities 108
Climate 21, 73, 206
    Earthquakes 22
Community 74
    Fees 124
    Maintenance & Repairs 125
    Management 125
    Properties 121
    Restrictions 125
Community Properties 121
    Advantages &
    Disadvantages 122
    Checks 123
    Cost 124
Completion 167
    Declared Value 168
    Final Checks 167
    Payment 168
    Registration 169
    Signing 168
Conditional Clauses 165
Contents Insurance 199

Contracts 163, 206
  Buying Through a
  Company 166
  Conditional Clauses 165
  Deposits 165
  Legal Advice 164
Conveyancing 161
Cost
  of Living 24, 119
  of Property 23
Country Properties 115
Crime 74, 217
Customs 175
  Non-EU Residents 175
  Prohibited & Restricted
  Goods 176
  Visitors 175

D

Declared Value 168
Deposit 165
DIY & Building Supplies 138
Driving
  Italian Roads 88
  to Italy 83
Duty-free Allowances 228

E

Earthquakes 22
Economy 22
Electricity 241
Embassy Registration 176
Emergency & Service
Numbers 232
Emilia Romagna 49
Employment 74
Estate Agents 103

Commission 104, 113
  Legal Advice 107
  Qualifications 104
  Viewing 105

F

Fax 233
Fees 111
  Estate Agent's 113
  Land Registry Tax 112
  Legal Costs 113
  Mortgages 112
  Notary 112
  Registration Tax 111
  Running Costs 113
  Utilities 113
  Value Added Tax 112
Ferry Services 88
Finance 98
Finding
  a Builder 139
  Help 176
Fiscal Code 181
Flights 86
Friuli-Venezia Giulia 50
Furnishings 208

G

Galoppino 97
Garages & Parking 126
Garden 74
Gas 245
Geography 41
Geometra 135
Getting Around 86
  Bus 87
  Ferry 88

Flights 86
Rail 87
Roads 88
Getting There 77
  Airline Services 78
  Airports 80
  Buses 83
  Driving 83
  Ferries 83
  Trains 82

H

Health 33
  Cover 202
Health Insurance 194
  Private 195
  Residents 195
  Visitors 194
Heating 218
Holiday Homes 200
Holiday/Travel Insurance 200
  Annual Policies 202
  Claims 203
  Cost 202
  Health Cover 202
  Visitors 202
Home
  Exchange 101
  Security 220
Hotels & Hostels 101
Household Goods 226
Household Insurance 198
  Building 198
  Claims 200
  Contents 199
  Holiday Homes 200
  Premiums 200
House Hunting 102

I

Illigal Building 97
Immigration 173
Importing & Exporting
Money 150
  International Transfers 151
  Obtaining Cash 152
Income Tax 182
  Allowances 185
  Credits 185
  Liability 183
  Payment 187
  Rates 185
  Returns 186
  Taxable Income 184
  Using a Commercialista 187
Inheritance Tax 189
  Wills 190
Inspections & Surveys 130
  Checks 131
  Swimming Pools 134
Insurance 193
  Insurance Companies 193
International Bank
Transfers 151
Internet 235
Italian
  Currency 148
  Homes 116
  Roads 88

K/L

Keys 209
Land Registry Tax 112
Language 32
Lazio (Latium) 52

Leaseback 128
Legal
  Advice 96, 107, 164
  Fees 113
Letting 205
  Advertising 211
  Brochures & Leaflets 212
  Doing Your Own 210
  Handling Enquiries 212
  Internet 212
  Letting Rates &
  Deposits 211
Liguria 54
Local Council 75
Location 71, 206
  Accessibility 73, 207
  Amenities 73
  Attractions 207
  Climate 73, 206
  Community 74
  Crime 74
  Employment 74
  Garden 74
  Local Council 75
  Natural Phenomena 75
  Noise 75
  Parking 75
  Property Market 76
  Proximity to Airport 207
  Radon 76
  Sports/Leisure Facilities 76
  Tourists 76
  Town or Country? 77
Lombardy (Lombardia) 55
Long-term Rentals 99

M

Maintenance 213

Caretaker 213
  Closing for Winter 214
Maintenance & Repairs 125
Major Considerations 17
Marche 57
Miscellaneous Matters 217
Mobile phones 234
Modern Homes
  Apartments 114
  Townhouses & Villas 114
Molise (Molize) 58
Money Matters 149
Mortgages 156
  Fees 112
  Procedure 158
  Second Homes 158
Moving House 171
Moving In 177

N

Natural Phenomena 75
Negotiating the Price 108
Noise 75
Non-EU Residents 175
Notary's Fees 112

O/P

Offshore Banking 155
Parking 75
Part-ownership 127
Permits & Visas 25
Pets 36
Piedmont (Piemonte) 59
Planning Permission &
Building Permits 136
Postal Services 222
Premiums 200

Professionals 97
Prohibited & Restricted
Goods 176
Property
    Cities 108
    Market 76
    Negotiating the Price 108
    Prices 107
    Rural Areas 107
    Tax 187
Public Holidays 103
Public Telephones 233
Puglia (Apulia or le Puglie) 60
Purchase Procedure 161

Q/R

Quotations 139
Radio 240
Radon 76
Rail Services 87
Regions 43
    Abruzzo (Abruzzi) 43
    Basilicata (Lucania) 45
    Calabria 46
    Campania 47
    Emilia Romagna 49
    Friuli-Venezia Giulia 50
    Lazio (Latium) 52
    Liguria 54
    Lombardy (Lombardia) 55
    Marche 57
    Molise (Molize) 58
    Piedmont (Piemonte) 59
    Puglia (Apulia or le
    Puglie) 60
    Sardinia (Sardegna) 61
    Sicily (Sicilia) 63
    Trentino-Alto Adige 67

Tuscany (Toscana) 65
Umbria 68
Val d'Aosta 69
Veneto 70
Registration 169
    Tax 111
Renovation & Restoration 135
    Building Permits 136
    Checks 136
    Cost 141
    DIY & Building Supplies 138
    DIY or Builders? 138
    Finding a Builder 139
    Geometra 135
    Italian or Foreign
    Builders? 139
    Planning Permission 136
    Quotations 139
    Supervision 140
Renting 99
    Long-term 99
    Short-term 100
Research 94
Residence Permits 29
Retirement 31
    Homes 126
Running Costs 113

S

Sardinia (Sardegna) 61
Satellite
    Radio 40
    Television 237
Security 214
Selling 143
    Presentation 144
    Price 143
    Using an Agent 145

Shipping Your Belongings 171
Shopping 223
   Abroad 227
   Duty-free Allowances 228
   Furniture & Furnishings 225
   Household Goods 226
   Opening Hours 224
Short-term Rentals 100
Sicily (Sicilia) 63
Signing 168
Sports & Leisure Facilities 76
Subrogation 98
Supervision 140
Swimming Pools 134, 207

T

Taxation 181
   Rates 186
   Returns 186
Telephone Services 229
   Alternative Providers 231
   Charges 231
   Emergency &
   Service Numbers 232
   Fax 233
   Installation &
   Registration 229
   Internet 235
   Mobile Phones 234
   Public Telephones 233
   Using the Telephone 230
Television 236
   Satellite Television 237
   TV Standards 236
   Videos & DVDs 239
Timeshare & Part-ownership
Schemes 127
   Leaseback 128

Part-ownership 127
Timesharing 128
Town or Country? 77
Trains 87
Trentino-Alto Adige 67
Tuscany (Toscana) 65
Types of Property 113
   Apartments 114
   Castles, Monasteries,
   Estates & Villages 116
   Country Properties 115
   Townhouses & Villas 114

U

Umbria 68
Utilities 240, 241
   Fees 113
   Gas 245
   Water 247

V

Val d'Aosta 69
Value Added Tax 112
Veneto 70
Viewing 105
Visas 27
Visitors 25, 175, 194, 202

W/Y

Water 247
Where to Live? 41
Why Italy? 17
   Advantages &
   Disadvantages 19
Wills 190
Working 30
Your Dream Home 93

Survival Books was established in 1987 and by the mid-'90s was the leading publisher of books for people planning to live, work, buy property or retire abroad.

From the outset, our philosophy has been to provide the most comprehensive and up-to-date information available. Our titles routinely contain up to twice as much information as other books and are updated frequently. All our books contain colour photographs and some are printed in two colours or full colour throughout. They also contain original cartoons, illustrations and maps.

Survival Books are written by people with first-hand experience of the countries and the people they describe, and therefore provide invaluable insights that cannot be obtained from official publications or websites, and information that is more reliable and objective than that provided by the majority of unofficial sites.

Survival Books are designed to be easy – and interesting – to read. They contain a comprehensive list of contents and index and extensive appendices, including useful addresses, further reading, useful websites and glossaries to help you obtain additional information as well as metric conversion tables and other useful reference material.

Our primary goal is to provide you with the essential information necessary for a trouble-free life or property purchase and to save you time, trouble and money.

We believe our books are the best – they are certainly the best-selling. But don't take our word for it – read what reviewers and readers have said about Survival Books at the front of this book.

Buying a Home Series

Buying a home abroad is not only a major financial transaction but also a potentially life-changing experience; it's therefore essential to get it right. Our Buying a Home guides are required reading for anyone planning to purchase property abroad and are packed with vital information to guide you through the property jungle and help you avoid disasters that can turn a dream home into a nightmare.

The purpose of our Buying a Home guides is to enable you to choose the most favourable location and the most appropriate property for your requirements, and to reduce your risk of making an expensive mistake by making informed decisions and calculated judgements rather than uneducated and hopeful guesses. Most importantly, they will help you save money and will repay your investment many times over.

Buying a Home guides are the most comprehensive and up-to-date source of information available about buying property abroad – whether you're seeking a detached house or an apartment, a holiday or a permanent home (or an investment property), these books will prove invaluable.

Living and Working Series

Our Living and Working guides are essential reading for anyone planning to spend a period abroad – whether it's an extended holiday or permanent migration – and are packed with priceless information designed to help you avoid costly mistakes and save both time and money.

Living and Working guides are the most comprehensive and up-to-date source of practical information available about everyday life abroad. They aren't, however, simply a catalogue of dry facts and figures, but are written in a highly readable style – entertaining, practical and occasionally humorous.

Our aim is to provide you with the comprehensive practical information necessary for a trouble-free life. You may have visited a country as a tourist, but living and working there is a different matter altogether; adjusting to a new environment and culture and making a home in any foreign country can be a traumatic and stressful experience. You need to adapt to new customs and traditions, discover the local way of doing things (such as finding a home, paying bills and obtaining insurance) and learn all over again how to overcome the everyday obstacles of life.

All these subjects and many, many more are covered in depth in our Living and Working guides – don't leave home without them.

The Expatriates' Best Friend!

Culture Wise Series

Our **Culture Wise** series of guides is essential reading for anyone who wants to understand how a country really 'works'. Whether you're planning to stay for a few days or a lifetime, these guides will help you quickly find your feet and settle into your new surroundings.

Culture Wise guides:

• Reduce the anxiety factor in adapting to a foreign culture
• Explain how to behave in everyday situations in order to avoid cultural and social gaffes
• Help you get along with your neighbours
• Make friends and establish lasting business relationships
• Enhance your understanding of a country and its people.

People often underestimate the extent of cultural isolation they can face abroad, particularly in a country with a different language. At first glance, many countries seem an 'easy' option, often with millions of visitors from all corners of the globe and well-established expatriate communities. But, sooner or later, newcomers find that most countries are indeed 'foreign' and many come unstuck as a result.

Culture Wise guides will enable you to quickly adapt to the local way of life and feel at home, and – just as importantly – avoid the worst effects of culture shock.

Culture Wise – the wise way to travel

The essential guides to Culture, Customs & Business Etiquette

Other Survival Books

Investing in Property Abroad: Essential reading for anyone planning to buy property abroad, containing surveys of over 30 countries.

The Best Places to Buy a Home in France/Spain: Unique guides to where to buy property in Spain and France, containing detailed regional profiles and market reports.

Buying, Selling and Letting Property: The best source of information about buying, selling and letting property in the UK.

Earning Money From Your Home: Income from property in France and Spain, including short- and long-term letting.

Foreigners in France/Spain: Triumphs & Disasters: Real-life experiences of people who have emigrated to France and Spain, recounted in their own words.

Making a Living: Comprehensive guides to self-employment and starting a business in France and Spain.

Renovating & Maintaining Your French Home: The ultimate guide to renovating and maintaining your dream home in France.

Retiring in France/Spain: Everything a prospective retiree needs to know about the two most popular international retirement destinations.

Running Gîtes and B&Bs in France: An essential book for anyone planning to invest in a gîte or bed & breakfast business.

Rural Living in France: An invaluable book for anyone seeking the 'good life', containing a wealth of practical information about all aspects of French country life.

Shooting Caterpillars in Spain: The hilarious and compelling story of two innocents abroad in the depths of Andalusia in the late '80s.

Wild Thyme in Ibiza: A fragrant account of how a three-month visit to the enchanted island of Ibiza in the mid-'60s turned into a 20-year sojourn.

For a full list of our current titles, visit our website at www.survivalbooks.net

📷 Photo Credits